# THE GREAT DIVIDE :

## MUSLIM SEPARATISM AND PARTITION

# THE GREAT DIVIDE:
## MUSLIM SEPARATISM AND PARTITION

*S.C. Bhatt*

GYAN PUBLISHING HOUSE
New Delhi-110002

**THE GREAT DIVIDE: MUSLIM SEPARATISM AND PARTITION**
[*History, International Studies, Law, Politics, Religion*]

**ISBN : 81-212-0594-8**



Published in 1998 in India by
Gyan Publishing House
5, Ansari Road
New Delhi 110 002

Laser Typeset at Akshar, Delhi
Printed at Mehra Offset Press, New Delhi.

# CONTENTS

# PREFACE

An attempt has been made in this book to deal with the perennial issue of relations between the Hindus and Muslims from a standpoint different from the routine one: lay the blame at one door or the other. Historical developments have been analysed and studied to arrive at conclusions not only on the continuing conflict but on the issue of what led to the partition of India.

In recent times, some of the media and intellectuals have tried to absolve the architect of partition, Mohammad Ali Jinnah, of some of his responsibility. The Fiftieth anniversary of India's existence as a free nation in modern times and of the completion of 50 years of Pakistan as a sovereign nation has come in handy for some of these self-appointed apologists of Jinnah to place part of the blame on others' shoulders. The book looks at his role in preparing the Muslim mind for taking power in a separate nation that he was carving out for them from India because he preached that the Hindus constituted a nation and the Muslims another.

The role of the great poet, Sir Mohammad Iqbal, has also been examined and his open advocacy of a separate Muslim state has been brought out to disabuse the minds of the people who still sing his "Sare Jahan Se Achha" with fervour. In the evolution of Pakistan as a separate state for the Muslims of the sub-continent, Iqbal had a big hand and he is rightly regarded and revered as Pakistan's national poet.

The book seeks to bring out that Jinnah and his followers had created a situation in which it was impossible to function as a single nation. Apart from the emotional and other support that Jinnah had for his demand for Pakistan, there were strong forces working for a separate state for the Muslims. It was clear that the kind of unity that we had dreamt of and which we realised in ample measure after partition was to be denied to us. A price had to be paid for salvaging the wreckage that the country was about to be reduced to by Jinnah and his supporters. Partition was the objective of Jinnah and his men as they were furiously working for it and it was finally effected by the British.

Pakistan has continued to harbour ill-will towards this nation and that is apparent to anyone except those who are blindly befriending it and supporting its allegations against India. Within less than twenty-five years of its creation, Pakistan lost a majority of its population as Bangladesh was created a sovereign nation. This was total rejection of the false doctrine of a separate Muslim nation.

But in the process of partition and re-partition the division of the Indian Muslims into three parts became inevitable. Jinnah's dream of a separate nation was bound to result in this three-way division and the Muslims were warned, above all by sane Muslim leaders themselves. The danger of Pan-Islamism exists even now. This became recently evident when large numbers of Bangladeshi cricket fans frantically supported the Pakistani team against India, although India did not lack some backing. Bangladesh has not been able to express its gratitude to the sacrifices made by the gallant officers and men of the Indian armed forces for the liberation of their country. The recent statement of apology by the Pakistan Prime Minister and his acceptance of the responsibility for what Pakistan did in 1971, leading to the separation of Bangladesh, could be a ploy or could be an attempt to rewrite and rectify history.

Pakistan is only one side of the problem that this nation faces. The other side of the problem will have to be resolved in the best interest of India and all its people, including the Muslims. The Pakistan issue casts its shadow and this aggravates the separatist feeling still entertained by a number of Muslims but this has to be understood if a proper solution has to be found.

Gandhiji did his utmost to weld the Hindus and Muslims into a single nation. Despite his supreme effort Jinnah succeeded in forcing partition on the country and he did not accept even the suggestion of the Father of the Nation for a "brotherly" settlement. The fact of Muslim separatism has to be faced. Many millions of them only want to live in peace with their neighbours and there are indeed forces of modernisation as many young men and women are trying to blaze a new trail. These forces have to be encouraged without closing our eyes to the "leaders" who are keen believers in separatism. Some of them wear an attractive garb which should not deceive anyone, although some uncritical people fall victims to it.

We cannot afford to sweep under the carpet the forces of separatism. One must look at the bright side but the dark forces must not be lost sight of. The problem has to be viewed in entirety and we have to recognise that votebank politics had dealt a severe blow to the fabric of our society.

It gives me great pleasure to acknowledge my gratitude to the Librarian of the library of the RR and T division of the Information and Broadcasting Ministry for his consistent help by way of supply of books.

Delhi.
March 1998

S.C. Bhatt

*Chapter 1*

# THE GREAT DIVIDE

Gandhiji, rightly revered as the Father of the Nation and Apostle of truth and non-violence, campaigned ceaselessly and worked assiduously for Hindu-Muslim unity all his life. Before he was killed mercilessly by a Hindu fanatic on January 30, 1948, as he was rushing to his daily prayer meeting, he had been planning to go to Pakistan to continue the good work which he had done in Calcutta and later in Delhi. He wanted to restore peace and good sense to a troubled sub-continent. Yet he had to admit: "I had realised early enough in South Africa that there was no genuine friendship between the Hindus and Musalmans."

We should remember that he had been taken to South Africa from his native Kathiawar (now called Saurashtra, part of Gujarat state of India) by a Muslim businessman.[1] Gandhiji had succeeded in welding the Indian community, in that white dominated and racial land, into a whole and the Muslims, including a hot-headed Pathan who once attacked him but later regretted, had generally cooperated with him. Many of them had gone to jail along with other Indians. That was a unique experience for a subject people. Gandhiji made jail-going look easy, although it was a difficult and painful experience, and gave the form of protest a patriotic fervour.

His observation that the Hindus and Muslims did not have genuine friendship for one another was of immense significance. There could not be two communities, like the Hindus and Muslims, who have so much in common in their habits, language and attitude to life as well as social customs, specially marriage ceremonies. Take the first night of the bride and the bridegroom together. It is referred to in northern India as 'Suhag Raat' or the night of bliss. The word 'Suhag' is a derivative of 'Saubhagya', good luck in Sanskrit. In the eyes of the people of India and Pakistan what could be more a matter of good luck than marital bliss? The wedding party is called a 'baraat', which again is a corruption of 'varayatra', the bridegroom's journey, which is accomplished on a white mare, in both communities, the bride being taken in a palanquin, now only symbolically and as a formality. All this points to a great deal of commonness.

Yet there is a large enough chasm dividing them. What obtains between the Hindus and Muslims is much more pronounced in the relations between India and Pakistan. The two countries have gone to war on three occasions to which you have to add the proxy war launched in Jammu and Kashmir state of India by Pakistan in 1989. This has been largely beaten back by the valiant Indian army and the paramilitary forces as well as the state police of Jammu and Kashmir; Pakistan had to eat the humble pie, although it would not admit it. Even after the Gujral doctrine of one-sided concessions to neighbours was enforced by India in 1996 and 1997, Pakistan tested the Haft missile and "invented" the Ghauri missile, with Chinese help, aimed at India. Bullets were rained on the Indian soldiers in Kashmir, along the Line of Control and the international border, even after a foreign secretary level dialogue began between the two countries. Whatever the Prime Minister, Mian Nawaz Sharif, may say — and what he says nowadays is not what he said when he was fighting the election to the Pakistan National Assembly — the shots are called by the army and the establishment of the foreign service and the civilians.

The hostility between the Hindus and Muslims not to be confused with the conflict between India and Pakistan, is a continuation of the lack of "friendship" that Gandhiji referred to, ever since the first contacts began or shortly thereafter. Islam came to India first in the form of Arab traders who reached the Kerala coast around 634 A.D. Then in the form with which we have been too familiar for ages, the appearance of the invaders. Mohammad Ibn-al Qasim, popularly known as Mohammad Bin Qasim, son-in-law of the Governor of Iraq, al-Hajjaj ibn Yusuf al-Thaqafi, invaded Sind in 712 A.D. and defeated and killed its King Dahir. His queen, Rani Bai, burnt herself along with several other women rather than fall a prey to the lust of the invaders. Before taking the last plunge the Queen said: "God forbid that we owe our liberty to outcaste cow-eaters. Our honour would be lost and our term of life has come to its close. As there is no hope of safety and liberty let us collect cotton and oil. The most expedient course for us, I think, is to burn ourselves and thus quickly meet our husbands."[2]

**First "Jauhar"**

What the last Hindu queen of Sind did was to be repeated many times over in different parts of India, although instances of Rajas marrying their sisters or daughters to Muslim emperors are also not lacking and there were a few genuine cases of love at first sight. The moment Mohammad Ibn-al Qasim had conquered Sind he imposed the Jaziya tax on the Hindus who, as non-Muslims, were declared second class citizens or Dhimmis by the Arab invaders. However, India withstood for nearly a thousand years Muslim pressure to convert itself to Islam. India was one of the few countries to resist the religious and cultural invasion, of all the countries conquered by the invaders. India had absorbed invaders in the past. This country had an advanced civilisation, more progressive than the undoubtedly advanced one the Muslim invaders brought with them, and this enabled the country to resist the pressure. This and the social system that the country had. Despite the constant running down of the caste system by many Muslims and some Hindus too, the social structure represented by it withstood the buffeting of the invaders who were keen proselytisers. Apart from the greed for worldly possessions and wealth and the lust for power, which in the first place, attracted the invaders, specially men like Mahmud of Ghazni who made repeated trips to plunder the wealth of the temples, sacked by him, conversion of people to Islam was one of the most dominant motives of the invaders.

The invaders who came to India before Mohammad Bin Qasim were absorbed in the Hindu order. The Greeks, Scythians, Kushans and Huns were among them. The Parsis came as refugees from the terror of Islam and were accepted as friends but preferred to live as a separate group. The authors of the *History and Culture of the Indian People* published by the Bharatiya Vidya Bhavan have this to say: "Unlike the previous invaders, the Muslims did not merge themselves with the Hindus and thus for the first time the population of India was divided into two separate units with marked distinctions. This was the historic beginning of the Hindu-Muslim problem that led, after more than six hundred years, to the creation of Pakistan."[3]

Gandhiji fought all his life against the forces which divide the Hindus from the Muslims and so did the Indian National Congress which stood for the betterment of all Indians, irrespective of caste or creed. The sad fact, however, was that the generality of Muslims in the country did not accept the Congress ideology, although many individual Muslims fought bravely, shoulder to shoulder with their Hindu brethren against the oppressive foreign regime. But, except during the interlude of the Khilafat agitation, which the Mahatma embraced and made his own, the Muslims generally kept away from the struggle waged by the leaders of the freedom movement. What is more, leading Muslims like Sir Syed Ahmed Khan, Ameer Ali, and later, Mohammad Ali Jinnah urged them to keep away from the path of "agitation" against British rule. The relevant points have been examined in detail in later chapters.

From the time the invaders began their rule, the kings and potentates were egged on by the Ulema, the Muslim religious men, and even by the Sufi saints, who were close to some of the rulers, to greater Islamisation of the country, suppression of the Hindus and increased fundamentalism eschewing any commonality with the indigenous people. It is customary in India to lay stress on the common features and emphasise the composite culture of India but many of the Muslim rulers looked upon India as a prized possession and the people as set targets for conversion. Only Aurangzeb, among the rulers, claimed to be more learned in religious lore than the Ulema and the Sufi saints and took his own decisions on increasing the measure of bigotry while his great-grandfather, the wise Emperor Akbar, steered clear of fanaticism, perhaps the only Muslim ruler to do so.

**Pragmatic View**

Often, however, the Sultans and Shahinshahs took a more pragmatic view of things and took practical steps, realising that they had to carry the Hindu population with them, adjust the dose of Islamisation to the needs of the situation and the reality, and be as practical as they possibly could in their day-to-day behaviour towards the people of the land. There were rulers and rulers and some whom we regard as wise were actually more intent on curbing the Hindus. We rightly revere the Mughal Emperor Shahjahan as the builder of the wonderful Taj Mahal, that great monument of love, but it should be remembered that he had banned the construction of temples. He was also the first ruler in India to introduce the celebration of the birthday of Prophet Mohammad. It fell to the lot of the government of Prime Minister V.P. Singh to declare the birthday of Prophet Mohammad in 1990 as a public holiday. There are thus four Muslim holidays in the Indian governments' calendar out of 17 annual holidays, only one less than the number of Hindu holidays.[4]

If the Hindu social system was as fragile as painted by some people it would have crumbled at the first impact of Islam, had the claim to equality held out by its protagonists been true and the Indian system unsustainable. Neither the Indian system was fragile nor the promised equality of all citizens a reality. What is more remarkable, the citizens of Sind asked the new ruler and got permission to keep their social order intact.[5] They were allowed by the conqueror, Mohammad Ibn Qasim, to get the Brahmin priests to perform their chores in temples and social and religious ceremonies and for the other castes to do their share of the work. It does not mean the Indian system did not have weaknesses, some of which persist to this day and have to be cured, and life was not hell for the so-called untouchables. The glaring inequalities led Gandhiji to launch a massive temple entry campaign and for the minimum human rights of the Dalits.

The promise of equality was a myth which actually helped the Hindus to hold fast to their system, among other things. The ignorant always talk of Islamic equality for all Muslims. But the reality is different. In the days of Mohammad Ibn Qasim and his successors, the converted Muslims were subject to almost the same iniquitous treatment. For one thing, the foreign Muslims, who came with the invaders or who kept on migrating held sway for a long time. Even in the days of the most liberal and thoughtful ruler like Akbar, as many as 70 per cent of the key officers of the army and civil service were foreign Muslims. Only fifteen per cent were from among the converted Indian Muslims and the remainder fifteen per cent were Hindus without whom the army and the administration could not carry on.

If equality is confined to the Friday Namaz it remains a myth. In the day-to-day affairs and social practices like marriage equality is given the goby. A maid's daughter, however intelligent and pretty, could never be the wedded wife of the Nawab's don, even if he is a wastrel and worthless successor to his father's wealth and power. She could, of course, end up as the concubine of the son, or one of the many of his father. The mythical Anarkali, recurrent theme and character of our films and TV serials, could not marry Prince Salim because she was a maid.

**Myth of Equality**

Even a person like Syed Shahabuddin, who is widely believed to preach separatism, had to admit: "In Islam, the measure of status is piety, not power or position or profession or wealth. Yet Muslim India has an in-built caste system, quite parallel to what exists in Hindu India. (Like Jinnah, Shahabuddin divides India into Hindu and Muslim). Caste came into Indian Islam with the converts who not only retained their traditional occupations but their inter-relationships as well. Their descendants account for the overwhelming majority of Muslim Indians. Islam could and did unite them within the Masjid and the graveyard, but not outside the Masjid, in the living society.

"Like the Hindu Savarnas, the Muslim elite, largely of foreign extraction (Iranis, Turanis, Afghans, Mughals, Arabs) but also including some converts from the Savaranas (Brahmins became Sheiks, Rajputs became Pathans) translated their proximity to the institution of the state into economic dominance, and social status, even monopoly of education and employment."[6] Jinnah, borrowing his ideas from Rahmat Ali, the first protagonist of Pakistan, used to say that the Hindus and Muslims did not intermarry or interdine, but the fact is that the upper crust of Muslims never deign to intermarry with the ordinary Muslims.

The roots of separatism are deep. There is no question of visiting the sins of the barbarous invaders on today's Muslims and Indian society cannot make progress or even exist in a climate of revenge, but the actions of the invaders have to be understood in their proper context because many of the descendants still claim their ancestry. Will Durant, in his *Story of Civilization*, has this to say: "The Mohammedan conquest of India is probably the bloodiest story in history. It is a discouraging tale, for its evident moral is that civilization is a precarious thing, whose delicate complex of order and liberty, culture and peace may at any time be overthrown by barbarians invading from without or multiplying within."[7]

The authors of the *History and Culture of the Indian People* say: "To these invaders nothing was sacred. The description given by Padmanabha in *Kahnadade Prabandha* (A.D. 1458, believed to be the first literary work in Gujarati) of what the armies of Ala-ud-Din Khalji did equally apply to the campaigns of the Turks:'The conquering army burnt villages; devastated the land, plundered people's wealth, took Brahmanas, children and women of all castes captive, and flogged them with thongs and raw hide, carried a moving prison with it and converted the prisoners into obsequious Turks."[8]

The same book goes on to quote a Muslim authority : "In the days of Mahmud of Ghazni, in the words of Utbi 'the blood of the infides flowed copiously and apostasy was often the only way of survival'."[9] Here is what the horse's mouth has to say about the fate of the Hindus who could survive if only they accepted Islam.

By the time the British divided the country, after bringing it under one roof, the Muslim population of India was 25 per cent of the total. India then had a Dalit population of 15 per cent. This means that the Muslims were not able to convert the downtrodden sections of the Hindu society after being in power over large parts of the country for more than six hundred years. This is significant because it exposes the theory that the Hindu system was so oppressive that many voluntarily offered to change their faith. Of course, people who had to hold on to their professions, like carpenters, washermen, masons and barbers who had to enter the *harem* of the rulers and their hangers on as well as the "nobles" had to accept the faith of the rulers. Then the Sufi saints, who ought to have been more concerned with the other world, converted many by their sweet words. In spite of all that, the bulk of the Dalits refused to be converted.

We have noted how kings and emperors celebrated for their great construction activities were not above anti-Hindu pogroms. Shahjahan's son and successor, Aurangzeb, was the worst culprit, although he had many noteworthy personal qualities. He destroyed the celebrated temples at Kashi and Mathura and built mosques over them, instead of protecting his subjects who worshipped at these temples. He was a much more capable military leader than some of his brothers but he ousted them and killed his eldest brother Darashikoh who was keenly interested in Hindu works like the Upanishads and described the philosophy contained in them as the mingling of the oceans because he found in them echoes of Islam's monism. Aurangzeb's cruel rule, in a way, hastened the end of Islamic domination over India because the height of bigotry and fundamentalism had been reached in his rule and the division between the Hindus and Muslims could not be more acute.

There were many others in his category although he excelled them all. Ferozshah Tughlaq and Sikandar Lodhi, both celebrated in Delhi with gardens and roads named after them, were known for cruelty. But it was left to Aurangzeb to try to extinguish any vestige of commonness so that India could be a completely Islamic state. He discontinued the celebration of Navroz, the Parsi festival of the advent of the new year in August which some Iranian nobles had brought with them to India. He also abolished the celebration of several other Hindu festivals which his great grandfather, Akbar, had introduced in the royal palace. Aurangzeb also closed the Hindu schools of learning in Varanasi, Multan and Thatta, dismissed Hindu clerks and prohibited the Hindus from riding in palanquins unless they were Rajput warriors. This was the only means of transport for the common people unless they could ride horses, for which you had to own them. He did not have to introduce the Jaziya tax on the Hindus. It had already been introduced by his grand father Jahangir, after the later's father, Akbar, had abolished it.

These "exploits" of Alamgir, as he is referred to by his biographer, are recorded by a man called Saqi Mustad Khan. He said: "The Hindus had not been degraded to such a degree in any other period."[11]

We have seen how some of the rulers took a more pragmatic view than the Ulema who instigated them to heap more and more indignities on the Hindus. Emperor Iltutmish of the Delhi sultanate was approached by a delegation of the Ulema, led by none other than his Sheikh-ul-Islam, Sayyid Nuruddin Mubarak Ghaznavi, a Sufi "saint", which asked him that the Hindus be given an ultimatum that they accept Islam or face death. Their reason for this outlandish advice was that being neither Jews nor Christians they were not 'Dhimmis' and , therefore, not entitled to protection by the government. The king, however, told his wazir to explain to the learned men of Islam and the Sufi, who belonged to the Suhrawardy order, that the Muslims were numerically so small that an adventure of that type would be the end of the sultanate. Neither this nor the suggestion made by the Sufi that the Hindus be disgraced, dishonoured and defamed was accepted by the king who considered the future of his sultanate more important than the display of bigotry, although he did not lack the ardour.[12]

Other sultans were also confronted with this problem. Alauddin Khalji told a delegation of bigoted religious leaders: "I do not know what is lawful or unlawful. Whatever I consider good for the state I decree." One of his predecessors, Jalaluddin Khalji, was not that strong but he also refused to accept the recommendation: "Oh you fool!... Don't you see that the Hindus who are the worst enemies of God and of Islam pass daily below my royal palace to the Jamuna beating drums and playing flutes and practise before our eyes the worship of the idols with all the rituals?"[13]

**"Sufi" Misconception**

Contrary to the popular misconception among many Indians, the Sufis, some of whom were close to the rulers, played a notable part in the job of Hindu-baiting. Those of Chisti and Suhrawardy orders were more orthodox than the others and were the first to introduce religious bigotry in the Delhi sultanate. The founder of the Chisti order was none other than Khwaja Muinuddin Chisti whose Dargah at Ajmer attracts thousands of pilgrims all the year round. Aziz Ahmed who wrote *Studies in Islamic Culture in the Indian Environment* says that Muinuddin Chisti was responsible for "acrimonious polemics against the Hindus."[14]

There was much coordination between the rulers and the Sufis and this helped in the process of the consolidation of their kingdoms and of the Islamic conquest. People like Muinuddin Chisti knew that to rule over India they had to learn the language of the people. He, therefore, studied the Hindi language before settling down in Ajmer. That did not prevent him from inviting Shahbuddin Ghori to invade India. He found that Prithviraj Chauhan, who was from Ajmer but ruled Delhi also, was an obstacle in his way. Ghori followed his advice but did not succeed in his first effort during which he was routed by Prithviraj. But Ghori made a second attack which was successful and he took the Chauhan prisoner and killed him after taking him to Kabul. The Sufi Khanquahs (establishment) went to south India in the wake of the capture of Deogiri by Allauddin Khalji. The Deccan rulers who had surrendered to the Delhi rulers had to provide for the Sufis some of whom were also given titles like "Kufarbhanjan" or destroyer of Hindus.[15]

But we cannot tar all the Sufis with the same brush. There were Several who were really philosophical minded Sufis and who were only interested in God and suffered for the sake of their beliefs. We have the case of Sheikh Sarfuddin Maneri two of whose disciples were awarded capital punishment for preaching the doctrine of Wahadutul Wujud or monism. Sheikh Nasiruddin preferred to live in the midst of the people instead of living in the court of a Sultan. They used Hindawi, or Hindi, in preference to Persian and Urdu. In 1485, the Shattari Silsilah was established by Shah Abdullah Shattari whose followers believed in the monistic doctrine of Sufism. Some of the Sufis helped Humayun who faced a series of difficulties and had to fight the fanatical Sunnis among the Afghan rulers. He had married a Shia princess in his years of exile. That the Mughal dynasty was more liberal than the other Sultans, at least in the earlier years, was due to the fact that they were influenced by a number of liberal Sufi Ulema.

Among the Indian Sufis who were only interested in God were great thinkers like Nanak who founded the Sikh faith and the great Kabir, who was probably born a Muslim but whose writings and work were all centred around the principles of Vedanta and Bhakti. Kabir was one of the greatest men produced by India whose worth has not yet been recognised. Several Muslim Sufis used to visit their Hindu counterparts and discussions were often held on the basic truth of life. Their interaction helped in maintaining a balance at turbulent times of fanaticism and bigotry. But the ignorance which prevails today is also annoying because many bigoted men who were essentially fundamentalists of Islam have been passed off as Sufi saints.

Many of the Sultans cared little for the principle of equality even among the Muslims. Sultan Balban dismissed all the non-Turkish nobles and low born government servants. His utter contempt for the low born is reflected in his remark: "I will not allow a low born person to occupy a high place. When I look at a low born person my blood begins to boil."[16] By low born is, of course, meant a converted Indian Muslim. Both Iltutmish and Balban looked upon with contempt on the "low born" converted Indian Muslims and bypassed the non-Turkish nobles of foreign birth. A theologian and historian of the period, Ziauddin Barani, supporting the rulers, said: "The merits and demerits of men have been apportioned at the beginning of time and allotted to their souls... If a man is pious there must be elements of aristocracy among his ancestors; but if his low birth is proved than his piety is mere pretence. It would be a scandal if the sons of butchers, weavers and shopkeepers have more honour in the eyes of Allah than the sons of Khans, Maliks and Amirs."[17] Is this the equality promised by Islam? It is not enough that you recite the *Kalma* and say prayers in the mosques five times a day and on Friday but you must also be a high born! Sultan Iltutmish dismissed 33 persons from government service because they were low born or converted Muslims from India.

**Jiziya and Shivaji**

There is considerable confusion over the special Jiziya tax imposed on the Hindus which signified their inferior status under

Islamic rule. According to Hafeez Malik, a Pakistani historian settled in the United States, Jiziya was imposed by Mohammad Ibn Qasim and was enforced right up to the reign of Aurangzeb. It was, however, abolished by the great Mughal Emperor Akbar and his son, Jahangir, and grandson Shahjahan did not enforce it but, says Hafeez, "reimposed all the other restrictions and liabilities that a Dhimmi suffered in medieval India. "Hafeez adds: "Shivaji's assertion that the Jiziya was something new is not true. From Mohammad Ibn al-Qasim to the reign of Aurangzeb, only Akbar abolished Jiziya. Although his son and grandson, as pointed out by Shivaji's letter, followed his example in regard to Jiziya they reimposed all the other restrictions that a Dhimmi suffered in medieval India." "Jiziya was relatively a light tax," explains Hafeez, but it was a symbol of an inferior status "and the Hindus were no longer prepared to live the life of second class citizens in their own homesteads." Hafeez Malik quotes Professor Hartz to establish that Shivaji's protest against the imposition of the Jiziya tax on the Hindus and his rejection of the iniquitious tax was like the Gandhian movement against the salt tax under British rule.[18]

Shivaji founded the Maratha kingdom and later the Marathas ruled over large parts of India, their sway extending up to Attock in the north and Cuttack in the east, although they had some control over Bengal at times. In the days of the later Mughals the Maratha armies provided the armed umbrella for the largely nominal emperors. In 1679, Shivaji addressed a strongly worded letter to Aurangzeb protesting against the reimposition of the Jiziya tax on the Hindus. He said:

"May it please your Majesty. That architect of the edifice of the empire, Emperor Akbar, reigned with full powers for fifty two years; he adopted the fair policy of perfect peace (Sulh-i-Kul) with all the diverse sects... So he became famous under the title of the world's preceptor (Jagatguru). Then His Majesty the Emperor Nuruddin Jahangir for twenty-five years spread his gracious shadow on the head of the world, and its people. Next the Emperor Shah Jahan for thirty-two years cast his blessed shadow... The splendour and power of these emperors can be easily gauged from the fact that the Emperor Alamgir fails in merely following their system. They too had the power of imposing the Jiziya, but they did not admit bigotry into their hearts. Therefore their wealth and fortune continued to increase.

"But in your Majesty's reign many of the forts and provinces have gone out of your possession and the rest will soon do because there will be no slackness on my part in ruining and devastating them. When poverty and bigotry have made their homes in the palaces of the Emperor and the princes the conditions of the amirs and mansabdars (nobles and military officers) can be easily gauged. It is a reign in which the army is in tumult, the merchants complain, the Muslims cry, the Hindus are being grilled.... How can royal generosity permit you to add the hardship of Jiziya to this grievous state of things? It will be proclaimed from east to west and recorded in history that the Emperor of India, envying the bowl of the beggars, takes Jiziya from the Brahmins, Jain monks, Yogis, Sanyasis, bairagis, paupers, beggars, ruined wretches and the famished...."

Shivaji added a few words of religious amity and Hindu-Muslim compatibility, something to which he was wedded, in his letter to the Islamic fanatic. In vain, of course, because they were anathema to Aurangzeb: "Well, your Majesty, if you believe in the true Heavenly Book (the Quran) you will find there Rabb-ul-Alamin (God of all men) and not Rabb-ul-Musalmin (God of Muslims only). Verily Islam and Hinduism are contrasted terms (lafz-ul-muqabil) used by the divine painter to blend his colours and produce harmony (of effect through variety...) To show bigotry to the creed and practice of anyone is like altering a word in the holy book; to draw lines on a picture is to find fault with the painter.... Not to speak of justice this imposition of Jiziya is an innovation in India and unsuitable."[19]

Shivaji is known as a bold and fearless man who created a kingdom out of nothing. But this letter reveals not only his boldness and fearlessness but also his wisdom and deep understanding of the religious philosophies of Hinduism and Islam. Alas, his words fell on deaf ears because Aurangzeb was neither wise nor tolerant. Being a bigoted fundamentalist he was not willing to listen to such sage words. That Shivaji who represented the best in the culture of India should be dubbed a Hindu revivalist by some writers instead of a successful rebel against tyranny and religious bigotry is a sad commentary on the secularists of India.

There is no question of applauding the thinking or action of some Hindu fanatics who harbour those memories and seek revenge today for the inequities and indignities inflicted on their remote ancestors or the Hindus in general by the fanatical rulers egged on by equally or more fanatical Ulema. Hindu tolerance or Indian tolerance, enshrined in the Constitution as equal rights in all matters including the practice and propagation of religion, will not allow it. No Indian dare raise his hand against a fellow Indian and only the law must take its course. As the wise first President of India, Dr. Rajendra Prasad observed, history cannot be rectified.[20]

But it is equally true that for many years before independence the Muslim psyche was influenced by the thought that today's citizens were heir to the rulers of the past and on that ground so many privileges were sought and ultimately the partition of the country was forced. In the welding together of all Indians this feeling would seem to stand in the way and many votebank politicians and leaders of the Muslim community, who profess to speak for it, as well as a number of Muslim writers still plough the separatist furrow. The continuous hostility preached and practised by Pakistan adds fuel to the fire.

Fortunately, a new generation has come up among the Muslims, specially the young men and women, who have taken to modern education in a big way and have sought no privileges for themselves. They want to face life much the same way as other Indian do. As Firoz Bakht Ahmed, journalist, says: "There was a time when it was difficult to find educated Muslims, but today though not up to the mark, there is no dearth of them. This class of enlightened Muslim youth is ready to lambast anything filled with religious bigotry, hypocrisy, conceit, ambiguity and fraud. They come down heavily upon the Muslim leadership which is selfish, egoist and semi-literate."[21]

And what has an eminent Muslim educationist got to say about some of these leaders? " Who does Syed Shahabuddin and Salman Khurshid represent?[22] Rajiv Gandhi should have posed this question to them during the Shah Bano controversy when they were busy mobilising the Muslims against the Supreme Court judgment and defending a retrogade piece of legislation. He did not do so. Let us now settle the issue in this fiftieth year of our independence through a nationwide referendum. Let us, once and for all, decide who represents whom. Otherwise a number of Muslim leaders and politicians, many of whom have been repeatedly humbled by the electorate would continue to act as the self-proclaimed conscience of Muslim interests."[23]

**History can't be Rectified**

It is in the hands of these young people of the Muslim community that the future seems to lie, of the community and perhaps also the peace and progress of India. They alone can wipe out the residue of the days of the freedom movement but the historical forces have to be understood in the proper context and no effort should be made to brush the controversial points under the carpet. Truth has to be faced by both communities and the people who take upon themselves the interpretation of events. There is a responsibility on the shoulders of the Muslims, specially the youth, but also of the Hindus who have to encourage these forces and not to rake up old issues. If the past cannot be ignored there should be no attempt to rectify it, as the wise Dr Rajendra Prasad said in an address as early as 1951. Some of them ask what would have been the condition of the people when some historical temples were demolished. If they seek to remedy that situation now we have to ask them why did they wait so long. It is like a politician, saying more than six years after the Babari mosque was demolished, that she was devastated by it.[24] Why, can we ask, did she wait for such a long time to share her feelings? Why not on the day of the demolition if she was really devastated? Are we to believe that she was devastated and yet she waited for this time? Was she in a state of devastation so long?

## NOTES

1. Dada Abdulla Sheth of Dada Abdulla and Company.
2. *Moslem Nationalism in India and Pakistan*, Hafeez Malik, Public Affairs Press, Washington D.C.
3. *History and Culture of the Indian People*, R.C. Majumdar and A.D. Pusalkar, Bharatiya Vidya Bhavan, Bombay (Mumbai).
4. There are 17 holidays in the government 's calendar, as testified by the official calendar and diary of the DAVP, Govt. of India. Three of

them are national holidays, Republic Day, Independence Day and Mahatma Gandhi's birthday, five Hindu holidays, Holi, Ramnavami (for Mahashivratri), Janmashtami (Krishna's birthday), Dussehra and Diwali, four Muslim Holidays, Id-uz-Zuha, Id-ul-fitr, Id-e-Milad (the Birthday of Prophet Mohammad), and Moharram, two Christian holidays, Good Friday and Christmas, a Sikh holiday, Guru Nanak's birthday, a Buddhist holiday, the day of the birth, Enlightenment and Parinirvana (death) of the Buddha, and one Jain holiday, Lord Mahavira's birthday. In a country in which the Hindus are 82 per cent of the population, the Muslims are 12 per cent, and Sikhs and Christians are less than two per cent, and Jain below one per cent, can there be anything more secular?

5. Hafeez Malik, *op. cit.*
6. *The Pioneer*, Delhi, March 24, 1997.
7. Quoted in *History and Culture of the Indian People.*
8. *Ibid.*
9. *Ibid.*
10. *Ibid.*
11. Saqi Mustad Khan's 'Maasir-i-Alamgiri', quoted in *Islam in India's Transition to Modernity*, M.A. Karandikar, Orient Longmans, Bombay.
12. *Ibid.*
13. *Ibid.*
14. *Ibid.*
15. *Ibid.*
16. *Fatwa-i-Jahandari*, quoted by Karandikar, *Ibid.*
17. *Tarikh-i-Firuzshahi*, Karandikar, *Ibid.*
18. Hafeez Malik, *op. cit.*
19. *Ibid.*
20. *Speeches of President Rajendra Prasad*, Publications Division, Delhi.
21. *National Herald*, Delhi, February, 24, 1997.
22. Syed Shahabuddin, once referred to before, was an Indian Foreign Service Officer, who retired prematurely and took up politics, championing Muslim Separatism. Salman Khurshid was a minister in the P.V. Narasimha Rao Government and is a noted Congress leader from U.P.
23. *Indian Express*, Delhi, June 28, 1997.
24. Sonia Gandhi's election speech at Hyderabad, Jan. 16, 1998. See *The Hindustan Times*, Jan. 17, 1998.

*Chapter* 2

# BRITISH BIAS

From the outset the British rulers of India were looking for opportunities to get solid support for their regime. They had great skills in warfare but greater still was their ability to win the confidence of the Indian rulers and princes, create dissensions in their ranks and promote palace revolutions. The flag followed the trade. Quite early in their dealings with India they had come to the conclusion that the way to succeed in India was to wield effective power. They also realised that one way of doing it was to keep the Hindus from the Muslims. They set about their task of grasping Indian territories with both hands and did not care, if in the process, they offended Hindus and Muslims alike.

The central Muslim power was on the decline and several Hindu states had come up. In Punjab a powerful and wise ruler, Maharaja Ranjit Singh, had set up a Sikh kingdom which held sway over large areas including Afghanistan. But his successors were not cast in the same heroic mould. The British in India had competition from the French and to a certain extent from the Portuguese but they were better in their system and had greater support from 'home', understood the Indian system better than their rivals from Europe and had a greater feeling for the Indian climate.

By 1857 India was almost ripe for a revolt. The British had embarked on a plan to annex as much Indian territory as possible. This had created frustration and a spirit of revenge among many Rajas and Nawabs, dispossessed of their kingdoms or principalities.

Those who had been thus deprived were smarting under the humiliation heaped on them. The Mughal emperor Bahadurshah Zafar was only an emperor in name, a pensioner of the East India Company. He was aware that he was called "Your Majesty", more out of courtesy and sometimes out of sneer than genuine respect or as a tribute to his position. Ranjit Singh's sons had been packed off to London after Punjab was annexed.

The Maratha empire, which had provided a shield to the tottering Mughal rulers of Delhi in the 18th century, lost its last Peshawa, Bajirao II, who was pensioned off by the British and exiled to Bithur, near Kanpur in Uttar Pradesh. His heir, Nanasaheb, was not given a penny of the pension. So ignorant were the British of Indian tradition and sentiment that they had not left Nanasaheb with any land and cows to be given away as 'mahadan' to Brahmin priests when Bajirao died. An old and loyal Sardar (a noble) had to come to his aid by donating his entire property.

Satara, Jhansi, Nagpur and Tanjore (now Tanjavur) had been seized by the British under Dalhousie's specious plea of lapse, which was a fashionable word for illegal annexation. The Carnatic nawabs, the Muslim rulers of Murshidabad, in Bengal, the Raja of Sambalpur, in Orissa, and others fared no better. Tipu Sultan's sons were sent away to Calcutta. On top of these annexations came the most unjust act; the grabbing of the territory of Oudh (Avadh, Central and eastern UP) for no better reason than the misrule of the pleasure loving Wajid Ali Shah. Any excuse was good enough to the grasping British, lack of a natural male heir, although adoption had traditional Indian sanction, alleged or real misrule or suspected disloyalty.

How did the British themselves view these illegal seizures? When Lucknow was besieged during the 1857 revolt and English were holed up in a small area, an English woman remarked: "The tribulations we are now in is just punishment to our nation for the grasping spirit in which we have governed India."

For the Muslims whose forefathers occupied top civilian and military positions and for those Hindus whose forbears were lucky enough to be conferred with such offices by the Muslim kings and those who had occupied such positions under Hindu rulers there was nothing left. They could at best aspire to junior positions as sub-magistrates, munsifs or subedars in the British Indian army. The landholders could not pay the excessive land revenue and had sometimes to sell off their land to pay the government its taxes. Many British traders became farmers overnight and emerged as monopolist growers of indigo, opium and other cash crops.

The rulers were smarting under their losses and insults heaped on them but the real revolt against the rising power of the British came from the ranks of the Indian soldiers in the British army in India, men who had served the foreign masters loyally and had borne the brunt in the fight for their various acquisitions. Many of them had gone abroad to Burma (now Myanmar) and Afghanistan. (Even now the Defence Ministry has no powers to order Indian soldiers and officers to go abroad and the Indian media have not caught up to it.) The soldiers, today's 'jawans', were called 'sepoys' and were paid a princely sum of seven rupees a month if they were foot soldiers and Rs. 27 a month if they were in the cavalry, called 'sowars'. The riders had to find their own mount and received no rations.

Every soldier had to pay a bribe to the European sergeant on recruitment and the fellow broke them in. The institution of bribe is an ancient one and the British were as much a party to it as the Indians. As much as 57 per cent of the annual expenditure of pounds 9,802,235 was spent on the British officers and men, no more than 51,316 in number, out of the total of 315,000 officers and men. The Indians were well treated in the beginning but later they were called 'niggers' or even 'suars', pigs, which caused special pain to the Muslims because they look upon the pig as 'an unclean animal'.

According to Pritchard, who wrote *Mutinies of Rajputana*, "the population of the country had no love for us. It would have been strange if they had. What did they owe to us? Nothing". By and large such honesty was confined to a few. The bulk of the Englishmen were self-righteous, disdainful of the 'natives' as they referred to the Indians, and enforced their rule with scant regard to Indian tradition and sentiment because they had a mission to 'civilise'. There was a general apprehension in the army that the British were out to convert the Hindus and Muslims to Christianity and there was no dearth of overzealous officers.

**Last Straw**

The greased cartridge was the proverbial last straw on the camel's back. In the course of changing to modern weapons from the less efficient rifles, the British had introduced a cartridge which had to be ripped open by mouth and there were strong grounds to believe that the cartridges were greased with beef or pig's tallow, forbidden to the Hindus if it was beef and the Muslims if it was pig's tallow. The suspicions were not removed in time and the order rescinding the breaking open by mouth were not implemented in time. The challenge to one's religion was a matter of life and death to a poor but proud people. When Mangal Pande rose in revolt in Barrackpore in Bengal in March 1857 it was a signal to others to do likewise. The British aggravated the situation by their self-righteousness when they hanged Pande.

The soldiers were already in ferment. They had been forced to go to Burma and Afghanistan against the terms of their contract.[1] Crossing the sea was then regarded as a sin by the Hindus. As for the Muslims it was no pleasure to fight fellow Muslims like the Afghans and the Hindus disliked going to Afghanistan because they feared that if they were taken prisoner by the Afghans they would be compelled to become Muslims, if they were not put to the sword by their captors. The basis of trust had thus been destroyed. On May 10, 1857, the baloon went up in Meerut cantonment. The sepoys rose in revolt and went to the nominal ruler of India, the Mughal emperor Bahadurshah Zafar, in nearby Delhi asking him to assume the leadership of the revolt against the British and help them drive the foreigners out of India.

They virtually forced a reluctant and weak, irresolute and infirm Bahadurshah to become their leader. It is a tragedy of Indian history that wrong heroes are singled out for adoration. In song, TV serials and in poetry, Bahadurshah is commemorated by Indians today as a great hero and freedom fighter and even a road is named after him in New Delhi. But, in reality, he was not at all interested in leaving his poetry and take up arms. He even tried to persuade some British officers nearby to 'control' the mutinous sepoys and come to his rescue. But no Englishman was ready to be slaughtered by the angered troops. A spirited subedar of the British army, Bakht Khan, was appointed commander of the revolting sepoys and Bahadurshah tried his best to maintain law and order. But his best was not good enough and, contrary to the romantic distortion of history by modern day Indians, Bahadurshah remained until the end an unwilling emperor in revolt. But he did a few decent things like the prevention of cow slaughter on Bakr-Eid on August 1, when the British who were now fighting back hard to stage a comeback, were ardently hoping that the Hindus and Muslims would slaughter one another following the killing of cows and that would make things easier for the foreigners.

Revolts broke out in many parts of India and the rebellious sepoys and Rajas and Nawabs fought well. But they lacked good leadership, discipline, coordination and organisation and the science of warfare, all points in which the British scored over the Indians. The British also had the modern means of communication, like the telegraph, so that they could get to know what was happening in different parts of India at a few hours notice. According to a British writer, the telegraph saved the British empire.

To cut a long story short, the first war of independence did not end in success. But the British rulers learnt a few lessons. One of these was that the Hindus and Muslims must be divided if they had to rule India for a long time. They did not recruit the Eastern UP and Bihar people, who constituted the bulk of their Bengal army, for a long time and introduced the bogus martial race theory which free India had to give up. Because the British even took the Bengal army even to Singapore and Malaya (now Malaysia) the people there used to distinguished between the fair-skinned Indians, drawn from the Bengal army, and called them 'Bengalis' and usually the dark-skinned as Indians. When I was in the area, in the early seventies, these distinctions, more popular than real, were still in vogue but now they are said to be disappearing, thank God. In the post-1857 recruitment, the British not only separated the Hindus and Muslims but introduced caste and community-based regiments. This advice was tendered by a great Muslim leader, Sir Syed Ahmed Khan, but the British had learnt the lesson themselves.

The objective of separating the Hindus from the Muslims and depending on the Muslims to perpetuate their rule was not realised immediately. The Muslims were sullen at the loss of power and refused to take to modern education with the same enthusiasm as many Hindus did. They resented what they considered to be their being deprived of their overlordship of India by the British and this feeling of hostility was being reciprocated by several British officers also. But gradually the British began to realise that they must favour the Muslims if they had to rule India.

**Blunt a Pioneer**

Whatever the importance of the factors which divided the Hindus from the Muslims, the British rulers added fuel to the fire. Interestingly, some pucca Englishmen, straight from England, were more anti-Hindu and pro-Muslim than those who had spent long years and seen the reality. Men like Wilfred Scawn Blunt and William Hunter not only spoke of the important role the Muslims could play in India but also appealed to them to realise their strength, and at least one of them sowed the seeds of partition. Blunt wrote after visiting India in the early 1880s and meeting a number of Muslim leaders: "I told them that if the Mohammedans only knew their power they would not be neglected and ill-treated by the government as they were now. In England we were perpetually scared at the idea of a Mohamedan rising in India and any word uttered by a Mohamedan was paid more attention to than that of twenty Hindus. "A former editor of the British-edited *Statesman* daily of Calcutta, Ian Stephens, who was hired by the Pakistan government to write a history (of Pakistan) in 1957 said: "In Pakistan's history, neither Hunter's role nor Blunt's seems to have been given due place. The latter sympathiser got so far, while in Calcutta in 1883, as to outline, pretty clearly, the Pakistani demand of the future".[2]

What did Blunt do that Stephens proclaimed him as a visionary of Pakistan even in 1883? Blunt told a Muslim friend: "He (his Muslim friend) asked me what I thought of the ultimate fate of India and I explained my view that it should be on the same footing as Australia, that is to say that each province should have its English government, supported by English troops, but that the whole civil administration, legislation and finance should be left to native hands; that the effect of this would be to put northern

India under Mohamedan, south under a Hindu government, a solution which pleased him much".[3] Neither Blunt, nor his Muslim friend could think of the British leaving the country in any foreseeable future but remarkably Blunt's mind was pointing in the direction of Pakistan, even at that point of time, to which Ian Stephens, a committed friend and now a paid employee of Pakistan, wanted to draw attention to.

The *Times* of London was the vocal exponent of the British establishment and was often wrongly considered as well-informed by several Englishmen, in the home country as well as India. Like most blue blooded English it was opposed tooth and nail to the Indian National Congress, founded in 1885 by a retired English civil servant, Alan Octavio Hume, and dubbed it, in the face of facts, as a Hindu body which was shunned by the Muslims. In an editorial on the birth of the Congress the paper ridiculed the demand for greater Indian representation in the affairs of the country and, *inter alia*, said: "But it was by force that India was won, and it is by force that India must be governed, in whatever hands the government of the country may be vested. If we were to withdraw, it would be in favour not of the most fluent tongue (typically the British felt small in the presence of the sharp Indian minds noted for their eloquence) but the strongest arm and the sharpest sword".[4] The meaning of the strongest arm and the sharpest sword was clear, the Muslims, the fluent tongue, of course, being reserved for the Hindus.

As early as 1821, 36 years before the first armed revolt against the British, a British officer, writing in the *Asiatic Journal*, had observed: "*Divide et Impera* (divide and rule) should be the motto of the Indian administration, whether political, civil or military". Another officer by the name of John Coke had said: "...*Divide et Impera* should be the principle of the Indian government". Lord Dufferin the Viceroy, had written to his masters in London: "The Hindus with their elaborate caste distinction and habit of submission to successive conquerors...and the Mohamedans, a nation of fifty million, their iconoclastic fanaticism and their remembrance of the days when they reigned supreme from the Himalayas to Cape Comorin (now called Kanya Kumari)...were as distinct from each other as the poles as under".[5]

**"Divide et Impera"**

There is the famous observation of Monstuart Elphinstone, after whom the centre of learning, the Elphinstone college, Mumbai, is named because he was then the governor of the Bombay Presidency. He had said in a minute dated May 14, 1859: "*Divide et Impera* was the old Roman motto and it should be ours".[6] Lord Olivier, once Secretary of State for India, said in a letter to the *Times* of London in July 1926: "No one with any close acquaintance with Indian affairs will be prepared to deny that on the whole there is a predominant bias in British officials in India in favour of the Muslim community, partly on the ground of closer sympathy but more largely as a make-weight against Hindu nationalism".[7] That is as honest an admission of British bias as one could get from a person competent to speak on the subject.

These quotations of the British viewpoint, opposing Indian nationalism and laying emphasis on dividing rather than uniting the Indians, could be multiplied and some would be offered later also. The British mind, by the time things had come to simmer, before coming to boil when Gandhiji arrived on the scene in 1918, had been made up. It was dead against composite Indian nationalism and virtually accepted the two nation theory even before it crystallised among the Muslim intelligentsia. The bedrock of British rule was built upon the two communities being kept apart from each other.

Lord Minto was the Viceroy of India when the famous Aga Khan-led deputation of a number of leading Muslims waited on him in 1906 in Simla (now called Shimla) then the summer capital of the British empire in India. The year was important because by then a strong streak of separatism had emerged among the Muslims. It was in that year that the All India Muslim League was also founded in the eastern city of Dacca (now Dhaka) which ironically is the capital of Bangladesh. That country rejected altogether the pernicious two nation theory of Jinnah and fought a war of liberation in 1971 to free itself of the clutches of the Pakistanis with Indian help.

What the Viceroy's wife, Mary Minto, said of the Aga Khan deputation being received by her husband is highly interesting: "This (October 1, 1906, the day of the deputation) has been a very eventful day; as someone said to me 'an epoch in Indian history'. We are aware of the feelings of unrest that exist throughout India and the dissatisfaction that prevails amongst people of all classes and creeds. The agitators (that is how the British, in authority, used to refer to the Indian National Congress) have been most anxious to foster this feeling and naturally done their utmost to secure the cooperation of this vast community (the Muslims). The young generation (of Muslims) were wavering, inclined to throw in their lot with the advanced agitators of the Congress, and a howl went up that the loyal Mohamedans were not to be supported and that the agitators were to obtain their demands through agitation".[8]

Rightly did the British establishment rejoice over the great success because the entire episode had been orchestrated and the deputation had been stage-managed by interested Britons, among them the British principal of the college at Aligarh founded Sir Syed Ahmed Khan. Sir Syed did monumental service to the Muslim community taking western education to them but he also worked all his life to keep them away from the Indian National Congress. He believed that nothing was to be gained by "agitation" and, more importantly, he firmly held that the Muslims were a separate nation.

## Bastions of Loyalty

The Aligarh institutions were noted as strong bastions of loyalty to the British rulers and key British personages took a great deal of interest in their advancement. Syed Ahmed never wavered in his dedication to the imperial power. The first principal of the Aligarh College (the Mohamedan Anglo-Oriental College, to give its full name) was Theodore Beck who had done plenty of homework on Muslim separatism before he landed in India and did his best to preach it to a largely receptive audience. His successor was another Theodore, Theodore Morrison. Beck had died, soon after Syed Ahmed, in 1893, when the Muslim leader ended his life's journey. But the good work was being carried on by his successors. Morrison's successor at the Aligarh College, Archibald, played a crucial role in arranging for the deputation to meet the Viceroy and took a hand even in drafting tye the memorial.

Before we deal with Archibald and the Aga Khan delegation let us record here the obituary tribute paid to Beck by a member of the British steel frame, the Indian Civil Services, ICS; "An Englishman who was engaged in the consolidation of the empire has disappeared from the scene". The men who kept the empire going were fully aware of each other's contribution and Sir Arthur Strachey, the author of the tribute, and other senior civil servants did not fail to praise the work done by a college principal. We are naturally proud of people like Deenbandhu (C.F.) Andrews, Annie Besant, Mirabehn and Sister Nivedita, people from Britain who served this country, but the early pioneers like Beck, Morrison and Archibald, who consolidated the empire, while they were only non-officials, should also be remembered in a different context. It takes all kinds to make this world.

It was Archibald who was in touch with the Viceroy's private secretary, another pro-Muslim Briton, and it was he who organised the deputation, calling back the Aga Khan, who was on his way to Europe for his usual sojourn in some western countries, to lead the delegation. He played a leading part in formulating the memorandum and fixed up the time for the delegation to call on His Excellency. The Viceroy was, of course, more than pleased to receive the Muslim delegation and had kept a reply ready, the memorandum having been submitted to him in advance. Archibald remained behind the scenes all the time. Such was the zeal and dedication of the empire builders and preservers that they pushed the Muslim leaders to the fore while they themselves remained behind the "purdah".

Apart from Archibald, the architect of the deputation was Nawab Mehdi Ali Hasan, generally known as Mohsin-ul-Mulk. He was born a Shia but converted himself to the Sunni faith and rose from the rank. He belonged to Etawah in Uttar Pradesh which was, in many respects, a cradle of separatist Muslim leadership and gave birth to Sir Syed Ahmed Khan of whom Mohsin-ul-Mulk was a close associate. Etawah, incidentally, is also the home district of Mulayam Singh Yadav, who is a great "champion" of Muslims these days and has even coined the slogan 'jawan, kisan, Musalman'. Mohsin-ul-Mulk belonged to a family which had provided several administrators to the Mughals. For his loyalty to the British during the 1857 revolt, he was offered a small job which he had to accept because of poverty. But he rose to high positions by his ability and hard work. He also served the Nizam's Hyderabad state where he rose to the office of Financial and Political Secretary. After Syed Ahmed's death he looked after the Aligarh institutions and revived the *Tahzib-ul-Akhlaq* and the *Aligarh Institute Gazette* both of which had been launched by Sir Syed.[9]

At Archibald's instance, Mohsin-ul-Mulk went to Simla and as planned by the former he drew up the memorandum with Syed Husain Bilgrami, a Hyderabad senior officer, whom he had come to know while serving the Nizam. He recalled the Aga Khan and collected the signatures of some 4,000 Muslims on the memorial to be presented to Minto. The people were chosen carefully so that an all-India representation could be assured. Mohsin-ul-Mulk also collected 35 prominent Muslim leaders to form the delegation under the Aga Khan.

**A Command Performance**

The delegation's work was called a "command performance" by a great Muslim leader, Maulana Mohammed Ali, who was a nationalist and also became President of the Congress. Mohammed Ali was in the forefront of the Khilafat agitation in the company of Gandhiji but later he turned a communalist. He was noted for great mastery over the English language and appropriately termed the Muslim delegation's performance as "command performance". Maulana Abul Kalam Azad, a great figure in Indian politics, had this to say of the Simla delegation: "I am a living witness to the fact that when, as a result of the agitation of the people, certain reforms were about to be conceded in 1906, the late Nawab Mohsin-ul-Mulk (he died in 1907 before he could receive the British title of KCIE) was sent for by telegram at Simla from Bombay where he was putting up with a friend. The result of the interview was that the Aga Khan who was on his way to Europe had to return from Aden. An address was then drawn up by Syed Bilgrami of Hyderabad (Deccan) on behalf of the Muslims of India asking for separate electorates. All this manouevred from Simla".[10]

Thus was a "command performance" accomplished. Principal Archibald played a prominent part in it from behind the scenes.

The British were the *maibaps*, the patrons, who had staged the drama. They managed a Muslim delegation to wait on them, meaning of course, the Viceroy and they made a big show of being just to the Muslims. Separatism was thus cultivated by the rulers and the title-holders of the regime, the feudatories, and other beneficiaries of British rule responded, in the name of the people, none of whom had elected them to the delegation and given them authority to speak in the name of the Muslims.

Those who want to defend the Raj could say that it did not owe anything to India by way of retaining its unity and they set about the task of finding willing tools for their policy of divide and rule. The Indian National Congress continued to voice a demand for greater Indian participation in the affairs of the country. The British, not willing to make such concessions, made a few cosmetic changes from time to time, usually after the time for any change had passed. The Indian National Congress was dubbed an agitator, which it was. But you have to decide whether it was a legitimate activity of a subject people or only an activity to embarrass the regime. The British, naturally, took this latter view, obviously a narrow and selfish view, and in their search for allies they found some Muslim leaders useful as they were ready to play the cards shuffled by the rulers and play the game according to the rules framed by them.

The British, as we have noted, looked upon the different Indian communities as so many nations, particularly the Hindus and Muslims, and, in their policy of divide and rule, they decided that the Muslims could be utilised as those who would defeat the "agitators", the Indian National Congress. What was a little sacrifice of the truth in the pursuit of this "noble" task of defending the Raj? For example, the *Times* of London wrote on the second session of the Indian National Congress that "the Mohammedan community appear to hold aloof from this kind of thing, on the ground that they prefer not to hamper the government of India at a time when it is doing its best for the natives of India. "Even the British-edited *Statesman* of Calcutta, where the second session was held, contradicted the *Times*. It said: "The Mohamedan community at Madras have sent delegates and so have the Mohamedans of Bombay, the North-West provinces, Oudh (both now in Uttar Pradesh) and the chief towns and cities of Bengal".[11]

In the second session of Congress of 1886, a Muslim delegate, Nawab Reza Ali Khan Bahadur of Lucknow, proudly declared that the "association that has done us the honour of deputing us is largely composed of leading Mohamedans, Nawabs, Wasikedars, political pensioners, and the scions of the royal house of Oudh and I assure you that our association and my brother Mohamedans, generally of Oudh, will utterly repudiate and condemn any unworthy attempt to create dissensions in our ranks by unfounded statements as to our supposed want of sympathy for the present movement. Hindus or Mohamedans, Parsees or Sikhs, we are one people now, whatever our ancestors six or eight hundred years ago may have been, and our public interests indivisible and identical".[12]

The fourth session of the Indian National Congress was held at Allahabad in 1888, right in UP which was the home of separatists like Sir Syed Ahmed Khan and leaders of his persuasion that the Indian people were a conglomeration of nations and abhorred the very idea of agitation against the British Raj while they considered the Raj as a protector of the Muslims. But the North-West Provinces, of which Allahabad and Aligarh were parts, sent more delegates to the Allahabad session of the Congress than some of the other provinces put together. In fact, the number of Muslim delegates was 221 as against 965 Hindu delegates. One of the Muslim delegates, Mohammed Hidayatul Rasul, told the Congress that the Muslim community was there in strength just to counter the hostile propaganda. He attributed it to the "kindness of our brothers in the Aligarh camp."

This did not convince Sir Syed who engaged in correspondence with Badruddin Tyebji, President of the third Congress session, held in Madras in 1887, who was trying to convince Syed Ahmed that it was in the interests of the Muslims to be in the Congress and, in fact, many had done so already. Badruddin was a judge of the Bombay High Court. Sir Syed told the distinguished Muslim: "I do not understand what the words 'National Congress' mean. Is it supposed that the different castes and creeds, living in India, belong to one nation, or can become a nation and their aims and aspirations be one and the same? I think it is quite impossible, and when it is impossible there can be no such thing as a National Congress nor can it be of equal benefit to all peoples."

Sir Syed was a founder of a number of institutions besides the Mohamedan Anglo-Oriental College, which later became the Aligarh Muslim University. Apart from his opposition to any participation in an agitation, like joining the Indian National Congress, he was also against the holding of the ICS examination in India and the very concept of competitive examinations. His preference was for nominations, which he calculated, would bring the Muslims many more senior positions than their numbers in the Indian population would justify. He ridiculed the idea the Indians, particularly those from an ordinary background, sitting for these examinations and rubbing shoulders with the people of noble birth. He said: "How can noble classes of Indians tolerate petty commoners, whose origin they know very well, as their administrators". He did not mind such ordinary people coming from England and ruling over the "nobles" because the people in India did not know what class they came from. He had another objection: England's was a homogeneous population and India consisted of several nationalities.

His thinking was not structured enough to visualise India splitting up into two states, India and Pakistan. For one thing, he did not envisage the British ever leaving India. But it was clear that he visualised that the Hindus and Muslims would be leading separate existence. He thought of Muslims as people from the higher classes and the Hindus as people mainly of the low classes, particularly the Bengalis who had taken to western education in a big way and had emerged as leaders in many fields. But, in his eyes, they did not count. He even dubbed the Congress as an organisation of the Bengalis, a misconception of which Tyebji tried to disabuse him as much as he could.

As we have noted, Sir Syed was greatly influenced by the British principals of the MAO college. With the help of the first English principal of the college, Theodore Beck, he had formed in 1888 the United India Patriotic Association, one of the several institutions founded by him. A number of Muslim nawabs and Hindu Rajas as well as some European officers, some retired and some serving, became its members. This body was to be the counterforce to the Indian National Congress, which he called the "so-called National Congress". One of the aims of the association was to educate "good" Englishmen, in India as well as England, about the wrong propaganda of the Indian National Congress that "all the nations of India" agreed with its objectives.

**More From Others**

Although Aligarh has made a significant contribution to the education of the Muslim community, and, indeed, it was founded with that aim in view, the fact is that Muslim education was making progress generally outside it. In the early years, the other universities, which carried no labels and which were open to all, made substantial contribution. During the years 1898-1902, the total number of Muslim graduates in India was 1,184 of which those who had come out of the Allahabad University as always a cradle of education in northern India, was as much as 410, Calcutta's not far behind at 398, Punjab's 255 and Aligarh's only 220. Between 1882 and 1887, the years in which there was a fierce campaign for the employment of Muslims in the government, Aligarh had produced no more than ten graduates.

Then, as now, the campaign was that the Muslims were a backward community and needed special attention by the government particularly. There is no doubt that the Muslims as a community are backward and in a poor country they are among the more poor. But there is also a myth of backwardness which is assiduously cultivated and there is no dearth of politically motivated campaign to cater to the exclusive interests of the community, like more Muslim or Muslim-oriented universities, while there is no restriction for any community in educational institutions from the primary to the higher educational levels.

Although a number of Muslims attended the annual session of the Congress, Sir Syed Ahmed and others of his ilk carried on a campaign against Muslim participation in "agitational" activities and coercing the people into loyalty to the Raj. There was at the same time a demand for special protection to the community and the British were too pleased to reward the loyal elements and the community as a whole. Before the stage-managed Aga Khan delegation, there were several delegations which waited on the Viceroy on behalf of the Muslims of Karachi, Calcutta and elsewhere. They were also led by prominent leaders of the community and the burden of the song was that the Muslims were different but backward and needed special care and protection. Needless to say that the Viceroy responded with more than the required enthusiasm on such occasions and the bond between the prodigal son and the *maibap* government was becoming firm and strong.

A delegation of the Central Mohamedan Association waited on the Viceroy, Lord Dufferin, at Karachi in November 1887. Dufferin told them that "owing to various circumstances and to historic forces over which they themselves had no control, the Mohamedan community in many parts of India hardly finds itself in that satisfactory position to which it has a right to aspire". In March next year a delegation of the same association called on the same Viceroy on the pretext of giving him a farewell address in which Ameer Ali[13] sought British protection for the Muslims of India. Dufferin's reply could not be more satisfactory to the Muslims: "The Mohamedans of India may rest assured that the government will view with the utmost sympathy and approval their endeavours to remove the peculiar impediments which hamper their efforts."

Many of the sentiments could be regarded as unexceptionable but the remarkable thing was that the British bigwigs were quite happy with the expression of loyalty and the bonds were further strengthened as the process continued. Dufferin's successor, Lord Lansdowne, received a deputation of 120 leading Muslims. If Ameer Ali had led a team to Dufferin for a farewell call this one was meant to welcome the new Laat Sahib. This helped the leaders to continue the relationship with the British government at the level where it mattered. The address to Lansdowne was read by the president of the association, Prince Farokh Shah, and dealt with the difficulties which the Muslims encountered in facing the competition of other Indians. That these worthies were not among the "agitators" facilitated the British rulers in accepting them as the true representatives of the Muslims. Lansdowne might have been new to the job but he knew that "you find yourself less strongly represented than you might have wished in the public service of the country."

The patronage was thus being extended but some peculiar provisions made in the Councils Act of 1892 also provided for special representation for the landed and commercial interests which actually reduced the representation of the Muslims. This was sought to be rectified by separate electorates for the Muslims which not only gave them a separate existence from the other Indians but also a higher representation than justified by their numbers in India. The stage was thus set for the Simla delegation to Lord Minto in 1906. Largely speaking the Muslims had adequate representation in government jobs. For example, in the North-West Provinces and Oudh, the present UP, they held 94 positions of Deputy Collectors to 116 held by the Hindus, and had eight out of 22 civil judges. Only in Bengal, where the Muslims were lagging behind in education, were they having less than adequate representation. The key then as now, was in more education but the leaders of the Community had other ideas.

There was no doubt that, despite the keenness with which many educated Muslims were actively participating in the affairs of the Congress, more and more of the landed gentry and the key figures among the intellectuals were opting for loyalty to the Raj. In these circumstances was created the All India Muslim League in 1906 at Dacca, the year in which the Aga Khan delegation was calling on the Viceroy in Simla. In between came the partition of Bengal by Curzon. The province, which was one of the three presidencies of India, the other two being Bombay and Madras, was one which the British knew more than any other, almost like the palm of their hand. Curzon did the foul action almost towards the end of his regime. He was full of hatred for the Indian intelligentsia. He tried to instigate the Muslims of Bengal as he launched his unwise act which had to be undone by his successor after it had ignited the fires and helped the nationalist cause.

**Favoured Community**

The partition also unleashed wanton forces of destruction and lawlessness in the eastern part of Bengal where many illiterate people came to believe that they had got a license to plunder and molest the Hindus. Not only their property was destroyed but also the womenfolk were subjected to indignities like abduction and forcible conversion. In his *Indian and Home Memories* Sir Henry Cotton, a Bengal civilian who served the province for many years and was later a member of the British Parliament, had this to say of the Bengal partition: "There was never any cause for quarrel between the Hindoos and Mohamedans as such... For the first time in history a religious feud was established between them by the partition of the province. For the first time the principle was enunciated in official circles: Divide and Rule! The Mohamedans were favoured in every way possible."[14]

The delegation that waited on the Viceroy at Simla in October 1906 was an important landmark in the history of Hindu-Muslim relations and a powerful link in the separatism which was to finally culminate in the partition of the country. The seeds of separatism left a perpetual wedge in the relations between the Hindus and Muslims which continued to haunt the ties between them even after the partition. Pakistan had no such problem, having evicted the entire Hindu community from its midst, in the western part, but it had other problems, apart from the separation of Bangladesh. We shall speak about both in later chapters.

The way of the Simla delegation was paved in the years which preceded it. There were some distinguished Muslims in this period, one of whom, Sir Syed Ahmed Khan, has been referred to earlier in one context or another. Among the others was Ameer Ali who was also knighted by the British, like Syed Ahmed, and ultimately made a Privy Councillor when he had settled down in England after his retirement from India in 1904. A grandson of a military officer of the plunderer of Delhi, the Persian Monarch Nadirshah, Ameer Ali was born in Chinsurah in Bengal. His grandfather had run away from Delhi when the Marathas invaded the city and had served the Nawab of Oudh who was finally dethroned by the British before the 1857 Revolt. Ameer Ali was among the first Indian Muslims to be called to the Bar in England where he had gone to study on a government scholarship. While Sir Syed laid great stress on the Muslims taking to modern education, Sir Ameer Ali stressed jobs for Muslims more and both said they must steer clear of the agitator Congress.

Ameer Ali founded the Central National Mohamedan Association of which he remained secretary for 25 years. He was a judge of the Calcutta High Court for many years and also a member of the Bengal Legislative Council and the Imperial Council in the years before the introduction of separate electorates under a law of 1909 after the Aga Khan delegation had asked for it in 1906 and Lord Minto had promised to introduce. Ameer Ali not only believed in the backwardness theory but was also a founder-president of the London branch of the Muslim League while he lived in Britain.[15]

Sir Sultan Mohammad Shah, the Aga Khan, who led the Muslim delegation to Minto, claimed that the delegation represented the "Mohamedan subjects of His Majesty the King Emperor". It also claimed in the memorandum that the delegation consisted of "nobles, jagirdars, taluqdars, lawyers, zamindars and merchants" besides others. They recognised that the Muslims of India numbered 62 million or between one-fifth and one-fourth of the total population of India. The memorial claimed that the "uncivilised" portions of the Indian population should be excluded and it argued that if the Hindus who are otherwise enumerated as such but are not "properly speaking Hindus at all" are excluded the proportion of the Muslims to the Hindus would be much larger. The Muslim leaders of the delegation and people like Maulana Mohamad Ali, an important figure of the Khilafat movement of the twenties, always looked upon the so-called untouchables as legitimate prey for Muslim aggrandisement. The delegation also wanted the tribals to be excluded because they were "uncivilised".

The memorandum then went on to stress the largeness of the Muslim population in India in absolute terms and said it was larger than the population of any first class European power except Russia. It then claimed that the position accorded to the Muslims should be commensurate with not only their numerical strength but also with their political importance. The delegation thus emphasised that the other factors like their contribution to the defence of India and the British Empire should be recognised as well as their political importance. Above all, the memorandum said that the position the Muslims occupied in India, as its rulers, of course, a little more than a hundred years ago, should be taken into account. The memorandum stressed that the traditions of that had not "faded from the minds of the Muslims".

Warning the rulers that representatives institutions be introduced with care and caution because the Hindus would not vote for anyone except the Hindu community, the memorial demanded that the Muslims must have a due proportion of government jobs, competitive element in recruitment must be eliminated, there should be separate representation for each community in the municipalities and a separate electoral college for the Muslims in elections to the legislative councils. (The provincial assemblies were then known as councils and the Imperial assembly known as the Imperial council.)

In his reply, the Viceroy paid handsome tribute to the glorious past of the Muslims and the services rendered by Sir Syed and his Aligarh movement and assured the delegation: "The Mohamedan community may rest assured that their rights and interests as a community will be safeguarded in any administrative reorganisation with which I am concerned". He did not indicate, as could be easily understood, what the nature of the government's dispensation would be, but said categorically that any arrangement which disregarded the beliefs and traditions of the communities composing the population of this "continent" was doomed to failure.[16]

**His Highness**

The Aga Khan was given the title of His Highness, without having any state, for his loyalty to the British. He was to say later in his memoirs in 1954, that "in 1906 we boldly asked the Viceroy to look facts in the face, we asked that the Muslims of India should not be regarded as a mere minority; but as a nation whose rights had to be guaranteed by statute."[17]

That great champion of Muslim interests, the second principal of the MAO college, Theodore Morrison, said of the claims made by the Aga Khan delegation that "the grounds on which the Muslims based their claim for weightage was that they did, in fact, command an amount of influence which was greatly in excess of their ratio to population—they owned much of the landed property in India, they still formed a large element in the public service and Muslim soldiers constituted a large proportion of the Indian army". These assertions were in total contradiction of facts, the backwardness theory, claims of poor representation of the Muslims in services, and Muslims owning a part of the landed property. Even the claim that Muslim soldiers constituted a large proportion of the Indian army was not true. Facts, however, did not bother either the British government or the partisan supporters of the Muslims among the non-governmental personalities like Morrison.

The British were thus directly encouraging separatism and helping its consolidation. The separateness was being crystallised through the separate electorates which continued until the very end of British rule which culminated in the creation of a separate Muslim nation, Pakistan. The concept that the Muslims constituted a separate nation, different from the rest of India, was being boosted with open encouragement by the British rulers. The seeds were sown by Sir Syed and the delegation which the Aga Khan led to Minto and the culmination achieved through the efforts of Sir Mohammad Iqbal,[18] Chaudhury Rehmat Ali and finally Mohammad Ali Jinnah, who gave shape and substance to the Pakistan concept. Blunt and the three principals of the Aligarh college had assisted in the birth of the separate nation at the conception stage.

In the imperial council the Muslims were given, by the Indian Councils Act, 1909, the first piece of legislation which gave effect to the demand for separate electorates, 26.6 per cent reserved seats as against their population of 22.9, and in Madras council 10 per cent of the seats against their population of six per cent, in U.P. (North-West and Oudh) 19 per cent against 14 per cent in the population.[19]

Separate electorates were combined with weightage which was not only granted by the British but insisted upon by the Muslim leaders. Robinson tells us that through the efforts of the Aga Khan and Ameer Ali in London, and the Muslim League and its leaders in India, the Muslim proportion was always on the rise "...between the tentative proposals of 1907 and 1908 and the passing of the Indian Councils Act (by the British Parliament) in 1909, the Muslim League won four additional seats in the Imperial council and in the provincial councils four additional seats in Bengal, four in Bombay and three in East Bengal and Assam."[20]

While the Congress leaders and Gandhiji put their faith in the freedom struggle and braved lathis, bullets and jail, the Muslim leaders like Jinnah and his predecessors keenly followed the British moves and sought to ensure for their community much greater representation than they would otherwise be entitled to. It was not for nothing that they had shunned the path of "agitation" as advocated by Sir Syed and followed right upto Pakistan by Jinnah and the others.

**A Mindset**

The British role of "divide and rule" might not have been well thought out and conceptualised but their minds were set. They looked upon the Muslim community as a separate nation which had to be pampered by separate electorates, weightage, nominations and the like. They were following the dictates of their minds, in England and in India, and this was deeply embedded in their thinking. S.A. Wolpert concluded that "British policy exacerbated Indian disharmony", but in defence of the British rulers he said that "it did so more out of ignorance (or innocence) than malice."[21]

Viceroy Minto's private secretary, Dunlop Smith's role in the success of the Aga Khan delegation to the Viceroy has been referred to. He and the Aligarh principal, Archibald, acted in concert and guided the delegation at all stages. Not only he regarded the Muslims as "manly" but even preferred a fairly ordinary person like Mohsin-ul-Mulk, in intellectual terms, to a giant like Gopal Krishna Gokhale.[22]

This bias was to manifest itself all through the remaining 41 years of British rule in India which were crucial to Indian independence. There were a few periods when the British were angry with the Muslims, as when they joined hands with the national leaders as Gandhiji took up the cause of the Khilafat agitation, or when Jinnah was still playing the nationalist role. He was then a thorn in their side but later as he turned a communalist and said there was a Hindu nation in India and a Muslim nation they loved him.

In Robinson's words "by 1909, a Muslim identity was finally established in Indian politics. The first stage in the process had been the creation of a Muslim political organisation... The result was the foundation of the All-India Muslim League. The second stage was the winning of a separate Muslim electorate in which the Muslim League persuaded the government to give Muslims representation which in most (provincial) councils took into account not only their proportion in the population but also their alleged political importance. But the key element seems to have been the assumptions that the British made about Indian society and Indian Muslims. The former was regarded as a collection of interests and groups. The latter formed one of these groups and were regarded, quite wrongly as separate, distinct and monolithic. The result was that the Muslims were also seen to be an important group and above all dangerous which had to be kept satisfied."[20]

This is strong condemnation of British policy towards the Muslims by a British author. The separate electorates were demanded, on prompting by some Britishers, by a group of Muslim leaders who soon came together to form the Muslim League. This indicates a cosy relationship between the British and the separatist leaders. One accepted their claim to represent Muslim opinion, the other asked for a separate existence for themselves.

## NOTES

1. This unconstitutional and illegal practice continues to this day as the Indian army has to go abroad as part of the UN peace keeping operations. There is, however, nothing in the Constitution nor in any law which could compel the jawans or officers to go abroad.
2. *Pakistan: Old Country New Nation*, Pelican Books, quoted by M. A. Karandikar in *Islam in India's Transition to Modernity*, Orient Longmans, Bombay.
3. See Karandikar, *Ibid.*
4. Quoted by Ram Gopal in *Indian Muslims A Political History*, Asia Publishing House, Bombay.
5. See Karandikar, *Ibid.*
6. Quoted by R. P. Dutt, *India Today*, cited by Ram Gopal, *Ibid.*
7. Ram Gopal, *Ibid.*
8. *Ibid.*
9. *Separatism among Indian Muslims*, Francis Robinson, Vikas, Delhi.
10. Ram Gopal, *Ibid.*
11. Quoted by Ram Gopal, *Ibid.*
12. These references are in Ram Gopal, *Ibid.*
13. See details about Ameer Ali later in this chapter.

14. Ram Gopal, *Ibid.*
15. See Robinson, *Ibid.*
16. For the text of the memorial see Ram Gopal, *Ibid.*
17. Quoted by Karandikar, *Ibid.*
18. See later chapters.
19. See Robinson, *Ibid.*
20. Robinson, *Ibid.*
21. Quoted by Robinson, *Ibid.*
22. Robinson, *Ibid.*
23. *Ibid.*

Chapter 3

# OPTING OUT OF STRUGGLE

The Muslim has always been torn between Islam and the land of his birth and that of his forefathers. He may be no less patriotic than any other Indian but with this divided loyalty he has often difficulty in giving his best to his country. Although 90 per cent of the Indian Muslims are converts from Hinduism (less if you include the Pakistanis), Islam has had a powerful influence on them and has affected their attitude to the nation in general.

Until the rule of Aurangzeb ended, and with it the dream of a central Muslim authority over the whole of India, this country was Darul Islam, the land of Islam. Once the decline began the question arose whether India was really Darul Islam or Darul Harb, a country which the Muslims had to bring under the yoke of the "only pure and the final religion" on earth, as the fanatics believed. To achieve this goal the Wahabi movement arose in many parts of India in the eighteenth century. It was founded by Shah Waliullah Dehlavi who blamed the converts from Hinduism for all the ills that the Muslims were heir to. He said the moral standards among the Muslims had declined owing to their contacts with the Hindus and with the converts in their midst. His complaint, in fact, was that the "Muslims had become Indians and had forgotten their links with the Muslim world."[1]

He was the first to raise the cry of Islam in Danger. This cry was to reverberate until Pakistan was created and even afterwards. He did not want the Muslims to consider themselves part of the general Indian society. To begin with, the Wahabi movement was against the Sikhs who, under Maharaja Ranjit Singh, had captured the whole of Punjab (on both sides of the present international border) and some adjoining regions, including Afghanistan at one time. Under Waliullah, and more so under his son, Shah Abdul Aziz, a jehad was also launched against the Sikhs. Waliullah, who was completely Pan-Islamic in his approach, even invited the Afghan adventurer, Abdally, to invade India so that the country could once again become Darul Islam. Abdally did invade India, with the help of Najib-ud-Daulla, the Rohilla ruler from Uttar Pradesh, and defeated the Maratha army in the third battle of Panipat in 1761. But, like his predecessor, the Persian plunderer Nadir Shah, Abdally also came, conquered, looted and left.

Waliullah's followers tried to defeat the Sikhs and attacked them from the North West Frontier Province side, after reaching there from Sind, with a Mujahid force, recruited from most of north India, but were badly beaten in the battle of Balakot in 1831. Now the movement acquired anti-British overtones and some leaders also gave it an economic edge because the Muslim weavers in the eastern sector, all converts from Hinduism, had suffered owing to the exploitative policy of the British rulers. Some even encouraged the Muslim landless cultivators to grab the lands of Muslim as well as Hindu landlords. But the emphasis on eschewing Hindu customs, like chewing of pan, consulting astrologers, and observing Hindu marriage customs which had penetrated Muslim society continued. The leaders called upon their followers not to celebrate Hindu festivals or join in the celebration.

As long as the movement was aimed at the Sikhs the British rulers closed their eyes to it and even encouraged participation. British planters would grant leave to their Muslim employees to join the jehad and the government forced the local bankers to release the funds deposited with them by the leaders and followers of the movement. Even a Muslim leader, Sir Syed Ahmed, a staunch advocate of staying away from the nationalist struggle and a votary of Muslim separatism, asked the British government whether it had not encouraged the Wahabis. He pointed out that the British had connived at the collection of arms by the Wahabis when they were planning a jehad against the Sikh ruler. Syed Ahmed also gave instances of the British administration giving direct help to the Wahabis. This only recalls the recent revelations that a number of prominent tea companies in Assam and even many ethnic Assamese, including government leaders, were giving aid and comfort to the ULFA (United Liberation Front of Assam) ultras to save their skin. As long as the trouble makers are aiming at someone else we can look the other way.

**Urge for Hegemony**

The British now turned on the Wahabis ruthlessly and hanged some of them and sent away others to the newly emerging penal settlement of the Andamans ('Kala pani' as it was popularly known) for a term of life imprisonment. Some writers are inclined to see in these instances of defiance of British authority the first signs of Muslim participation in the freedom struggle. A freedom movement is, however, not a one-time phenomenon, not a blue moon syndrome and it is a mistake to term the Wahabi resistors as such. They were, no doubt, anti-British but their motivation was different. It was to establish Darul Islam in India and restore Muslim hegemony. For record, we have to note that Sher Ali, a Wahabi, assassinated Viceroy Lord Mayo in the Andamans in 1872.

These names are included in Professor Santimoy Roy's booklet, published by none other than the Communist Party of India's People's Publishing House. The fact is that the undivided CPI had played a prominent role in popularising Jinnah's demand for a separate Pakistan state, as part of the reds' campaign to mobilise the Indian people to support the war effort because the (late) Soviet Union had entered the second world war on the side of the British and the Americans.

It is, therefore, natural for the Communists to help the professor to publish his monograph. They are no longer talking of the theory of separate nationalities, on the basis of which they justified the partition of the country, but they are conscious of the need of the Muslim vote being preserved for the leftists. In the years leading to partition, the Communists talked of separate nationalities and Jinnah talked of a Muslim nation different from a Hindu nation. From nationality to nation was a small step.

It is very good to recall the glorious deeds of sacrifice when the nation in whose cause the sacrifices were made has been divided for 50 years and almost everyone is reconciled to it and even Pakistan has been divided into two nations (a repudiation of the reds' pet theory or shall we say a reaffirmation of the two-nation theory, albeit in a different context). But we do not have to be reminded that the Muslims had a share in the freedom struggle, both in the mass movement which was led by Gandhiji, and in the revolutionary struggle waged by some young men and women. The community was, however, led by people who condemned the struggle and asked the Muslims to stay away from it and, in fact, they followed the advice.

How the Muslim leaders got together a powerful delegation to call on the Viceroy in Simla in 1906, under the "dynamic" leadership of the Aga Khan, and how it laid the foundation of separate electorates from 1909 onwards has been dealt with in an earlier chapter. The delegation made an attempt to tell the British rulers that the Muslims were different and had their own platform. Many of the leaders were title holders and the Aga Khan himself was a 'Sir'. So was Syed Ahmed who always insisted that the Muslims must stay away from the nationalist struggle. Even at the time of the advent of freedom, and thereafter in Pakistan, many of the prominent leaders of the Muslim League were title holders and landlords.

There were, indeed, high minded Muslims who defied the advice of people like Syed Ahmed and refused to be led by the landed gentry and the title holders. The third session of the Indian National Congress was presided over by a distinguished Muslim from western India, Justice Badruddin Tybeji. Another eminent Indian, drawn from one of the smallest Indian minority of the Parsis, Dadabhai Naoroji, was the president of the second session of Congress. Maulana Abul Kalam Azad, who was in the throes of the struggle from his young days, was president of the Congress thrice. He was, in fact, at the helm of affairs in the crucial days of 1945 and 1946.

**Shining Example of Rafi Sahib**

Spirited young men like Rafi Ahmed Kidwai gave up a life of ease and comfort, which he really loved, to serve the nation in whose cause he embraced poverty so that he could go to jail at the Mahatma's call. He eventually became a key minister in his native

Uttar Pradesh and later rose to be one of the outstanding ministers of free India in the first years of independence until his life was cut short. He nationalised the airlines (now being denationalised under a regime of which the Communists are part) introduced the all-up airmail service and gave the hardworking postman his weekly Sunday off. He ended the food ration regime.

There was young Ashfaqullah from Uttar Pradesh who joined the revolutionary movement and was hanged along with his colleagues in the Kakori case. A number of young men also took part in the mass struggle, the Salt Satyagraha of 1930 and the Quit India movement of 1942. Unfortunately, we have it on the authority of Rafiq Zakaria, a noted Muslim writer and former Congress Minister in Maharashtra, that he was hounded out by his co-religionists for his participation in the Quit India movement. In the armed struggle waged by Netaji Subhas Chandra Bose from outside the country, under his INA (Indian National Army) banner, there were Hindus, Muslims and Sikhs among the soldiers of freedom. Shah Nawaz Khan was among the three top officers of the INA chosen for court martial proceedings by the British in the Red Fort in Delhi. Unwisely, the British chose as the accused three top officers, a Hindu, a Muslim and a Sikh, and told the world that Netaji's army had all the communities and it was fully representative.

**Red Fort a Symbol**

One of his significant achievements was his ability to blend people of different religions into one single whole and do away with the distinctions of caste, creed and community. He gave the slogan, 'Jai Hind' to the nation, which Nehru later popularised without acknowledgement, and it was he who introduced the concept of the Red Fort as a symbol of Indian aspirations and of India's freedom. Before he brought in the Red Fort in the songs of the marching columns and in slogans, there was no mention of it in any Congress resolution or statement and no Congress leader or delegate referred to the place. Today no one acknowledges the debt to Netaji in such vital matters while a needless controversy has been allowed to simmer over his death. It has never occurred to the people who seem to have a stake in keeping the controversy alive nor to the media that a fiery leader like him would have surfaced long ago whether he was in the Soviet Union or anywhere else much before he was too old to be of any service to the nation.

I was one of the few to visit (in 1969) the Renkoji temple outside Tokyo in Japan where his ashes are kept. The Japanese priest of the Buddhist temple made piteous pleas to me to tell the Indian government to allow his ashes to rest in India where they belonged and should be kept in great honour. All that the Congress leaders have done is to exploit his name and memory and the Leftists of Bengal have done a complete *volte face*. From calling him a quisling (anyone who fought against their beloved Soviet Union and supported the Axis powers was a quisling to the Communists) and an agent of Japan they joined the big crowds of Netaji supporters and even acknowledged the Forward Bloc, founded by him, as an important Leftist party to be always kept along with them in the Left Front.

**Distortion of History**

Distortion of history goes on all the time. Only the real scholar tries to find out the truth. Nehru not only plagiarised the "Jai Hind" slogan but donned the black robes of a (briefless) barrister, perhaps for the first time in many years of non-practice, when the three INA officers, Sehgal, Dhillon and Shah Nawaz Khan, were court-martialled by the British in the Red Fort. Nehru had done a lot in popularising the INA's cause but he had no real role in the INA trial as a lawyer. It was Bhulabhai Desai who spear-headed the legal brains and who deftly conducted the proceedings of the trial but whenever the event is recalled the media always refer to Nehru donning the robes of a lawyer.

Surprisingly, Jinnah who was a great lawyer, had nothing to do with the INA trial in which the nation's best lawyers, including Bhulabhai and Tej Bahadur Sapru, were involved. He and the other Muslim League leaders allowed the Congress to exploit the event because they knew they could do little about it and, in any case, the Muslims were not much affected by it. Many Muslim soldiers and officers had shed their blood and even given their life in the cause of Indian freedom while serving the INA, and Jinnah could have brought it out by associating his party with the INA trials. If he was really interested in upholding the rights of the Muslims in India here was an opportunity *par excellence*. According to Santimoy Roy's calculations 40 Muslims had died fighting for the INA against the British and their allies. Contrary to the image sought to be projected by some pseudo-intellectuals of Jinnah as a great nationalist leader, the man was only concerned with glory for himself, not for the country nor for glorifying those who gave their lives for it.

Jinnah, in fact, was opposed to all mass action which he abhorred and when the Congress, under Gandhiji, became a mass organisation he walked out of it. He never forgave Gandhiji for transforming the Congress from a petitioning body to a fighting mass organisation. Gandhiji, on the other hand, blended idealism with pragmatism. When he realised that the Muslims were apathetic to the freedom struggle despite their patriotism, he enlisted their sympathy for the non-cooperation movement, launched by him on behalf of the Congress, by embracing the cause of the Khilafat movement which was gripping the Muslim mind.

The Khilafat agitation thus brought a galaxy of high minded Muslim leaders into the vortex of the mainstream Indian political movement and Gandhi deserved all credit for it. He saw in this decision a way to forge Hindu-Muslim unity, which was always dear to his heart, and transform the Muslim awakening into a nationalist urge and direct the energies of the Muslim masses into the channels of the freedom movement. He was successful to a great degree.

**Risk of Pan-Islamism**

But there are those who hold the view that by adopting a Pan-Islamic movement as his and India's own, he was running great risks of making the Muslims more communal. He also indirectly acknowledged the fact that all Muslims, irrespective of national boundaries and transcending the loyalties imposed by one's allegiance to India, were one. While one would not like to inject conflict where there was none, one has to be realistic and recognise that the interests of a nation were paramount and they sometimes could be in conflict with the interests of another nation whatever its composition. That question is more relevant today when

Pakistan, avowedly an Islamic nation, is constantly at loggerheads with India and Indian Muslims, numbering about 110 million, have to be loyal to India.

What was the Khilafat agitation about? The religious leaders of Islam in India were greatly agitated by the ill-treatment of Turkey by the British government in London during the first world war and immediately afterwards. The unjust post-war scenario was being written by British and French leaders who had won the war with considerable Indian blood. Turkey is now firmly aligned to the anti-communist west, particularly the United States for whom it is like a colony, but it was on the wrong side in the first war, that is, it was on the side of the Germans who were challenging the might of the British and the French. It was truly speaking a colonial war and the victorious British and French parcelled out African and West Asian areas among them and their friends. They made use of the instrumentality of the League of Nations for a peace settlement to suit their national interests.

The Turks were bound to suffer in the process. Turkey had under its control the west Asian regions of Saudi Arabia, Syria and others. After the death of Aurangzeb, Indian Muslims would take the name of the Turkish Sultan in their Friday prayers. It was natural for them to resent the ill-treatment of Turkey by the British and the French after the first world war and see the biggest Muslim power being reduced to a skeleton of its previous self. They claimed that Lloyd George, the British Prime Minister, had promised during the war and the crucial post-war years that Turkey would not be broken up. Since the British and their French collaborators were looking at the problem from their respective colonial point of view they could not appreciate the sentiments of the Indian Muslims who were looking for a strong Muslim power to which they could swear allegiance. If the Arab nations had been given their independence straightaway Mecca and Medina would have come under the sway of Saudi Arabia and this could have satisfied the Indian Muslims. Neither was Turkey able to hold on to its possessions nor a substitute Muslim power was visible to replace it.

The Muslim masses, under the sway of the Ulema, threw themselves heart and soul in the Khilafat agitation for nearly a year. The religious leaders were, in any case, in the forefront and thus grew up an anti-British freedom movement of the entire Indian people, Hindus and Muslims. Looking at the spontaneous Hindu support for their demands, some of the Muslim leaders were so moved that they offered to voluntarily abandon cow slaughter. Maulana Abdul Bari and others were prominent in this move. Sentiments often clashed when some Muslims made a demonstration of cow slaughter and some Hindus objected to it because the cow was holy to them while to the Muslims it was only good meat. There would be riots sometimes and (human) heads would roll over cows. Now it was different and even though Gandhiji said the offer looked like a price for Hindu support the Ulema insisted on it.

Maulana Bari said that the Mahatma saying so was all right for him. "That does credit to him and to our Hindu brethren. But the Muslim honour would be at stake if they forget the cooperation of the Hindus... As a Maulvi I say that in voluntarily stopping cow slaughter we shall not offend against the canons of our religion. Nothing has so helped Hindu-Muslim unity as the Hindu cooperation with us on the question of Khilafat".[3]

For a few months there was complete identity of views. Gandhiji was the common leader of the non-cooperation movement and the Khilafat agitation. Prominent Hindu leaders like Swami Shraddhanand and the Shankaracharya of Sharadapeeth spoke from the platform of big mosques by invitation. Not only the Congress but the entire country came under the Gandhian spell, as never before and never since, because after the failure of the Khilafat movement the Muslims went their own way.

The Khilafat agitation is viewed by many observers as a throwback and an atavistic and reactionary movement which did not involve the real interests, specially the economic interests of the poor Muslims, of the poor in general. The final blow came in the form of the abolition of the caliphate (Khilafat) by the Turks themselves under the leadership of the revolutionary Kamal Ataturk in 1924. Gandhiji had also called off the non-cooperation movement in February 1922 after the Chauri Chaura (not Chaura Chauri, and not in 1919 as stated by an "eminent" journalist in the *Indian Express*) incident in which more than a score of policemen were massacred in this small town of Gorakhpur, UP. He was himself arrested and tried by the British in the same year. He was sentenced to six years in jail but released earlier on health grounds. As already stated, the Turks had themselves gone through a revolution and the Khilafat itself was abolished by the revolutionary leader. The British had not yielded on the question of Turkey's fate either.

Incidentally, the revolution led by Kamal Ataturk has survived despite some setbacks. Turkey was proclaimed a republic with the abolition of the sultanate and a modern and forward-looking society was founded by him which has withstood the vicissitudes through which the nation has passed. Although an Islamic party has also emerged, Turkey remains dedicated to democracy. On the other hand we have the example of Pakistan where the elite is all westernised but subscribes to a fundamentalist outlook and pretends to be Islamic, with women being barred from sports and male broadcasters having to keep a distance from their women colleagues, covering of the head by women employees, in other words suppression of women which is the most evident form of Islamisation as in Afghanistan under the Pakistan-aided Talibans. The elite, of course, leads a high life on the western pattern. Practise modernity but preach orthodoxy is their watchword. The women of Turkey were liberated in 1924 and have remained so even to this day. The women of Pakistan have been striving to break the shackles imposed on them by the menfolk in the name of Islam. Despite claims made on its behalf by writers in India, Islam, as understood by the Pakistanis and many even in India, means the veil, triple talak, lack of alimony on divorce, freedom for the male to marry four wives and, in Pakistan, many loopholes for the rapists. It is, no doubt, a travesty but there it is.

**Grave Consequences**

The failure of the Khilafat movement in India had grave consequences. Some Muslims had taken up the concept of an Islamic upsurge so seriously that many thousands tried to migrate to Afghanistan, an Islamic country they thought would welcome them. They suffered in the process because you cannot enter another country simply because you are a Muslim. The euphoria of Hindu-Muslim unity evaporated and Gandhiji's dream lay shattered. The Moplas of Kerala, Muslims by faith and fanatical in their belief, rose in revolt, first against the British, but it soon developed into a violently anti-Hindu movement. There was much forcible conversion and abduction of Hindu women whom some of the Moplas married after forcible conversion.

The Congress failed to condemn it in strong terms as even radical Muslim leaders like Maulana Hasrat Mohani justified the conversions on the specious plea that the Hindus had the choice of death or conversion and hence the Moplas could not be blamed. Mohani was such a radical that he had brought a resolution on complete independence at the Congress session in 1921 at Ahmedabad and but for Gandhiji's strong plea that this was a matter for gradual evolution it would have even been carried. It took the Congress eight years more to formally adopt Purna Swaraj, or complete independence, as the goal of the nation. Radicalism on the one hand, where it costs nothing, goes hand in hand with communalism where it is a matter of life and death for the Hindus. But the tradition survives because the leader of the mass conversion of the Hindus at Meenakshipuram in Tamil Nadu in the early eighties was also a Muslim Congressman.

Even great leaders like Maulana Muhammad Ali, who was a fiery speaker, wrote well and had much sacrificing spirit but was somewhat wayward in his behaviour, turned communal. He was a great admirer of Gandhiji and, along with his brother Shaukat Ali, did a great deal for the cause of freedom for a couple of years. But how communal one can grow is illustrated by what Mohammad Ali said at Aligarh in 1924, and repeated at Ajmer (then spelt the British way 'Ajmere'): "However pure Mr Gandhi's character may be, he must appear to me from the point of view of religion to be inferior to any Mussalman, even though he be without character.

This was reported by a leading paper, *The Times of India*,[5] then well known as the authentic voice of His Majesty's government, being completely under British ownership and thumb, and the authenticity of such a communal statement could hardly be doubted. Also, the paper, because of its British ownership, like its eastern India counterpart, the *Statesman*, which was also British-owned, refused to call Gandhiji as Mahatma Gandhi. This was until August 15, 1947 when both suddenly changed their front. The Muhammad Ali quotation, therefore, seeks only of "Mr Gandhi".

This was in accord with Jinnah's policy of calling Gandhiji "Mr Gandhi". Even in his left-handed tribute to Gandhi on his assassination, the Pakistani leader used this term, although by them the two British owned papers (one had changed its ownership) had begun calling the Mahatma as such. Jinnah had hated Gandhi for the metamorphosis he had carried out in the Congress and at the time of the Khilafat agitation had no sympathy with mass movements or with the Ulema. If the movement had come when Jinnah himself had turned Islamic in his approach he could have possibly supported Khilafat or any Islamic agitation. In later life, he had posed as a great champion of Islam. But he could not bring himself to spin, wear khadi, the "livery of freedom" as Nehru called it, or go to jail like any Congressman. People who are keen to find alibis for Jinnah say he left the Congress because Gandhiji talked in terms of "Ramrajya" but the real reasons were what we have stated here, his dislike of mass action being the most important. It is another matter that he authorised the Muslim League's direct action in 1946 which killed 5,000 people in Calcutta and set off a chain of communal clashes. After all, Westernised Muslim has also to change if he was to become the leader of the Indian Muslims and achieve his goal of Pakistan.

As stated, the failure of the Khilafat movement had made many Muslim leaders seek refuge in communalism. People like Sir Abdur Rahim, President of the Muslim League in 1925, proudly declared that no Muslim had joined the Indian revolutionaries although the Santimoy Roy booklet of the People's Publishing House would have us believe the opposite. Rahim even said that non-cooperation was bad for the country and advocated the presence of English servicemen in India. Such ultra-loyalist views voiced from the platform of the Muslim League, even in 1925, showed that despite. Jinnah capturing the League in the thirties, the majority of League leadership was in the hands of title holders and landlords and Jinnah apparently liked their company. Naturally, like their leader, they also detested the Gandhian ways.

**Jallianwalla Massacre**

But they had the support of the Muslim masses, intellectuals and even the Ulema, although some remained anti-British till the very end. This support was growing and snowballing although many individual Muslims participated in the freedom movements. That, however, did not amount to enthusiastic Muslim participation in the freedom struggle. The shining example of Ashfaqullah was not emulated by many nor was there large scale support for the Gandhian movement either. Santimoy Roy's booklet would have us believe that at least 59 Muslims died in the Jallianwalla Bagh massacre by the British officer, Brig. Gen. Dyer. He should not be confused with Sir Michael O'dwyer, who was then the Governor of united Punjab and was killed much later in London by Udham Singh for which Udham Singh was hanged by the British. Dyer, according to his own statement, had killed 379 persons by just firing his bullets. But many more had been killed in the stampede and the figure of 2,000 who lost their lives in the massacre and its aftermath is not off the mark.

If 59 people out of 2,000 were Muslims it could only prove what we have been saying all along, that there were always Muslims in one or the other freedom movement. Otherwise in a province where the Muslims were in a majority and in Amritsar where they were in large numbers in 1919 this figure was not something to be proud of.

If we talk of the Frontier Pathans, under the leadership of the Frontier Gandhi, Khan Abdul Ghaffar Khan, what do we find? These usually volatile people, many of them watchmen or moneylenders in Bombay (now Mumbai), but also possessed of some admirable qualities, immortalised by Tagore in his Kabuliwallah, were taught the primary lessons of non-violence in their home province of NWFP. He established the Red Shirt movement, also called the Khudai Khidmatgars, volunteers of God, who faced much repression including British bullets. In 1930, soldiers of the Garhwal Rifles, an important wing of the British Indian army, refused to open fire on them while the civil disobedience movement was in progress. This incident in Peshawar city was a bitter pill to swallow for the British rulers. For many years the Frontier Province was the sole preserve of Abdul Ghaffar

Khan and his brother, Dr Khan Sahib. In the elections for provincial autonomy in 1937 and even in the elections in 1946 the Congress was returned to power in this Muslim majority region. By 1946, however, the Muslim League had made some inroads in this province too.

In that poll, the League won 17 seats against 19 of the Congress, including two captured by its ally, the Jamiat-ul-Ulama-i-Hind. Obviously the Pakistan fever had penetrated the NWFP also. The tragedy of turning over the province to "wolves", as Badshah Khan put it, was to follow when the partition of the country was to take place in the following year. The NWFP had stood like an oasis in the sea of communalism but even that was to be engulfed in the tragedy of partition. Unfortunately, many Pathans had gone over to the side of the Muslim League, as evidenced by the results of the 1946 elections, although in the unnatural referendum on whether the NWFP wanted to join Pakistan or not only 50 per cent opted for the partition of the country. Khan Abdul Ghaffar Khan had not taken part in the referendum because the choice of joining Pakistan or remaining in India would have been difficult to follow for the ordinary people in this remote area of the north-west of the country. Badshah Khan was naturally bitter but this was a price paid for the partition of the country.

The Muslim League juggernaut was almost stopped by the non-violent Pathans but the 1946 polls proved that the Congress had failed to win the confidence of the Muslims at large. Its score was only five Muslim seats in all the Indian provinces put together, except the NWFP, which showed that the large majority of the Indian Muslims wanted Pakistan. The electorate was communal and the franchise limited. But in 1939 the Congress had still managed to get 56 Muslim seats and now its tally was a meagre five. This easily demonstrated that the Muslims were steeped in separatism and irrespective of the consequences, which neither they knew nor their leader, they had taken the plunge for partition.

### Equation Mania

Voting is a good index of the support of a political party among the people. The rapid decline of Congress strength among the Muslims was contrasted by the overwhelming support of the

Congress among the Hindus who constituted about 75 per cent of the population of undivided India. This is also a disclaimer of the argument of some Marxist writers that Hindu communalism had taken deep roots in the country as had Muslim communalism. If this was true the Hindu Mahasabha, the only Hindu political party in India at that time, would have won a sizable number of general seats, if not a majority. I happened to be in Delhi when the Central Assembly elections were held in 1946 and a Hindu Mahasabha candidate, an old revolutionary, Ram Singh, lost to a Muslim Congress leader, Asaf Ali. In those days, only Muslims could stand for an election from a Muslim seat but in a general constituency anyone, including a Muslim, could contest although the Muslims would not be voters in that constituency. Despite all that the Muslims wanted their pound of flesh, Pakistan.

The Hindu Mahasabha had prominent leaders like Madan Mohan Malaviya, founder of the Banaras Hindu University and, what is not generally known, of the newspaper the *Hindustan Times*, Lala Lajpat Rai, Veer Savarkar, who had taken part in the revolutionary movement, and others. But its lack of popular backing is a slap in the face of those theorists who may call themselves historians but who knew little of history when they talked of two kinds of communalism. The equation disease, a phenomenon of the freedom struggle days, has been carried over to the post-partition era because the self same theorists now equate India with Pakistan.

That despite the strong disapproval of the Indian National Congress by the Muslims in general, the Congress continued, under Gandhi's leadership, to be secular in approach is proof of the fact that the large body of Indians have always been tolerant and went to the extent of forgiving the people who blindly followed a destructive leader. Despite the aversion of their co-religionists for the Congress, some Muslims of strong will took part in the various struggles. It is not easy to do so and withstanding the boycott of fellow Muslims must have been a difficult proposition for people like Rafiq Zakaria who joined the Quit India movement despite this boycott. He said as much in an article in the *Indian Express*.[6]

According to Santimoy Roy's studies, a number of Muslims faced army and police bullets in the Gandhian movement of Civil

Disobedience or Salt Satyagraha in 1930. In that movement some 45 Muslims gave their lives. The people and the film media devote exaggerated importance to revolutionaries who faced the gallows after throwing bombs but people who died silently and far from the glare of publicity for a noble cause were no less patriotic and deserved all the praise one can shower. Many of those who sacrificed their lives in the 1930 movement were the non-violent Pathans of the NWFP who proved to be faithful disciples of the Frontier Gandhi.

The Quit India movement saw some 25 Muslims, mainly in Bihar, participating in the struggle and laying down their lives while many others suffered imprisonment. The learned professor is, however, misled into counting a Hindu, Ashrafi Lal of Deoghar, Bihar, among the Muslims who embraced death during the Quit India movement. Anybody with a name like that would appear to be a Muslim to a person not acquainted with the peculiarities of this great country. The catholic Hindus give their offspring names like Ashrafi, Iqbal, Daulat, Zinde Lal, Darya Lal and so on, names which would appear to be those of Muslims to Santimoy Roy, when there is no dearth of purely Hindu names. Many Christians give their children Hindu names which means the parents have no religious prejudice, something more than you can say of the Muslims.

But apart from the shining examples of a small section of Muslims, the community in general avoided the national struggles like plague. Why should they join these movements when their leaders knew that they could extract the best advantage for their community from any dispensation that the British had in view. If there were loaves and fishes of office to be distributed the Muslims would get their share and if somehow they did not they could demand for a greater share and get it in the next round. They were certain that their leader, Jinnah, would snatch from the British more than their due share and they trusted him to get Pakistan when the final shots were called.

One could almost say cynically that the Muslims believed that their leader would ensure a place for them under the sun, actually more than that, while the Hindus, Sikhs, Christians, Parsis and some hotheaded Muslim young men and the religious leaders, fought it out with the British rulers. So why bother to go to jail, face lathis and bullets, and face the wrath of the foreign masters when Jinnah was there to get them their share and more. Jinnah was a master of excuses and even now Indian intellectuals and some mediamen are taken in by his communal propaganda, like that Gandhi was a Hindu—he was certainly one of the greatest of Hindus but that not detract from his Indianness—Vande Mataram was offensive to the Muslims, the Congress was advancing the cause of the Vidya Mandir scheme, even though the author of it was Dr Zakir Husain, and so on.

The truth was that from the late nineteenth century leaders of the community like Sir Syed Ahmed wanted the Muslims to keep away from the national movement and advocated the loyalty platform. Many Britons, like the indefatigable principals of the Anglo-Oriental College at Aligarh, founded by Sir Syed, and many civilians as well as Viceroys like Minto and Curzon, fanned this separatism. The Muslims were rewarded with separate electorates, nominations in civil services, and prized positions under the government for non-participation in the freedom struggle. So why bother to join the mainstream, specially when leaders like Jinnah would get them all this and much more without ever going to jail.

## NOTES

1. For details of the Wahabi movement see *"Islam in India's Transition to Modernity"*, M. A. Karandikar, Orient Longmans, *Ibid*.
2. *Role of Indian Muslims in the Freedom Movement*, Santimoy Roy, People's Publishing House, New Delhi, Ahmedabad, Bombay, 1970. The book carries a foreword by the then General Secretary of the CPI, P. C. Joshi, who says "Hindu" historians must be answered. (Quotation marks his.)
3. As quoted in Ram Gopal's book, *Ibid*.

*Chapter 4*

# FROM CONCEPT TO REALITY

In a previous chapter we have noted how a Briton, Wilfred Scawn Blunt, who was in India in 1883, had given his own outline of a future set-up of India from the Muslim standpoint and how he had visualised Pakistan in the process at a time when no Muslim leader had given a thought to it. Of course, when we talk of separatism we know that the idea of a separate state was also rooted in that consciousness which gradually took hold of the Muslim mind as important leaders of the community nourished it and the British rulers vaguely encouraged them to think of it. The latter were, of course, more concerned to keep the Muslims as loyal subjects of the Raj who would not join agitational activities for reforms in India, by which they meant that the Muslims would not participate in the doings of the Indian National Congress.

How this sense of separatism strengthened the Muslim resolve to find a state of their own in India, without the presence of the British authority, and how this dream was translated into action is a painful yet fascinating story. It would be wrong to suppose that there was a deliberate and conscious drive with a set goal in mind so that the homeland could become a reality and there was some kind of a devilish plan. But the seeds of a separate state to be carved out of a future free India, to serve only Muslim interests, existed in the seeds of separatism, carefully nursed from the earliest times, by men like Syed Ahmed Khan, and developed into a campaign by Mohammed Ali Jinnah in the late thirties and early forties, when Jinnah maintained that there existed a Hindu nation and a Muslim nation in India.

At first it was only a vague thought, not worked out in detail, but the idea had been planted in the minds of many Muslims. The two basic concepts were : the Muslims had ruled over India for centuries and could not be reduced to, what Jinnah said, a numerical minority, and they were different from the Hindus. It was inchoate in the beginning and later, when Jinnah demanded Pakistan, he would generally refuse to define its boundaries and whether the state conceived by him would be an Islamic state or one based on democratic principles. Generally these ideas gather a concrete shape and flesh and blood as the idea itself is propagated and accepted. It is never defined in a clear cut manner and it acquires substance and reality as the movement itself proceeds along.

The plan has to touch the vital chords in the hearts of the people concerned and there has to be a leader who would give it a big push. In the beginning the idea did not evoke much response but as the principal protagonist went on hammering the theme and the British rulers encouraged him the acceptance was bound to come and the others were also concerned about it.

**The Progenitor**

The word "Pakistan" was first used by Chaudhry Rahmat Ali an Indian student in Britain. That was in 1933 and Rahmat Ali was also the first person to define what his concept stood for. Others like the great poet, Mohammad Iqbal, had already spoken of it, as we will see, but Rahmat Ali was more specific and used the word Pakistan also. In a pamphlet—NOW OR NEVER—Rahmat Ali demanded three independent Muslim states in India, Pakistan, Usmanistan and Bang-i-Islam. According to him, the name Pakistan itself stood for the provinces of Punjab, Afghania, or the North-West Frontier Province, Kashmir, Sind and Baluchistan. He wanted Hyderabad, now part of India's Andhra Pradesh state, to become an independent Muslim state and called it Usmanistan because it was ruled by the Nizam, Sir Usman Ali. His Bang-i-Islam included the whole of Bengal, that is, the present Indian state of West Bengal and the present sovereign Bangladesh.

Rahmat Ali was dead against Indianness and called the concept of Indianness as a soul-killing cult. He declared: "We are Moslems, not Hindus, Pakistani, not Hindustani". He called the Muslims Asians, not Indians. His scheme was the first one which gave some details of the boundaries of the proposed sovereign Muslim states. The scheme was ambitious but it was not clear whether he wanted the three states to be part of a whole or at least having some kind of relationship. He was naturally not concerned with the rights of the Hindus, or else he would not have made the Hindu majority Telangaga area into a Muslim state. For him it was enough that the area was under the rule of a Muslim Nizam but he violated his own principle when he ignored that Kashmir was then ruled by a Hindu maharaja. When you are out to grab territory and laying down a grand scheme you are not bothered about small things like the Hindu majority in Hyderabad.

His scheme was, however, dismissed by most Muslim leaders of the day as a "student scheme", meaning a raw, immature product of a young mind, under emotional strain, which men of the world would not touch with a pair of tongs. But at least three years before Rahmat Ali authored his "student scheme", the poet Iqbal, wrongly revered by many in India, as Allama Iqbal, had put forward almost the same scheme as President of the Muslim League in Lahore in 1930. He had, of course, not named the country he had envisaged as Pakistan. Curiously, the man had also written the song, "Sare Jahan Se Achha Hindustan Hamara", which is much loved by all Indians but we forget that it was before he had put forward his plan of a Muslim state.

There is no dearth of half-baked Indians who admire Iqbal as Allama, a learned man, which he really was but we have to recognise that he envisaged a Muslim India within India. If a man is revered as a national poet in Pakistan, as Iqbal is, how can Indians also look upon him as a great champion of India? The song "Sare Jahan Se" is a beautiful one and is liked by a lot of people but let us not forget that Iqbal was not the one to uphold Indian unity. The Hindu and Sikh delegates at the 1931 Round-Table Conference in London convened by the British government were perturbed by Iqbal's presidential speech at the Muslim League conference in which he had put forward his pet scheme.

**Iqbal's Pakistan**

He said in that famous speech[2] : "India is a continent of human beings belonging to different races, speaking different languages, and professing different religions. Their behaviour is not all determined by a common race consciousness. Even the Hindus do not form a homogenous group. The Muslim demand for the creation of a Muslim India, within India, is, therefore, perfectly justified. I would like to see the Punjab, the North-West Frontier Province, Sind and Baluchistan amalgamated into a single state. Self-government within the British Empire or without the British Empire, the formation of a consolidated North-Western Indian Muslim state appears to me to be the final destiny of the Muslims, at least of the North-Western India".

Of course, Bangladesh could not live with the Punjabi-dominated West Pakistan and the men in Islamabad have not yet succeeded in their designs to grab Kashmir but Iqbal's words had a prophetic ring. That Iqbal who belonged to the Punjabi part of the country cared little for the Indian Muslims who were to be left behind in the Hindu majority provinces could be understood; why should he bother about their fate? But at least, Mohammad Ali Jinnah who belonged to Bombay, now called Mumbai, and was a Gujarati Muslim, should have asked himself what would happen to these people once his Pakistan dream was realised.

Ten years before Jinnah persuaded the Muslim League in the same city of Lahore to accept his "Pakistan" resolution the great poet had set out in clear terms a separatist demand. That people like Gujral still rever him—he referred to Iqbal as "our poet" in December 1997 when talking to the Indian-American woman astronaut, Kalpana Chawla—is India's tragedy but Iqbal fathered the separate Muslim state idea even before Rahmat Ali had stirred the minds of Muslim young men by his "Now or Never" pamphlet.

Iqbal had moved away from the concept of a united India long before Pakistan was eventually born. He had said that the Indians are a conglomeration of different races and the Hindus and Muslims have different destinies. That the Hindus are not homogenous is a theory which several Muslims love even today because they see in it the possible fulfilment of their dream that the vast Indian population could one day be converted to Islam and then India could become all Muslim, something which the invaders and Sultans failed to achieve for many centuries.

How homogenous the Muslims are was proved when Pakistan was broken into two in December 1971 when Bangladesh was born. The Shias and Sunnis of Pakistan are still at loggerheads and often there are violent clashes and a number of people lose their lives. The Indian Urdu-speaking Muslims have not been accepted by the Punjabis in Pakistan and still go about as Muhajirs. The Ahmediyas stand excommunicated. Are they part of Islam, if there is such a thing as Islamic unity? The myth of equality under Islam has been fully exposed.

If Iqbal spoke of the immortality of Indian civilisation—*Ek bat hai ke hasti mitati nahin hamari*—he lived to denounce his own views. In the same address he said:[3] "That which really matters is a man's faith, his culture, his historical tradition. These are the things, which, in my eyes, are worth living and dying for, not the piece of earth with which the spirit of man happens to be associated." Iqbal was, in the early part of his career, an advocate of Wajudia Sufism or monistic mysticism. From 1905 he gave up both Sufism and nationalism. Towards the end of his life, he attacked nationalism as a false god and pleaded for Muslim internationalism or Pan-Islamism as a federation of independent Muslim countries. He had great admiration for the Muslim Brotherhood or Ikhwan party of Egypt.[4] That modern Egypt looks upon the Brotherhood as a curse and does everything in its power to put it down is proof of the romantic but erroneous approach of Iqbal. But then there was great urge among the Indian Muslims for a separate homeland and even a hard-headed lawyer like Jinnah worked assiduously for it because he knew that thereby he could emerge as a great leader of the Muslim community.

**Connecting Letters**

That there was an important connection between the two is proved by Iqbal's letters to Jinnah to accept the goal of Pakistan and work for it. In a letter on March 20, 1937 the poet wrote to the lawyer asking him to declare clearly and strongly that the political objective of the Indian Muslims was a distinct political unit in the country. He wrote again and again to Jinnah to adopt the goal of a separate state for the Muslims. Iqbal realised that of all the Muslim leaders Jinnah had the capacity to attain the goal. Jinnah knew little of Islam and less of Urdu, which were the poet's strong points, and there was not much in common between the atavistic

Iqbal and the modern Jinnah but Jinnah was the man who could deliver the goods and the poet knew it well.

The orthodox Muslims, many of whom were associated with the Congress, denounced Jinnah and even called him a 'kafir' and non-Muslim, perhaps because they knew that his Pakistan would not be a proper Islamic state. The Ulema, like Maulana Hussain Ahmad Madani, and Maulana Mazhar Ali Azhar, leaders of the Majlis-e-Ahrar, another Muslim nationalist organisation, were intensely patriotic but they wanted an Islamic order to be created in India and were far more Islamic in their approach than the modernistic Jinnah. Mazhar Ali Azhar had even composed a limerick about Jinnah's marital status because he had a Parsi wife. She was probably converted to Islam, as is the practice almost universally followed even today of a Hindu woman becoming a Muslim on marriage with a Muslim male and, in many cases, a Hindu male becoming a Muslim on contracting a marriage with a Muslim woman, but this was not to satisfy the Ulema. The Maulana's couplet ran like this:

*Eek Kafira ke waste Islam ko Chhoda,*
*Yeh Quaid-e-Azam hai ki Kafir-e-Azam.*

(He, Jinnah, abandoned Islam for the sake of a Kafir (non-Muslim) woman. Is he a Quaid-e-Azam, leader-in-chief, Jinnah's popular title, or is he a great infidel?)[5]

Yet another Ahrar leader, Ataullah Shah Bukhari, who was an orator *par excellence*, used to tell a story of a girl in Punjab who went to a grocer and asked for more oil than her small container could hold because it was customary to ask the trader for a little extra after he had measured out the right quantity. Bukhari used to utter the proper Punjabi word for the practice ('Jhoonga', sometimes also called 'Boonga') and compared Jinnah with the young girl. When the Congress leaders were prepared to yield everything he wanted within a united India he still wanted Pakistan.

In the story the girl emptied her small container to receive something extra.[6] Nowadays, neither in India nor in Pakistan, this could be practised because of high prices and modern packaging and not many go out to buy oil in a small container. But the audiences enjoyed Bukhari's jibes at Jinnah, although the Muslims still supported Jinnah in his Pakistani demand. Bukhari perhaps knew this but he could not resist the temptation of attacking Jinnah and pointing out that Jinnah's scheme would leave the Indian Muslims divided into three parts. How prophetic of him to visualise that Pakistan would split up and there would be three nations in this sub-continent, India, Pakistan and Bangladesh, and each would have its Muslim component. As stated, the audiences relished the carping criticism but gave their vote to Jinnah. By the time Ataullah Shah Bukhari was speaking in Delhi in 1945 the tide had already turned. By the time of the Cripps Mission in 1942 and later, when the field was clear for Jinnah as the léaders of the nation, Gandhiji and people like Nehru, Patel and Maulana Azad, were all in jail, he could ask the Muslims "give me your votes, I will give you Pakistan".

In his presidential address to the annual session of the Jamiat-ul-Ulama at Jaunpur, UP, in 1940 Maulana Hussain Ahmad Madani, said: "These days the Pakistan movement is very popular among the masses".[7] In other words, he admitted that despite the intense efforts of people like him and his organisation and others like the Majlis-e-Ahrar, and some eminent Muslims, like Maulana Azad in the Congress, the Muslim masses were going all out to support Pakistan.

Jinnah had never believed in nor had patience for mass action which is why he showed his back to the Congress as soon as Gandhiji assumed command. Gandhiji had not only launched the non-cooperation movement in 1919 but also roped in prominent Muslim leaders of the time when he allowed the Khilafat movement to be joined with the non-cooperation movement. Gandhiji had felt there was justice in the Muslim demand that the Khilafat must be protected in Turkey by the British rulers in the U.K. and he also saw that by joining mass action the Muslims would remain with the mainstream.

Many writers have blamed Gandhiji for allowing himself to be a party to a purely Pan-Islamic movement but under the circumstances of the time he saw no alternative. There would have been a Khilafat agitation in any case and it was thought appropriate by the Mahatma, who had nothing but the good of the country and the Muslim community in his heart to be part of it. Even staunch Hindu leaders like Swami Shraddhanand had joined the movement and was invited to address Muslim audiences in mosques. The use of religious places, mainly mosques, for political activity has been an Indo-Pakistan tradition and the Khilafat agitation had acquired universal acceptance, only men like Jinnah keeping away from it. Swami Shraddhanand was later to be assassinated by a Muslim.

That was when the agitation had lost all validity. For one thing Gandhiji had called off the non-cooperation movement because of the violent and harrowing incident in Chauri Chaura, near Gorakhpur in Uttar Pradesh in 1922, and himself had been tried and jailed by the British rulers, and for another Turkey had removed the basis of the agitation when the great reformer and moderniser of Turkey, Kemal Ataturk, had abolished the Khilafat and the Turkish kingship altogether in 1923. Gandhiji was at the receiving end of much flak because he had called off the campaign as he was severely criticised by some Muslim leaders and leaders of the Congress. But subsequent events, like the Mopla riots in Kerala, proved that the communal spirit had taken hold of the Indian mind once again.

The events of the anti-partition agitation of 1909-10 in Bengal were repeated. During that movement the spirit of Swadeshi and nationalism had been aroused on a mass scale for the first time since the awakening of the Indian mind. But some elements in the part of the country which later became East Pakistan and Bangladesh had taken the instigation of the author of partition, Lord Curzon, literally and allowed themselves to swoop on the hapless Hindus who were subjected to plunder and killing, abduction and forcible conversion. Some of them thought that Curzon having told them the that he was giving them a Muslim majority province of their own they had acquired a licence to rob and kill. The ghastly events of the partition of the country in 1947, again in the same pattern but on a vastly larger scale, proved that the antagonism between the Hindus and Muslims lies just below the surface and requires only an excuse, sometimes no excuse, to burst at the seams. It is a violent rebuttal of the goody-goody commonality theory of Indo-Pakistani Bhai Bhai movement, practised by Gujral and his friends, who do not know that the roots of separatism are much deeper.

By 1940, Jinnah had won over large numbers of Muslims in the country to his way of thinking and acting. The Muslims of the non-Muslim provinces, people who would never see Pakistan in the north-west, had already been won over by him and now the people of the majority areas in Punjab and Bengal were coming over to his side as their leaders were terribly afraid of him and the Frankestein he had aroused. The British had also adopted him as a darling. He had been earlier hailed as a nationalist in the second decade of the twentieth century when the people of Bombay (now Mumbai) had built a People's Jinnah hall (subsequently shortened to P. J. Hall) to honour him. He was, of course, holding the membership of both the Congress and the Muslim League in those days, double membership being practised by many those days and also permitted by the two bodies. On several occasions Jinnah took a rational stand and the British were among those who did not like it a bit.

His failure to gatecrash into the Congress ministries, particularly in U.P., under provincial autonomy, made him realise that unless he took an extreme posture he would not win the support of the Muslims. Now he was elected a lifetime president of the Muslim League. Many mediamen and women are sarcastic when Shiv Sena chief Bal Thackeray was elected president of the Sena for life but Jinnah himself set the precedent which is no laughable matter. The British accepted him as the sole spokesman of the Muslims, although this was not formal. Jinnah got the Muslim League as President to adopt a resolution asking for Pakistan at the Lahore session of the League in March 1940.

Mian Fazlul Huq, the Bengal leader, often called the tiger of Bengal, more a wayward fox than a tiger, moved the Pakistan resolution although he was to go against the League even after that brave action of his. That was when he formed a new government in his native Bengal without the league, and what is more, a coalition with a section of the Congress, in the form of the Forward Bloc. He even said partition would not apply to Bengal which was a blatant lie.

**Pakistan Resolution**

But in moving the Pakistan resolution Huq was as effusive as possible and threatened "everyone of us is a tiger and a lion". The

Muslim Leaguers revelled in comparing themselves to animals, the more ferocious the better as a threat. Whatever might be Fazlul Huq's intention the audience of Muslims from different parts of the country lapped it up.

The League's resolution said in parts: "Resolved that it is the considered view of the session of the All-India Muslim League that no constitutional plan would be workable in this country or acceptable to the Muslims unless it is designed on the following basic principle, viz. that geographically contiguous units are demarcated into regions which should be so constituted, with territorial readjustments, as may be necessary, that the areas in which the Muslims are numerically in a majority, as in the north-western and eastern zones of India, should be grouped to constitute "Independent States" in which the constituent units shall be autonomous and sovereign."[8]

The resolution, while putting forward the long nourished Muslim ambition of an independent and sovereign state of their own, was somewhat vague on important points. For example, it spoke of "Independent States", one in the north-west and one in the east, although what Jinnah achieved was a unified Pakistan. Ultimately, of course, Bangladesh freed itself from the Punjabi Muslim domination and Mujibur Rahman, the founder of Bangladesh could have claimed that the Pakistan resolution of the League itself envisaged two separate states.

Also, the League's insistence on calling itself "All-India" Muslims League was quite in fashion those days when every institution tried to arrogate this appellation even if its all-India character was nominal. When Lionel Fielden was the boss of the radio in India about the same time, he cajoled the British Viceroy into accepting the name ALL INDIA RADIO, instead of the cumbersome Indian State Broadcasting Service, by playing up the all-India image of the national network.[9]

Chadhury Rahmat Ali's dream was thus acquiring some flesh and blood, although another seven years were to elapse before Pakistan was born. Incidentally, Rahmat Ali was not alone when he circulated his pamphlet "Now or Never", in which he set out the Pakistan scheme. There were some others with him—Mohammad Aslam Khan, Mohammad Sadiq and Inayatullah—

although the scheme, as we saw, was dismissed as a student scheme by many wise Muslim leaders. Now Jinnah, as we will see, even echoed some of the words and arguments used by Rahmat Ali.

In his presidential address to the Lahore session Jinnah said: "They (Islam and Hinduism) are not religions in the strict sense of the word, but are, in fact, different and distinct social orders and it is a dream that Hindus and Muslims can ever evolve a common nationality. The misconception of one Indian nation has gone far beyond the limits and is the cause of most of our troubles and will lead India to destruction if we fail to revise our notions in time. The Hindus and Muslims belong to two different religious philosophies, social customs, literature. They neither intermarry nor interdine together and indeed they belong to two different civilisations which are based mainly on conflicting ideas and conception".

Here we can see how Jinnah had borrowed ideas and words from Rahmat Ali, without acknowledgement, of course. Jinnah was often called a gentleman; whether it is true or not he was essentially an egoist and could not bear to see that his words depended on the student Rahmat Ali for their originality. Rahmat Ali's pamphlet had said: "India is not the name of one single country, nor the home of one single nation. It is, in fact, a designation of a state created for the first time in history by the British...We do not inter-dine; we do not inter-marry. Our national customs and calendars, even our diet and dress are different".[9]

**Indian Unity pre-British**

There is hardly any need for us to expound how erroneous was Rahmat Ali in his thinking and, indeed, how wrong was Jinnah, who heavily depended on the young Cambridge University Under-graduate, when he talked of two nations. India has always been one, long before the British set foot on the soil of India. When Kalidasa spoke of India, in his *Kumarasambhava* as a country which has the mighty Himalayas in the north, which has arisen from the oceans on the right and left, he was not conscious that some later day thinkers would invent a theory of the British conferring unity on India.[10] Kalidasa could not have lived later than the fifth century A.D. When the great Adi Sankara, in the course of a short life of 32 years, established four different maths (religious orders) in the extreme north in the Himalayas at Badrinath, east on the Bay of Bengal in Jagannathpuri, in the west at Dwarka again on the sea, and in the south at Sringeri or Kanchi, he was not obligated to the British for the unity of India he forged in a unique way.

Emperor Asoka travelled in his territories from the east to the west and north to south, erecting pillars and monuments on which he inscribed his immortal message of peace, tolerance and brotherhood. He lived in the third century B.C. and did not show any awareness that his concept of Indian unity suffered from any fault. Even the Mughal rulers tried to enforce their rule over the whole of India, whether they succeeded in it or not. Most of the Muslims sought and secured their separate state but for pursuing their demand they need not have invented the fiction that Indian unity was a gift of the British. True, India is a vast country and, therefore, there is always a possibility of diverse forces and rulers trying to carve out a separate existence for themselves and their kingdoms. There was thus chaos and confusion and the Marathas tried to enforce some order in the eighteenth and nineteenth centuries when the Mughal ruler was under their protection. The British took advantage of the situation and grabbed substantial territory, ultimately leading to the establishment of their rule.

Jinnah, as we have seen, took full advantage of the absence of the Indian leaders, who had been placed in detention, Gandhiji in the Aga Khan's palace in Poona (now Pune) and Nehru, Patel, Azad and others in the Ahmednagar Fort, after the Quit India resolution was adopted by the All-India Congress Committee at Bombay (now Mumbai) on August 8, 1942. Jinnah not only opposed the resolution but also asked the Muslims to stay away from the movement. He went on strengthening the Muslim League movement and consolidating his stronghold on the Muslim mind. The British were only too glad to do business with him while the Congress leaders were safely behind the bars.

### In Three Parts

We have referred to the Aharar leader, Ataullah Shah Bukhari, accusing Jinnah of dividing the Indian Muslims into three parts. An enlightened Indian Muslim leader, Dr Rafiq Zakaria, who was a minister in the Maharashtra government, had this to say: "That is why even as a student, I stoutly opposed Jinnah's pernicious two-nation theory. I participated in the Quit India movement despite the ire of my co-religionists who damned me as a traitor to Islam. The harm that Jinnah did is incalculable. I have repeatedly said even the worst Muslim ruler in the middle ages did not alienate the Hindus from the Muslims so badly as the so-called Quaid-e-Azam had done. The Congress, instead of confronting him, succumbed. The mess that this created has not been cleared even 50 years after partition."[11]

A romantic group of people, also calling themselves liberals, are inclined to blame the national leaders of the time for the partition of the country. Rafiq Zakaria is among them although he had a few home truths to tell us about Jinnah some of which have been quoted above. The issue has been examined in some detail in another chapter where the false assumptions made by the romantics have been exposed and, therefore, they are being touched here only in a limited way.

In the atmosphere that existed in India in the forties during which the author also lived, the Pakistan demand and the movement led by Jinnah was a real threat to the fabric of Indian society. To imagine that if Jinnah had been propitiated over the demand for the inclusion of his Muslim leaguers in the Congress Ministry in U.P., he would not have demanded Pakistan is to display lack of political understanding. Jinnah was not a child that if he was denied ministerships he would jump and begin voicing his utterly separatist demand. As we have seen, Pakistan was the culmination of a separatist urge which Jinnah gave expression to and channelled into the Pakistan movement. The second world war was coming to a close and it was clear that the British would quit India, sooner or later, sooner rather than later. Were we prepared to pay the heavy price of unity by yielding to Jinnah's demand for parity between Hindus and Muslims, supposing that he would have then given up his Pakistan demand? Partition, in the circumstances, was inevitable.

When we talk of a united India we naturally think of Indian unity as it now exists or had existed for the first five decades after independence, with the states having a substantial measure of internal autonomy but a strong centre, able to lay down the law, enforce article 356 of the Constitution, so that the centre could dismiss a state government in given circumstances, and having the authority to plan for the economy of the entire country. The Muslims, as represented by Jinnah, were bent upon having their pound of flesh and with a separate electorate they could and surely would have held India to ransom. Now we have joint electorates and adult franchise while Pakistan is an Islamic state and for half its existence the country was under the jackboot of the army.

There was a time when the country was faced with separate electorates even for the scheduled castes and Gandhiji had to fast and risk his life to prevent the breakup of the Hindu society. Ironically, B. R. Ambedkar, who then stood for the so-called communal award and had to be persuaded by a Gandhi on deathbed (from which he was saved) to agree to a joint electorate for the Hindus, was the draftsman of the Constitution, indeed, the chairman of the drafting committee of the Constitution and architect of the glorious Indian constitution as a whole. Joint electorate is the cornerstone of the Ambedkar-made constitution. These are not small matters. Gandhiji prevailed upon Nehru to include Ambedkar in the first cabinet of free India as Law Minister and he could have continued even beyond 1952 if he had so desired. It was not a favour to him but a recognition of his value and his worth. One cannot imagine Jinnah or any of his Leaguers agreeing to joint electorate and agreeing to abide by all the unity amid diversity that we have now.

The Cripps mission of 1942 had conceded the right of secession of the provinces which virtually meant acceptance of the demand for Pakistan. The talks then broke down over the fact that the British, always myopic in their outlook until 1947 when they were in a hurry to leave, were not prepared to give the Indians any substantive powers. What is more, the British would never have agreed to any arrangement under which the Muslims were not largely satisfied and that meant that Pakistan would be granted by them in some form of or the other. The Muslims then meant virtually the Muslim League. Even the Cabinet mission plan provided for groups, two of the three of which were Muslim majority areas, (wrongly including a non-Muslim majority Assam in Group C) and the provinces had the right to secede after some time, if they so wished.

Under the C. Rajagopalachari plan the concept that if the Muslim majority areas wanted to form a separate state of their own they could do so was assured. Incidentally, Rajaji, as Rajagopalachari was endearingly called, had opposed the Quit India resolution and he had stayed away from the struggle which ensued. In today's partisan politics this would be taken as defiance and the worst punishment would be visited on the person advocating it. The leader and his followers would be all expelled and castigated as splitters. This would apply equally to all political parties because they are all equally intolerant.

Half-educated critics are blind to this democratic system that prevailed in an India still struggling for freedom. Not only was Rajaji allowed his freedom of expression but he openly advocated the acceptance of the demand for a separate Muslim state but with some linkage with India. Naturally, his attitude was resented by a lot of people and he was often strongly criticised but the important thing is that Gandhiji listened to him, apart from the fact that his daughter Lakshmi had married Gandhiji's youngest son, Devadas Gandhi who rose to be a successful editor of a leading newspaper, the *Hindustan Times*. Gandhiji's son Ramadas was an engineer and another son Manilal remained in South Africa. Only his eldest son, Harilal, was a problem progeny and it is strange that a Muslim theatreman should have made much play of the issue.

**No Brotherly Settlement**

Rajaji had talked to Gandhiji during his fast in the Aga Khan palace detention in February 1943 and had obtained his clearance for his plan. After his release from jail in 1944, Gandhiji sought talks with Jinnah and went on bended knees to the latter's palatial house in the Mount Pleasant area of Bombay. He sought to bring round Jinnah to a common formula so that the British could be confronted with it and conceded the substance of Jinnah's Pakistan demand but the separation sought by him was to be avoided. Jinnah was not forthcoming. He even refused to agree to Gandhi's proposition that there should be a settlement "as between brothers".

In a letter to Jinnah, on September 22, 1944, Gandhiji wrote: "Let it be a partition as between two brothers, if a division there must be". But Jinnah would have none of it. Jinnah wanted the Muslim League to be recognised as the sole representative body of the Indian Muslims. If he was not prepared to accept "the division as between brothers" who else could be blamed for the horrors of the partition that followed in 1947?

What about the patriotic Ulema many of whom disliked and even hated Jinnah. Many of them had supported the Congress and had gone to jail by participating in the various struggles. The Jamit-ul-Ulama had, of course, been demanding preservation of Islamic culture and full rights for the Muslims to practise and propagate their religion. When the Pakistan demand was becoming more and more acceptable, even popular in the words of the Jamiat chief, Maulana Hussain Ahmed Madani, the Jamiat convened an Azad Muslim Conference in 1940 to find an alternative to Pakistan. And what did the conference ask for?

Apart from religious freedom, which can be easily understood, the conference also demanded full autonomy for the provinces, with the centre having only those powers which the provinces would leave for it, and, above all, parity with the Hindus, 45 per cent seats in the proposed federal legislature, for the Hindus and Muslims. This was at a time when the percentage of the Muslims in undivided India did not exceed 25. Until the provincial autonomy days, both the Muslim League and the Jamiat had demanded only 33 per cent representation for the Muslims in the federal legislature. Now the nationalist Muslims, who supported the Congress and opposed the Muslim League, wanted parity with the Hindus. Not only in the federal legislature but also in the Supreme Court, in the services, and a veto on any bill considered communal in nature.

These were the circumstances facing the Congress and the national leaders in the early forties and what else could they do? Those who lived through those terrible days, from 1944 to 1947, knew that partition was inevitable and a price which India had to pay in order to preserve the unity of the country, minus Pakistan. The British rulers who had always treated the Muslims as special were in no position to resist the demand. What Jinnah ultimately got was indeed a moth-eaten and truncated Pakistan but the British could not tell him "thus far and no further". If they had told him to behave in the earlier years things would have been different. But they looked upon and envisioned Jinnah and all the Muslims as breakers of the freedom movement. The nation had to move towards freedom and a price had to be paid.

## NOTES

1. See Ram Gopal, *Indian Muslims: A Political History*, for more details.
2. See Ram Gopal, *Indian Muslims: A Political History* and M.A. Karandikar, *Islam in India's Transition to Modernity*, for more details.
3. *Ibid*.
4. Quoted by Karandikar, *Ibid*.
5. *Ibid*.
6. Recalled by the author who was present at the meeting.
7. Quoted by Karandikar, *op. cit*.
8. See Ram Gopal, *op. cit*.
9. Refer to author's book, *Satellite Invasion of India*, Gyan, New Delhi.
10. *Kumarasambhava*, by Kalidasa, first verse of Canto One— "Asti Uttarasyam Dishi Devatatma Himalayo Nama Nagadhirajah, Purvaparau Toyanidhi avagahya sthitah Prithivyah iva Manadandah".
11. *Indian Express*, Delhi, August 14, 1997.

*Chapter 5*

# PARTITION

We saw how even the Jamiat-ul-Ulama, an organisation aligned to the Congress because the religious men were intensely patriotic although they were generally backward looking, had demanded 45 per cent representation for the Muslims in the proposed federal body of undivided India. (Of course, it never materialised.) In February 1943, three members of the Viceroy's Executive Council -- Sir Homi Mody, M.S. Aney and Nalini Ranjan Sarkar -- resigned in protest against the British government's refusal to release Mahatma Gandhi from detention even when he had undertaken a 21-day fast and his life was endangered.

The Viceroy, Lord Linlithgow, promptly accepted the resignations and went on to fill up the vacancies in a manner which would appear to concede Jinnah's demand for parity of the Muslims with the Hindus. The voice of leftism in Britain, the *News Statesman and Nation*, now defunct, wrote in its issue of March 8, 1943 : "The newcomers are not an impressive team but the most significant point about them is that the composition of the Viceroy's Executive now realises Mr Jinnah's ideal of parity in numbers between Muslims and Hindus. When once this precedent is established it will be claimed by the minority community as a vested right. This seem a reckless innovation."

Jinnah also succeeded in breaking the unity of the Ulemas and won over a strong section of the Jamiat led by Maulana Shabbir Ahmed Usmani. This body took up the cause of Pakistan although some of the Ulema, like Maulana Maududi, founder of the Jamaat-e-Islami, who later went over to Pakistan, went on chanting that Jinnah was irreligious. He even said that a lemon tree could not bear mangoes, not knowing that biological sciences had advanced rapidly and anything was now possible. The important thing was that Jinnah was now able to convince everyone that the Muslims were solidly behind him.

Jinnah was quite aware that he had to counter the Ulema's propaganda against him and he was gradually winning over the loyalty and support of important groups and individuals who could sway the doubting thomases among the Muslims to his demand for a separate state for the Muslims. A judicial report in Pakistan, written seven years after its formation, penned by Justice Munir, pointed out that the Muslim League, before partition, had made a bid for winning over the Pirs and Mashaikh "who command considerable following" for its Pakistan campaign. Accordingly, a Mashaikh committee was set up by the Muslim League in 1946 consisting of 12 members some of whom were religious leaders of "unquestionable position", like the Pir Sahib of Muski Sharif, Pir Jamaat Ali Shah, Khwaja Nizamuddin of Tuansa Sharif, and Makhdum Raza Shah of Multan.

"But the amusing part of it is," says Justice Munir, "that even men like Iftikhar Hussain Khan of Mamdot, Sirdar Shaukat Hayat Khan, Malik Feroze Khan Noon (who later became Governor General of Pakistan) and Navab Mohammad Hayat Qureshi, who were not much known for their religiosity, were also included in the committee and religious designations were assigned to them. Khan Iftikhar Hussain Khan of Mamdot was described as Pir Mamdot Sahrif, Sirdar Shaukat Hayat Khan as Sajjada Nashin of Wah Sharif, and to top it all, the secretary of this committee, Mr Ibrahim Ali Chisti, was designated Fazil-e-Hind Sajjada Nashin of Paisa Akbar Sharif."[1]

This was a decision of the Muslim League over whose destinies Jinnah presided. It is a poor reflection on an individual who is held up by some people as an epitome of personal integrity. There was transparent dishonesty in nominating known politicians to a religious committee by giving them fake religious identity to exploit their political positions when they had no religious function whatsoever to perform. The dishonesty in using the position of religious men to propagate a political goal is another despicable act. What else was it than exploitation of religion for achieving a political target. That all this is quoted by a high court judge long after partition means that the usual plea of being misrepresented with a *mala fide* intention cannot be availed of here.

**False Charges**

Some people accuse the Congress leaders— Gandhiji, Jawaharlal Nehru, Sardar Patel— of betraying the cause of the country because they were greedy for power and could not bear any further delay. Gandhiji never enjoyed power and was in Calcutta to quell communal passions when freedom dawned. But even the other leaders, Nehru, Patel and the rest of them, had fought the British all their life and suffered long imprisonment and other privations while men like Jinnah never sullied their hands in the cause of the poor of their own community, what to talk of courting imprisonment. A little over two years prior to partition, and the transfer of power, the Congress leaders were in the Ahmednagar fort, a hastily converted military establishment into a detention camp, from August 1942 to March 1945. Men like Nehru had spent some 15 years in British prisons. Gandhi himself had been in prison in South Africa and thrice in India. Other Congress leaders endured the hard prison life for years and years.

All this while the Muslim League's landlord politicians and their top man, who was a reputed lawyer, lived in palatial houses and often in airconditioned comfort. There is, indeed, no comparison between the hard life led by some Congress leaders and the life of luxury which the Muslim Leaguers led for whom there was no fear of British jails. Gandhi lived in a village which he called Sevagram, village of service, in the heart of India where the summer temperature would often be above 45 degrees Celsius and a mudpack was his only antidote to the extreme heat. His lifestyle only provided for a typewriter and a telephone as modern gadgets while some of his closest followers made fun of his "poverty", while the Muslim Leaguers led an easy life.

The practice of instigating the naive followers to go out and face bullets and lathis and often to loot and burn and to raise hell, resorted by Muslim "leaders" in free India, is only a continuation of what the archtypal leaders of the League, and Jinnah himself, did when they instigated the Muslims to resort to "direct action" in 1946 while the leaders watched from their ivory towers.

The Congress leaders continued with their policy of placating the Muslims, often called "appeasement", in order to avoid a final rupture. Even as early as 1916 the Congress leaders of the era had accepted the evil system of separate and communal electorates, under the Lucknow pact, in the hope that thereby the British could be confronted jointly and told to leave this country. But this could not succeed, as indeed no policy of appeasement could ever succeed, as Jinnah went on asking for more like Oliver Twist, under his 14 points and in the form of a share in the provincial governments formed by the Congress while his League had not won a single province, not even the Muslim majority provinces of the north or east, which, in fact, had disowned him completely. Gandhiji went to the extent of converting his noncooperation movement into a Khilafat movement which was blatant pan-Islamism in action. The hope again was that thereby the Muslim masses would be drawn into the mainstream of the freedom movement and the British would be presented with a hundred per cent unity of purpose.

But nothing seemed to succeed and Jinnah was leading the bulk of the Muslims into separatism and towards the goal of a separate state, as broadly enunciated in the Pakistan resolution in the Lahore session of the Muslim League in March 1940. The Ulema were also turning in favour of Jinnah whom they had so long called a "kafir". It was at that time that the Congress leader, C. Rajagopalachari, accepted the principle of self-determination of the provinces and later the same was adopted by Gandhiji. But the North-West Frontier Province, which had rejected Jinnah's pernicious two-nation theory even in the 1946 elections, was left out of this scheme. The Rajaji scheme, endorsed by Gandhiji, did not envisage a complete separation of the two nations, and it kept the unity of India intact, not in the form we have now, but not total separation.

This was, however, not acceptable to Jinnah. During the Gandhi-Jinnah negotiations in Bombay in 1944 he even rejected out of hand Gandhiji's plea that there should be "a division as between brothers." This would have ensured that there would be free access to each other's country and the kind of partition which left half a million people dead and many millions of Hindus and Muslims refugees in each other's country and millions of women subjected to indignities which can hardly be described would have been avoided.

**Interim Government: A Farce**

The Interim Government was formed in September 1946 by the Congress because the Muslim League did not join in the first instance. But a lover of power like Jinnah could not bear to be outside and soon found a way for his League to join in, but only to sabotage it from within. Maulana Azad, who was not in the interim government but knew what was happening, has dispassionately analysed the situation in his book *India Wins Freedom*. According to the Maulana, senior Muslim officers of the Finance department, headed by Nawabzada Liaquat Ali Khan, who was to become the Prime Minister of Pakistan in less than a year, provided the points on which every proposal of the Congress Ministers was shot down or delayed. The Ministers were then called members of the Viceroy's Executive Council, of which Nehru himself was Vice President and Sardar Patel member for Home and Information and Broadcasting. Nehru held the portfolio of External Affairs and Commonwealth Relations. Later the words "Commonwealth Relations" were dropped after independence but Nehru kept the Foreign Office with him during all the 17 years as free India's first Prime Minister.

There were virtually two parallel governments although it was called "the Interim government". There was an India and a Pakistan in every section in the two blocks of the Central Secretariat. Muslim officers were encouraged to report to the Muslim League ministers privately. How was a coalition government possible under the circumstances? As we have noted, India was not divided in the circumstances of today, when despite difficulties, the writ of the Central government runs over all parts of the country. Under article 356 of the Constitution of India, a state government could be dismissed by the Centre.

By now India was divided within the government and outside. The British officers, who still controlled many areas and had the entire army under their control, were, with some honourable exceptions, pro-Pakistan in their outlook and behaviour. The Labour government in London was fair, fairer than any of its predecessors in Whitehall, but the men in the field in India who had to carry out its wishes were openly pro-Muslim by and large.

Among the exceptions was Penderel Moon, an ICS officer of the old school, who was posted in undivided Punjab and served the state of Bahawalpur in the crucial pre-partition and post-partition years. Bahawalpur became part of Pakistan on partition and Moon who was Revenue Minister in the state helped thousands of Sikhs and Hindus to leave Pakistan for India in some kinds of honour although without any of their belongings. He knew the three communities--Hindus, Sikhs and Muslims—in Punjab like the palm of his hand but with a British outlook. Eventually he opted for service in India and retired as a member of the Planning Commission. His love of the province of Punjab comes through his book *Divide and Quit*[2]. He analysed the problem of partition as dispassionately as possible, from the standpoint of a British officer, but with remarkable objectivity.

Describing the state of affairs after the feuds had broken out in the Interim government on the entry of the League in the government, Moon says in his book: "The country at large, not fully aware of the inner discords, hailed the League's entry into the government (the League had joined nearly eight weeks after the Congress formed the government) with relief and its immediate effects were tranquillizing. But it soon became apparent that Jinnah's assurances were of no value. The League had entered the government not to cooperate with the Congress but simply to prevent the Congress from tightening its hold on the whole government machine at the League's expense. The Interim government became in fact a dual government. There was, as Liaquat Ali Khan put it, a Congress bloc and a Muslim bloc, each functioning under separate leadership. Each began to attract to itself its own supporters from among the civil servants and build up its own separate and exclusive empire. As a coalition government it was a farce."[3]

The Constituent Assembly began its session in Delhi on December 9, 1946 but, under Jinnah's directions, the Muslim League members did not attend. If proof was needed that Jinnah wanted to sabotage the entire scheme and his real intention was not to run a coalition government but wreck it from inside, here was more than a handful. He made a desparate attempt to get the assembly postponed *sine die*. How could an assembly which had not met even once be postponded *sine die*? Jinnah did not relish to answer such uncomfortable questions.

Moon observes: "The Congress leaders wanted a strong united India; the League a divided or divisible one. The Çongress aim had never been in doubt and accurately reflected the wishes of the Hindu community. The League's aim, only proclaimed in 1940, may not have reflected any real or rational wish of the Muslim multitude but at least accorded with their blind impulses." Further analysing the real motives of the parties Moon says: "Jinnah at an early stage became convinced that the Congress would never tolerate the weak, easily divisible, union of India such as he desired. And it gradually dawned on the Congress leaders, especially after their experience of the attitude of the League representatives in the Interim government, that the price which the League would extract for preserving the unity would be too high."[4]

The British author cautions his readers not to conclude that the Muslims in Pakistan were the villains of the piece and the Hindus and Sikhs their victims from his narrative which is concerned with the fate of the Hindu-Sikh minority in Bahawalpur of which he was a top official. He says this was not the complete story as in East Punjab (the Indian Punjab) the roles were reversed. According to him the Sikhs and Hindus there were guilty of excesses against the Muslims "which equalled and, in my judgement, exceeded in scale and severity, the outrages perpetrated by the Muslims in West Pakistan."[5]

**Evenhanded**

This is quoted here to show that Moon was evenhanded in allocating responsibility and fair in his observations. In fact, he had in him a substantial measure of the British pro-Muslim bias. His assessment is, therefore, important because he was an indepedent witness to the scene who had the capacity to read between the lines and form an unbiased judgment. He says: "In retrospect, it is perhaps less surprising that Pakistan came, as it were, with such a rush at the end as that it was at the beginning such a slow starter; for as far back as 1888 Sir Syed Ahmed, the great Muslim leader of the nineteenth century, had laid down the premises which lead naturally perhaps even necessarily, to the idea of Pakistan. India, he had said, is a country 'inhabited by two different nations and there would necessarily be a struggle for power between them, if the English were to leave India." Is it possible', he asked, 'that under these circumstances two nations—the Mohamaddan and the Hindu—could sit in the same throne and remain equal in power? Certianly not.' In that eventuality he foresaw a Muslim Victory over the Hindus."[6]

The urge for separate nationhood was at the root of partition and even Syed Ahmed had forseen it. Those blaming the Congress leaders for it are not only ignoring the forces of history but misleading others and those advocating the line in the media are guilty of misleading their readers. No matter what the Congress leaders did to appease the Muslims and give them 45 per cent of the federal assembly seats or even parity, the Muslims insisted, with the blandishments of Jinnah, on having their pound of flesh. And this remark of a sane leader like Syed Ahmed, held up sometimes as a nation builder, shows that they visualised nothing short of a Muslim state, if not a Muslim dominated state in the whole of India.

That powerful leaders like Sir Sikander Hayat Khan, Chief Minister of Punjab, (then called Prime Minister) had to bend to Jinnah's will, knowing full well the latter's destructive nature, because the rising tide of Muslim opinion was with Jinnah, is well known. To quote Moon : "One day in October 1938 during a conversation with Sir Sikander, I began talking to him rather enthusiastically about the merits of the Pakistan idea and suggested that after all it might be the best way of dealing with the communal problem. Sir Sikander, usually so calm and sauve, after listening for a few minutes turned upon me, his eyes blazing with indignation, and took me to task in these words : 'How can you talk like this? You have been long enough in Western Punjab to know the Muslims there. Surely you can see that Pakistan would be an invitation to them to cut the throat of every Hindu bania[7]".

A bania is only one of the Hindu castes but many Muslims contemptuously referred to the entire Hindu community as bania, which stands for shopkeepers who sometimes acted as moneylenders.

Moon put forward the hostage theory, that is the Hindus in the Muslim majority areas, to which Sir Sikander said: "I do hope I won't hear you talk like this again. *Pakistan would mean a massacre.*"[8] (Emphasis in the original.) Yet within 18 months of this conversation Sikander Hayat Khan subscribed to the March 1940 Pakistan resolution although be continued, until his premature death, to be the Chief Minister of the Unionist party government of the province of Punjab in which were included Muslims, Hindus and Sikhs. He disliked Pakistan so much that he called it Jinnistan and had even said that if Pakistan meant a Muslim Raj here and a Hindu Raj elsewhere he would have nothing to do with it. His remarks that Pakistan meant nothing but massacre and every Punjabi Muslim would cut the Hindus' throat in Pakistan should answer the critics of the Indian leaders. A wise man like him could forsee what was coming and Jinnah knowing it as well still wanted Pakistan and would not agree to a peaceful transfer of power, Gandhiji's suggestion for a settlement "as between brothers."

Sir Sikander died in 1942 at an early age. He knew that some of his followers were leaning towards Pakistan and did not have the courage to withstand the Jinnah pressure. So outwardly he kept good relations with the Muslim League but he knew that the destiny of Punjab could be safe only in the combined effort of the middle level farmers of the three main communities, Hindus, Sikhs and Muslims, and only his Unionist party was capable of achieving it. He was often rightly accused of being all things to all men but he was a pragmatist and knew that Pakistan would spell disaster for his beloved Punjab.

Leaders like Sikander and Fazlul Huq walked the razor's edge and pursued one line while they did lip service to the Pakistan goal of Jinnah. The latter also kept a close watch on the power game and changed his tactics from time to time, although he remained steadfast in the pursuit of the Muslim separatist goal. Jinnah had, in the circumstances of 1946, no option but to join the interim government eight weeks after the Congress had formed the government but, as we have seen he went about systematically demolishing it.

**Pakistan an Alluring Prospect**

The situation was highly complex. Sikander Hayat Khan knew that Pakistan would mean a massacre but still supported it. Fazlul Huq moved the Pakistan resolution at the League's Lahore session in March 1940 yet he formed an anti-Muslim League government in united Bengal. Some apologists of Jinnah say that even he had reservations about Pakistan and would have settled for less, although this is not true. That was because he knew, along with some other Muslim leaders, that the Muslims in general believed that Muslim Raj would be established in India in the form of Pakistan. This is what Moon has to say in this connection : "To the Muslim masses this held out an ill-defined but alluring prospect of looting the Hindus. With greater clarity of vision, ambitious politicians and civil servants, as also some professional men, perceived that under Muslim Raj, with the crippling if not the elimination of Hindu competition, they could rise to positions of power and affluence unattainable in a single mixed Hindu-Muslim state. Thus the cry for Pakistan appealed to excited powerful appetites and individual hopes, and these once aroused, would not be readily assauged."[8]

This brings to the mind of the author the case of a Pakistani, Quereshi,[9] whom he met at Indiana State University in the United States, at the town of Bloomington. I was then in the promised land for a nine-month Indo-US study-cum-participation course. Quereshi was also there doing an M.Ed. degree course under a joint Punjab University (Pakistan) and Indiana state programme. He had, of course, put in a number of years as a teacher in his native (West) Punjab. We became well acquainted and he would often complain that the American students, who dominated an otherwise international postgraduate complex (called 'graduate' by the Americans), were used to bathing in the nude, although, as he said, the Americans made plenty of cloth. The residents of each hall (or hostel) had their own rooms but they had to share the bathrooms.

Quereshi said frankly he would not have been in the United States but for Pakistan. The scholarship, which had brought him to a foreign university at no extra cost to him, would have gone to some "Puri or Swaminathan" and not to him if the country had not yet been divided, he told me in confidence. The year was 1964 and for a middle aged man like Quereshi the memories of undivided India could still be fresh. So, many of those who prospered because of partition would not have been so fortunate if the country had not been divided. Why did, in fact, so many intelligent Muslims from India-- doctors, lawyers, engineers, senior secretariat men in the government and other professions-- opt for Pakistan and why did so many Bombay and Gujarat businessmen migrate to Pakistan? The answer is : they became the bulwark (and their sons stepped into their shoes) on arrival of the economy of a new country. Gujarati, the mother tongue of the migrant businessmen, is an important minority language of Pakistan in which a daily newspaper and magazines are published and radio and TV programmes are presented. The daily papers are perhaps not in print now but the language used by the people and their journals is standard Gujarati, sometimes even better than the language of some of the papers in Gujarat and Mumbai. Jinnah himself was a Gujarati and in the musical chairs being played in Pakistan in the late fifties a Gujarati Muslim originally from Mumbai, Ismail I, Chundrigar, also became for a while the Prime Minister of Pakistan.

People like Chaudhury Khaliquzzaman swore loyalty to India in the Constituent Assembly in Deihi and later, when reportedly summoned by Jinnah, quietly left for Pakistan never again to set foot on Indian soil. Some of the fictional characters in films made in India, sympathetic to the Muslims, (no films sympathetic to the Hindus were made in Pakistan), like *Garm Hawa*, also left Khaliquzzaman style, for Pakistan after swearing eternal loyalty to India. It is true that many Muslims in north India were under pressure from their own community people or the Hindus, some of whom were hardly above board, but by and large the people remained rooted to their homes. A lot, however, rushed to Pakistan to make a fortune in the promised land but most of them lived to rue the day as they had to eke out a living as perpetual Muhajirs, or migrants. They found to their discomfiture that the land was not half as alluring as it appeared from a distance.

There was a time when India appeared to be denuded of Muslim intellectuals and entrepreneurs because many of them had migrated to Pakistan, either by force of circumstances or by the force of temptation. But the situation was soon retrieved as a number of young men (and some women) came to the fore and occupied high positions in the professions and even in trade and industry. Those in south India and some other parts were not much affected in any case. But the fact that many had gone away in the hope of making it big (and found the going rather tough) cannot be obviated. The lure of "positions of power and affluence", as Moon mentions, has much force and validity.

**Provincial Autonomy**

Let us go back to the period of the late thirties when provincial autonomy was introduced in India by the British rulers and both the Congress and the Muslim League took part in the elections to the provincial assemblies with the goal of getting into the seats of power. Like other parties they had earlier contested elections to the Central Legislative Assembly or under the diarchy in the provinces also but the prospects of power that the 1937 elections held out were unprecedented.

The Congress had approached the provincial autonomy polls with deep suspicion and had grave doubts whether the British rulers would not play foul and prevent the Congress from enjoying the fruits of the elections. The doubts, however, proved baseless as the Congress assumed offices in the provinces, after an initial hesitation. The party had seven of the ten provinces under its belt while the Muslim League, led by Jinnah, had not won a single province. Thereby hangs a tale because Jinnah thought he had a pre-emptive claim to power and must have his pound of flesh.

What were the election results? The Congress won 715 out of a total of 806 Hindu or general seats. The polls were held on separate or communal electorate laid down by the British since 1909. It also won 26 of the Muslim seats out of 58 it had contested. The total number of Muslim seats was 492. The Congress was able to form its governments in the provinces of Bombay, Madras, Central Provinces and Berar, Bihar, Orissa, Assam and in the North West Frontier Province which was to vote for the Congress again in 1946. Despite its claim to speak for the entire Indian people and its transparent sincerity in voicing Muslim feelings and demands, the Congress had failed to win any significant number of Muslim seats except in the NWFP. The election results also showed that the Hindu organisation, the Hindu Mahasabha, failed to win any sizable number of Hindu seats, although it had good leaders and the British in their desire to keep the country divided had nominated a number of Hindu Mahasabha leaders to the Round Table conferences in London. The Marxist historians who revel in equating Muslim separatism with Hindu communalism had a big slap on their face.

Since its formation in 1906 the Muslim League had claimed to speak for all Indian Muslims and ever since Jinnah assumed sole leadership of the party in the thirties this claim was louder and louder. But the League succeeded in only 108 of the 492 Muslim seats. It also suffered a rout in the Muslim majority areas of Sind, Punjab, Bengal and NWFP. Those who blame the Indian leaders for not accommodating Jinnah after the 1937 polls have to bear in mind that his claim to Muslim leadership was quite hollow. But it is equally true that in the few years after that he had won over the large bulk of Muslim support by making Pakistan a central issue for Indian Muslims and letting loose a propaganda blast against the Congress governments in the seven provinces. His propaganda skills were substantial indeed but what appealed to the Muslims more was the demand for a separate state voiced by Jinnah and the Muslim League since March 1940.

**Jinnah's Claim**

Of course, despite its rather dismal performance, the Muslim League, as a party, was next only to the Congress in the overall Indian context. Its tally of 108 seats was the result of its good showing in such provinces as Bombay, Uttar Pradesh (then called United Provinces, UP still) and some other Hindu majority provinces, having been rejected in the Muslim majority provinces. Govind Ballabh Pant became the Prime Minister of UP as the Congress party was invited to form a government by the British Governor on the basis of its majority.

By strange logic or no logic at all, Jinnah claimed that some Muslim League MLAs should be made cabinet ministers in UP although the Congress and League had no coalition arrangements before or after the polls. Neither was the League ready to merge itself with the Congress, an offer having been made after he staked his claim. Although the total population of the Muslims in the province was not more than 15 per cent, the Muslims always thought of UP as the fulcrum of their politics.

The Congress had won a few Muslim seats and some Independents, who were the most numerous of the Muslim MLAs in UP and even in the whole of India, had also joined the Congress party. Great Muslim leaders of the Congress, like Rafi Ahmed Kidwai, who played a noticeable role even after independence in the Central government (until his premature death in 1954) had won a Muslim seat in a by-election. So had another nationalist Muslim, Hafiz Mohammad Ibrahim, who had resigned his Muslim League seat and won as a Congress candidate from the same constituency. Both had been appointed Ministers in the Pant cabinet. Hafiz had won on the basis of his personal popularity and even Jinnah once was a member of both the Congress and the League.

The Congress had waged a series of campaigns for India's freedom and Congressmen had undergone imprisonment on the account. The League could not boast of such a record. Its leaders were either big landlords or British title holders or both. Titles were anethma to the Congress. If the Muslim electorate had put more faith in independents than in the Leaguers it was no fault of the Congress. The Congress's own efforts to win a sizable number of Muslim seats had not been crowned with success because the separate electorate made it difficult for the Congress candidates to become the highest bidders for communal rights and it was easy for the rivals to walk away with seats on the basis of such claims. After the failure of the Khilafat agitation the Muslim masses had not actively participated in any freedom campaign. Individually, of course, many fine people had been associated with one or the other freedom movement.

The fact has to be acknowledged that the Congress failed to make an impact on the Muslim voters in the provincial assembly polls except in the NWFP. The Congress launched a Muslim mass contact programme which did not yield any satisfactory results. The Muslim League objected to such a programme as it did not want any encroachment on its field of activity. To cut a long story short, the Congress in UP had good and efficient Muslims to assume the role of ministers, like RafiAhmed Kidwai and Hafiz Mohammad Ibrahim. In the normal circumstances that should have been a perfectly satisfactory arrangement but failed to satisfy the Muslim League and Jinnah who wanted their own Muslims Ministers.

But how could landlords be in the government when the abolition of the zamindari (landlordism) system was one of the principal goals of the Congress in assuming office, an objective it attained, really speaking, after independence. Perhaps that was at the back of the minds of the Congress leaders as they held fruitless talks with the League on the latter's demand to enter the government.

If the Governor could have interfered, in the name of protecting the minorities interests, they would surely have done it because the British had more than a soft corner for what they deemed Muslim interests. But in the face of facts that the Muslims were being well looked after by the Congress government in UP and elsewhere they could not very well do so. This is cited as proof of the Congress's Muslim credentials. In fact, after the Congress ministries had resigned when the British unilaterally declared India as a belligerent power on the start of the second world war, in 1939, the UP Governor said that the Congress in power had not ignored the interests of the Muslims.

**Only "My Nominees"**

The Muslim League, however, was determined to make the fullest propaganda use of the situation in which its MLA's could not become Ministers as if the Muslims themselves were being denied something. In its eyes, people like Rafi Ahmed Kidwai and Hafiz Mohammad Khan were not real Muslims. This attitude was kept up by Jinnah all through the years until the partition of the country by always insisting, and often getting away with it, that only his nominees were the real Muslims. After he was frustrated in getting them into the UP government, he launched a bitter propaganda campaign against the Congress. The campaign began in the right royal fashion when the Congress governments had hardly been a few months in office. At the annual session of the League held in Lucknow in October 1937, when there were no specific instances of discrimination against or harassment of the Muslims in Congress-ruled provinces, an outburst against the "Hindu" Congress was let loose. The only instance that the League could cite was that Vande Mataram (also referred to as *Bande Mataram*) was being sung everyday when the provincial assembly began its session. The Muslim League then and later raised a hue and cry against the national song simply because it says, "I bow to the Motherland" and according to the League, the Muslims could not bow to anyone other than Allah.

Bowing and folding hands in 'Namaskar' or greeting is a common practice not only among Indians but even among Christians and Buddhists and many eastern nations right upto Japan. The rituals of the Christian faith everywhere provide for folding of hands. For ages, from the time of the anti-partition agitation against the Curzon regime in the early years of the twentieth century, Vande Mataram had become a battle cry. The revolutionaries, among whom were Sikhs and some Muslims, made it their principal slogan and in the Gandhian mass movements for freedom it was on the lips of all freedom fighters when they faced the repression of the British rulers and their Indian policemen or braved their bullets. They did not remember the origin of the song nor indeed did anyone in the assemblies which used to sing the song everyday.

What was wrong with it then? But, no, the Muslim League must have its way and must raise endless objections in the name of religion. Jinnah may have been an agnostic and a 'Kafir', as some patriotic Ulema would say, but he knew that religion could be exploited and it was good for that purpose. Vande Mataram was originally composed by Bankim Chandra Chatterjee, the great Bengali writer, as part of his novel *Anand Math*. Bankim Chandra was a non-ICS senior officer of the British administration in the nineteenth century and perhaps in order to keep his official position secure made the Sanyasi revolt of the eighteenth century as though it was against the Muslim rulers of Bengal rather than the British intruders who were his real targets. But, in reality, the historical background was never in the minds of the freedom fighters, the followers of the Mahatma, or the revolutionaries who believed in violence, when they made it their battle cry. They were only concerned with the two magic words, 'Vande Mataram', I bow to the Motherland, and the shortened version of the Bankim song which is a fine Sanskrit lyric.

But anything was grist to the propaganda mill of Jinnah and his League. They appealed to the religious sentiment of the Muslims by telling them that the song involved bowing to somebody other than Allah. They did not care that the song was addressed to the Motherland, the one full of water and fruit, cool like the breeze from the Malaya mountain, bright like the moonlight, smiling and sweet speaking. Unfortunately, some Muslims are not even now reconciled to the bowing to the Motherland and some think they would not remain Muslims if they fold their hands. In the Urdu language the words, "I fold my hands to you", are often used as a sign of submission but when it comes to folding one's hands to the President of India, a Muslim film song writer, miscalled a lyriscist in films, refused to fold his hands while accepting the Dadasaheb Phalke award. Folding one's hands is a sign of humility and humility is not a vice or sin.

But making a grievance where none existed was a speciality of the League under Jinnah. Within a few months of Congress ministries being in office the opposition to the song Vande Mataram was the starting point of the League's propaganda campaign against the Congress, a virtual 'Jihad' or religious war. The Muslim League called the song anti-Islamic, idolatrous in inspiration and ideas and, surprisingly, as "subversive of the growth of nationalism". Surprising because Jinnah cared two hoots about nationalism and his concern would have been touching were it not so utterly false. This poison was sought to be spread to the street corners, mohallas and the ghettos in the urban areas where many Muslims lived then and unfortunately live even now.

**Pirpur Report**

Not content with this propaganda campaign the Muslim League appointed a committee. This was known as the Pirpur committee because Raja Mohammad Mehdi of Pirpur was its chairman. It was set up in 1938 and soon gave its report on the League's grievances and complaints against the Congress governments. The committee concluded that parliamentary democracy, as practised in Britain, was unworkable in India. Surprisingly, the conclusion of the Jinnah appointed committee reverberates through his Pakistan where the military ruled for nearly half its existence and the President had, until recently, the powers to dismiss a national government and indeed exercised the powers thrice. Pirpur was right at least on that point as the experience of Pakistan as a free nation shows. But if he was right then Mian Nawaz Sharif must quit and hand over to the army led by Gen. Jahangir Karamat. If parliamentary government was not right for the poor Indians of the 1930s how could it be right for the Pakistanis brought into being by Jinnah himself?

Those Indian intellectuals who find fault with the Indian leaders would do well to ponder over the findings of the Raja of Pirpur who thought that the Muslim League must be given a share of the government in UP but parliamentary democracy could go to hell. Jinnah, however, did not say anything about parliamentary democracy not being suitable when in two years time he led his League to demand Pakistan and, of course, he was silent over the unsuitability of parliamentary form of government subsequently also. It was all right to be used as a propaganda weapon against the Congress. In 1939, when Jinnah was still leading a propaganda blitz against the Congress governments, Dr Rajendra Prasad, who became the first elected President of India after independence, was President of the Congress.

Rajen Babu, as he was endearingly called, made a highly reasonable offer to Jinnah that all the complaints of his League against the Congress governments be referred to the British Chief Justice of India, Sir Maurice Gwyer, for inquiry. The offer was made in October 1939 and if Jinnah was interested in getting justice and a judicial verdict on his grievances rather than scoring points of propaganda he should have accepted the fair offer. Instead he rejected it saying airily, "now the matter is under His Excellency's consideration and he is the proper authority to take such action and adopt such measures as would meet our requirements and restore complete sense of security in those provinces where the Congress ministries are in charge of the administration."

The confidence reposed by Jinnah in "His Excellency", the Viceroy was not repaid on this occasion because the 'Laat Sahib', as many Indian would refer to the supreme lord of India, did not concede his demand for an inquiry nor did he condescend to make a statement giving his own verdict on the complaints of the Leaguers. Nor did the British concede Jinnah's demand for a royal commission to investigate his complaints. Perhaps they did not deem it necessary to go into such flimsy complaints. Jinnah apparently had less confidence in a British Chief Justice, although he should have known as a lawyer that they could sometimes take an independent view. The Indian intellectuals are also silent on the Maurice Gwyer offer of Rajendra Prasad.

In any case, the British, going by the remarks of Sir Harry Haig, Governor of Uttar Pradesh during the relevant years of Congress rule, were least convinced by Jinnah's baseless complaints. In his years of retirement, after the Congress ministries in UP and elsewhere had gone out of office, Haig said:" In dealing with communal issues, the (Congress) ministers in my judgment, normally acted with impartiality and a desire to do what was fair. Indeed, towards the end of their time they were being seriously criticised by the Hindu Mahasabha on the ground that they were not being fair to the Hindus, though there was no justification for such a complaint."[10]

Jinnah's desire for a share in the government of UP and possibly some other provinces under Congress rule could be understood as a genuine aspiration if he had accepted the Congress offer of joining the Congress legislature parties. He was, however, not prepared to accept it lest his Leaguers lose their identity and their claim to sole representation of the Muslims could be lost. Jinnah wanted the cake and eat it too. What was the guarantee that once inside the government his MLAs would not have behaved as Liaquat Ali and Company did in the interim government, that is, sabotage it from within?

The Indian intellectuals who think that but for this denial Jinnah would not have gone to the extent of demanding and getting his pound of flesh, Pakistan, exhibit utter naivette and lack of any capacity to think. The League had no *locus standii* as it had not emerged as a majority party even in the Muslim majority areas of Punjab, Sind, NWFP and even Bengal, nor had it got any coalition agreement with the Congress in the seven provinces where the Congress had a majority, including the NWFP. If for this denial you rush to the other extreme of Pakistan, a separate and independent country when you have not yet established any foothold in the northern and eastern areas, you are either out of your mind or your earlier demand was not justified. These individuals should rather understand the objective conditions, specially the manner in which the Muslims of the sub-continent gave their support to Jinnah when he pitched for a separate Muslim state.

**Rajen Babu's Offer**

The complaints against the Congress governments were flimsy because he would not accept the Rajen Babu offer of a Maurice Gwyer inquiry. The Viceroy, sorry 'His Excellency', would not bother to appoint a royal commission as Jinnah had demanded. Nor he himself pursued these demands. Instead he concentrated on the separate state demand. Even the most pro-Muslim Prime Minister of India, Inder Kumar Gujral, who became a care-taker in December 1997, seven months after he had assumed the high office, did not agree to drop the Vande Mataram as demanded by the Muslim separatists. Gujral had shown himself a great lover of everything Muslim, including Urdu, Iqbal whom he continued to refer to "as our great poet", but he had to know the limits to which he could go to pander to separatism. What do the other separatists have now to say about Vande Mataram?

How could the scheme of basic education, authored by an eminent Muslim himself, Dr. Zakir Husain, who later became the President of India, be called a Hindu system simply because it was called the Vidya Mandir scheme in the CP and Berar province? What is wrong if Muslim children, along with the Hindu boys and girls, learn to spin and weave while at school so that they could earn a living after leaving school which is what basic education is about? Are there no weavers among Muslims and how much have the Muslim "leaders" and the intellectuals done for the Muslim weavers of Varanasi (Benares) or for that matter for the Muslim artisans who do the fine chikan work in Lucknow, anything more than the governmental agencies of the Centre and the state or some NGOs, consisting mostly of Hindus, or even as much?

A hue and cry was raised about the Vidya Mandir scheme, the main grievance in the Pirpur report, because the word Mandir was used there. Any Sanskrit scholar would tell you that 'mandir' only means a house. The original word for temples was 'Devmandir', house of God, but later only the word mandir was used. Hindi had long been suppressed by Muslim rulers and when a British governor of UP, Macdonnell, made it compulsory for all employees to learn the Hindi (Devnagari) script, along with the Urdu (Persian and Arabic) script, there were loud protests by the Muslim employees and the press. That was in 1900 and the divide has persisted.

Such is the stuff of what Jinnah called his Pakistan movement. There is no use mourning now the fact that there was an inevitable and inexorable march towards the separatist goal. Partition should have, ideally speaking, been avoided, specially the forcible transfer of population and the mass killings of innocent people and the indignities inflicted on the womenfolk. But any fight against the partition of the country would have led to a massacre when the demand was being supported by the bulk of the Indian Muslims, although the large majority of them were never destined to see it, when the new nation was created or even after it. The continuous pressure on fair-minded Muslims to accept the large majority's view, the fate of Sir Sikander Hayat Khan and his successor, Malik Khizar Hayat Khan Tiwana and of wayward people like Fazlul Huq, the enthusiastic support to the unreasonable demand in the Central Secretariat by its Muslim employees, the great success of the Muslim League in the 1946 elections to the provincial assemblies and consequently to the constituent assembly, the failure and farce of the Interim government, the great Calcutta killing in which some, 5,000 people, more Muslims than Hindus, lost their lives, causing a chain reaction affecting large parts of India, and the strange reluctance of the British officers holding key positions to do anything to arrest the march to anarchy— all this and more was leading inevitably to the partition of the country. It is very easy to say Gandhiji should have stood by his word "Partition over my dead body" but was anyone ready to listen to him and could he also have arrested the march? Jinnah had let loose forces over which neither he nor anyone else had control.

Those were the fateful days of 1945, 1946 and 1947 and partition was a price—a heavy price indeed—which India had to pay if the foreigner had to be pushed out and the destiny, of the large part which still remained in India, was to be taken in hand.

The romantics talk of the aged Congress leadership which was tired of the obstructive behaviour of Jinnah's followers, the frustration of power being denied after they had struggled hard for years and so on. These romantics must invent some theory in support of their argument that partition could have been avoided. In lieu of partition, would they have supported Jinnah's demand for parity between the Muslims, represented by his Leaguers and Leaguers alone, and the Congress representing the Hindus, when the population ratio was 25:75 for the Muslims? Forty-five per cent representation for the Muslims was the demand of nationalist Muslims, not merely of the divisionists in the Muslim League and their leader, Jinnah.

We have referred to the great Calcutta killing and its evil consequences. There were also the terrible killings in undivided Punjab in March 1947 when Jinnah's Muslim League was denied the chance of forming a government and the unionists got ahead of them with Congress and Akali support. Women, Hindu and Sikh, were kidnapped in large numbers and there were the inevitable forcible conversions. There was large scale migration from West Punjab to places like Hardwar, Delhi and east Punjab, the present state of Punjab in India. In the light of these happenings could partition have been still prevented?

### "Aged" Leaders

The Congress had gone to the utmost extent in accommodating Jinnah and a separation as between brothers had been offered by Gandhiji to him when the former went on bended knees to the man who claimed sole representation of the Indian Muslims for himself. Jinnah got a vital little more but in the process the Indian Muslims were divided into three parts. Who was to blame for it but the Muslims who had given such massive support to Jinnah. If, even according to Rafiq Zakaria, the Muslim sentiment for a separate state was so strong that he was dubbed a "traitor to Islam" for supporting the "Quit India" movement, in 1942, how could partition have been avoided? Jinnah did not have to "browbeat" the aged leaders of the Congress.

And were the Congress leaders really aged or ageing? Jawaharlal Nehru was Prime Minister of India for full 17 years after independence. He was only 58 years old when freedom dawned and was in perfectly good health and remained so except for the last year of his life and tenure. Some of his successors were even older when they entered office, Inder Kumar Gujral became Prime Minister at the age of 77.

Yes, Sardar Vallabhbhai Patel was an old man, 71 years of age in 1947, and died on December 15, 1950. But those three and a half years were, in a way, the best years of his life as he achieved the complete political and emotional integration of 550 odd Indian princely states with the rest of India and showed Pakistan the way to be followed with regard to its own Bahawalpur and other princely states. What about the other prominent leaders of the Congress? Dr. Rajendra Prasad was first the President of the Constituent Assembly of India while he still functioned as Food and Agriculture Minister in the Nehru cabinet. Then he was interim President of India from January 26, 1950 to March 1952 when he was elected to the same high office and again reelected in 1957, the only President so far to enjoy the available two terms.

Maulana Abul Kalam Azad, the tallest Muslim under the Congress umbrella and a fine Muslim anywhere, lived for eleven years after independence and he was India's first Education Minister all these years. Rajaji performed many roles, first as Governor of West Bengal, then as Governor General, then as Chief Minister of Madras, again as Home Minister of the Union, and finally led a Swatantra movement which envisaged the economic liberalisation practised even by the United Front government, supported from outside by the Congress with ultimately pulled it down. A veteran like Bidhan Chandra Roy was a medical practitioner and the longest serving Chief Minister of West Bengal until Jyoti Basu arrived on the scene. All of them lived for a long time after independence and this completely debunks the ageing leadership theory.

Even Mahatma Gandhi was in good health and undertook two major fasts, in Calcutta and Delhi, in the interest of communal harmony. He wanted to live for 125 years but fell to the assassin's bullet when he was 78 and in good health.

## NOTES

1. Quoted by Karandikar, *Islam in India's Transition to Modernity*.
2. *Divide and Quit*, Penderel Moon, Chatto and Windus, London.
3. *Ibid*.
4. *Ibid*.
5. *Ibid*.
6. *Ibid*.
7. *Ibid*.
8. *Ibid*.
9. As recalled by the author.
10. Quoted by Ram Gopal, *Indian Muslims: A Political History*.

*Chapter 6*

# AND ITS AGONY

The elections in 1946, the last to be held before the country became free, produced results which gladdened the hearts of the Muslim Leaguers. The results were substantially different from the rather dismal record of the Jinnah League almost a decade earlier in 1937. Then the League, under Jinnah's leadership, had failed to gain a foothold in the Muslim majority provinces like Punjab, Sind and Bengal and some of the Hindu majority provinces also. No doubt, the League had emerged as the poor second of the Congress with an overall tally of 131 seats out of 495 Muslim electorate seats in the country as a whole but even then the large majority of Muslim seats had been won by candidates contesting as independent Muslims.

Now the fortunes were almost reversed. They reflected the real strength of the Muslim League which had won over the bulk of the Muslim population in the years in between by its policy of largely untruthful propaganda, bluff and bluster, by laying emphasis on Muslim separatism, a slogan to which the Muslim masses as well as the intellectuals, barring some honourable exceptions, responded as Jinnah dwarfed the other Muslim leaders and bamboozled the British who were ready to be fooled. He went on harping on the theme the League was the sole representative of the Muslims in India. It was no longer a question of refuting the Congress claim to being an all-India body although the Congress maintained its stand until the end. Now for Jinnah there was also a question of bringing into submission the provincial and other leaders of the Muslim community.

Among them was a tough man, Khizar Hayat Khan Tiwana, who had succeeded as Punjab Chief Minister the equally powerful but more pragmatic Sir Sikander Hayat Khan, who died prematurely. Khizar defied the Muslim supremo, although curiously he was even then a member of the Muslim League. Muslims who were not openly with the Congress carried a Muslim League badge even if they followed policies which were diametrically opposed to the League's ideology. Khizar's heart was, however, in the Unionist party of Punjab, which had Muslims, Hindus and Sikhs, all of them landholders, as its members. The party had ruled Punjab, even in the days of diarchy in the twenties and early thirties, when the founder, Sir Fazle Hasan, ruled the state, followed by Sikander Hayat Khan, followed by Khizar.

In the 1946 elections to the provincial assemblies, the League's victory in Punjab, Sind and Bengal was emphatic as opposed to its lackluster or dismal performance in 1937. In Punjab, it had won 73 of the 86 Muslim seats and as many as 113 out of 119 seats in the Bengal assembly and 27 out of the 34 seats in Sind. Its score was also high in the Hindu majority provinces: in UP it won 54 of the 66 Muslim seats, 34 out of 40 in Bihar, all the Muslim seats in Madras and Orissa (29 and 4 respectively), all the 30 in Bombay, 31 out of 34 in Assam and 13 out of 14 Muslim seats in the C.P. and Berar. In the NWFP, the writ of Khan Abdul Ghaffar Khan still ran and the Congress got 21 seats, including two won by the nationalist Jamiat-ul-Ulama but the League's tally was also an impressive 17. The Congress haul in the Frontier province was praiseworthy but in the rest of the country put together the Congress got just five Muslim seats.

The old difficulty of asking the Muslim voters, exposed to separatist appeals, to vote for a composite party, secular and fighting for India's independence, had to be faced by the Congress again. The Muslim League, on the other hand, appealed to separatism and stood for the rights of Muslims and for a separate state of their own. Now it could brook no rivalry. The objective situation, as reflected in the assembly results, is a slap in the face of those who argue that notwithstanding Jinnah's shenanigans the Indian leaders should have stood firm and not allowed the partition of the country. Apart from the danger of conceding Jinnah's parity demand, between the Hindus and Muslims, which could not have been accepted, how could the demand voiced by the Muslim electorate be ignored?

Here was an electorate, however circumscribed and limited it might be, which believed that the 25 per cent Muslim minority could dictate terms to the whole country. They believed, with their leader, that the Muslims had ruled over the whole country for centuries and were thus entitled to a state of their own. Jinnah had told them that they were a nation apart from the Hindus and they had reposed faith in his leadership. It is a different matter that the Muslims did not hold sway over the whole country at any time, although under the Mughal empire the Central authority had control of large parts of the country. But that authority was in decline from the 17th century onwards and the British had begun to dominate large parts of India.

**Past Recalled**

But the rabble rousers appeal to the popular imagination from time to time and public opinion is not concerned with the facts of history or with logic. It is, of course, true that from the time of Mohammad-Ibn-al-Qasim's invasion in the eighth century to the decline of the Mughal empire in the later part of the 17th century, Muslim power had dominated large parts of India. Although many of the Sultans were at loggerheads and fought against one another and many Muslim rulers had to make compromises, meaning that they could not entirely rule by force and subjugate the Hindus, however fanatical and staunchly Islamic in their approach they might be, with the shining exception of Akbar, the popular imagination is only concerned with the broad fact of Muslim domination.

Make no mistake, the sentiment of Muslims, in general, being heir to the Sultans and emperors of the past was freely aired by the newly elected Muslim MLAs of the League. At a convention of the League legislators this was voiced by Ismail I. Chundrigar, who as we have noted, became for a while the Prime Minister of Pakistan. He told the MLAs that the British had no right to hand over the Muslims to a subject people over whom they had ruled 500 years. (He was modest in calculating the number of years.) Hayat Khan, from Punjab who was once a minister and was Sir Sikander's son, said the Muslims, if given a chance, would give a rehearsal now when the British army was still in India. Sir Feroze Khan Noon, who later became Prime Minister of Pakistan, went even one step further. He said if the Muslims were forced to fight a central government or Hindu raj, "the havoc the Muslims would play will put to shame what Chengis Khan or Halaku did."[1]

The apologists of Jinnah would dismiss such bellicose statements as just one of those things, not to be taken seriously and literally. But remember that the threats were given by responsible people who later rose to high positions in Pakistan. The threats could cause consternation and panic among the Hindus and Sikhs in the northernmost parts of Punjab and in the NWFP particularly, as it did. We shall presently see it but let it be recorded that the convention of League MLAs reiterated in 1946 the demand for Pakistan from which they surprisingly left out Kashmir.

In the wake of the election results, Jinnah had little difficulty in installing Muslim League governments in Bengal and Sind but he was thwarted by Khizar Hayat Khan in Punjab. Here Khizar succeeded in forming a Unionist-Congress ministry although Jinnah had secured an overwhelming majority of Muslim seats which was, however, not sufficient to earn the League a clear majority in the Punjab Assembly. Pakistan had not yet been formed and he had to have the support of the Hindu and Sikh minorities whose voice he could not easily suppress. The logic of a coalition thwarting a big party was repeated in India in May-June 1996 when the United Front cobbled up a coalition of thirteen parties, some of which had fought the recent Lok Sabha elections against one another and certainly against the Congress, which was now extending the UF outside support. The BJP was the biggest party in the new Lok Sabha but it did not have a clear majority with it and the Congress was not supporting it. If precedents are to be found for the League being kept out by the Unionist-Congress coalition there were others too. A number of Indian intellectuals exulted when Gowda (followed ten months later by Gujral) was able to keep the BJP out of power. Would they also challenge the Punjab Chief Minister, Khizar Hayat Khan, who kept Jinnah at bay?

**Khizar Ministry**

But the Muslim League supporters challenged him in the only way they knew by looting and killing the hapless Hindus and Sikhs. They were venting their ire over the League being denied a chance to rule, the Hindus and Sikhs being set targets for venting the anger. The League's strength of 75 Muslim MLAs was further augmented by four Muslim independents joining it. But Jinnah could not get the support of the Hindus or Sikhs who were, in any case, enemies (a different nation) for the Leaguers. So, Khizar, with just nine Muslim seats, but with the backing of the Congress and the Akali Sikhs, whose leader at that time was Sardar Baldev Singh, who was free India's first Defence Minister, formed a government and the Governor, Sir Bertrand Glancey, did not utilise his own powers under section 93 of the Government of India Act and swore in Khizar's ministry. The British, by that time, had become strangely resigned and the attitude of the big bosses had rubbed off on the district officials.

Neither the British top men in the districts nor the subordinate police officers and constabulary, 75 per cent Muslim, defended the Hindus and Sikhs against the marauders of the League. A foretaste of what was to follow in August 1997 was thus provided in the vital Punjab province in March itself. The pretext was that Khizar Hayat Khan had formed a government with Hindu and Sikh support and the League had been denied its legitimate right. The denial was unfortunate but how were the ordinary Hindus and Sikhs to be blamed if Jinnah was thwarted by Khizar?

The Unionist-Congress coalition was an uneasy affair as the Leaguers chaffing at the denial of power were thirsting for taking it out on the Hindu and Sikh minorities. It did not matter to the League and its supporters that the government was headed by a tried and highly efficient Muslim of unimpeachable character. Why did the League supporters wait for February and March 1947 when the government was formed in 1946? The answer is to be found in some of the steps taken by Khizar's government. The Leaguers were getting ready for a showdown and were collecting arms throughout the province. Not to be outdone, the Hindus and Sikhs were also engaged in the same activity at some places.

In January that year, the Khizar government banned both the

National Guards, a "volunteer" force of the Muslim League and the Rashtriya Swayamsevak Sangh, RSS, a volunteer force of the Hindus. The RSS had become popular with the Hindus in Punjab because being a minority in the province, and in small numbers in the remote northernmost districts of West Punjab, they looked upto it for protection. We have seen that the British district officers were reluctant to do their duty and the Muslim policemen were denying the people the required protection. There were, however, demonstrations against the ban on the Muslim League force and by the end of the month it was withdrawn.

It was becoming obvious to Khizar that his position had become untenable, although he was meeting out justice even-handedly, as evidenced by his ban on the RSS at the same time that the Muslim League's National Guards were also deemed to be illegal. He, therefore, resigned on March 3 and invited the League to form a government with the help of other parties. The League was, however, in no position to do so as neither the Congress nor the Akalis would come forward to lend their support to it, although there were rumours that a League government was about to be formed.

**Sachar Procession**

The Hindus and Sikhs took advance action to register their protest against the League coming to power and the Finance Minister in the outgoing Khizar government, Bhimsen Sachar of the Congress, took out a procession in Lahore. The Sikh leader, Master Tara Singh, was also there to take part in the march and drew his sword to proclaim that the Sikhs would rule.[2] Although this was just a routine statement and gesture, it was utilised by the Muslim League to engineer large scale riots by its cadres on the pretext that they had been "provoked." The arms which had been collected in the past few months now came handy. More than five thousand people, mostly Hindus and Sikhs, were killed in Punjab. The violence was widespread but the brunt was borne by the remote districts of Rawalpindi and others where the minorities were hopelessly outnumbered.

Even Amritsar, the holy place of the Sikhs, was in the grip of anti-minority violence since the whole of Punjab was one and the Muslims were in large numbers even in this central Punjab town.

Migration soon followed in the wake of these riots and hundreds of thousands of people, who had no godfather in the British and Muslim-dominated administration, abandoned their hearths and homes for safer places like Hardwar, Delhi and the southernmost areas of Punjab itself. Even a Leftist writer, like Bhisham Sahni, had to face facts and his play, later serialised for the TV and made into a film, as *Tamas,* had to admit that scores of Sikh women in west Punjab killed themselves by jumping into a well to escape death and dishonour at the hands of the communally minded Muslim Leaguers.

Undivided Punjab was on fire and in the eastern sector Jinnah's deputy Suhrawardy had let loose a massive 'Direct Action' which had now spread to Bihar and the eastern part of Bengal, now in Bangladesh. Gandhiji camped for days together in Noakhali, in east Bengal, travelled barefoot from village to village to bring solace and cheer to men and women many of whom had been abducted and forcibly converted. The fires lighted by the great Calcutta killing had spread to Bihar also and ghastly scenes of violence and abduction were witnessed in that large province. Suhrawardy's plan had misfired as after the first two days of Muslims in indulging in loot and murder of the Hindus and Sikhs, many of the latter in the transportation and taxi trade, retaliated in a massive manner. Those days there were no Srikrishna Commissions to find out what had happened and who had been responsible for spreading the violence, as we have in free India.

The effect of all this was that the people and leaders of the country came to the firm conclusion that the British had, no doubt, seen reason and finally decided to quit but it would not be possible to carry on in future with the Muslim League. The Interim Government had resulted in virtual two administrations, the Central government was a mute spectator to the falling apart of things and the British officers still in key positions were unwilling to move their little finger. Their motto, as Moon said, was "to divide and quit".

Only a stupid optimist or an utter fool could think, under the circumstances, that India could any longer carry on as one nation. Jinnah had succeeded beyond measure and beyond his own imagination. Even so, the Pakistan offered to him was really moth-eater and truncated, words which he had used when Rajaji and Gandhi himself had given it to him on a platter. This was in spite of the great deal of negotiations, visits of the British Cabinet Mission and earlier by a bigger parliamentarian group, visit of Indian leaders to London and Mountbatten's quick-fix solutions. Not only India was being divided but Punjab and Bengal also. Assam, which was earlier included in the Muslim majority group C by the Cabinet Mission, was now to go to India except a Muslim majority district.

The Pakistan of Rahmat Ali's dreams and even of Iqbal's conception was not what finally emerged. The Hindus and Sikhs of undivided Punjab voted for being part of India and the Hindus of Bengal voted likewise for India, not Pakistan. The whole of East Punjab and West Bengal were lopped off Jinnah's Pakistan since the people's representatives so desired. The district, rather than the province, thus became the basis of partition. Under the Rajaji formula the province was to become the basis. The majority enjoyed by the Muslims in Punjab and Bengal was, in the first place, the *raison detre* for Pakistan and for the Jinnah demand.

Unfortunately, the Hindus and Sikhs of Punjab, rather many of them, clung to the view that city of Lahore would be part of India. Many for that reason did not move out to safer areas in India while the going was good. They were to learn a little later that this was not to be as the Radcliffe Commission gave its award but at least in the east the fair city of Calcutta remained in India while many had to give up their fond habitation in their lovely Lahore. In the east Gandhiji had been putting out the fires of communalism by abjuring power and perquisites, comforts and prerogatives that should have been his for the asking. He was the eternal naked fakir who kept away from the portals of power. He had worked as no other man had to achieve Indian independence but when it came he was in a crowded bustee of Calcutta devoted to his task of bringing peace and tranquillity to the city's poor and harassed middle classes.

**Gandhi Ignored**

It has never occurred to our intellectuals and historians that Nehru and his colleagues should not have taken it for granted that

Gandhi could not have been interested in assuming office as Prime Minister. The office should have really speaking been offered to him on the transfer of power, even for formality's sake. The Mahatma was in perfect health and was to undertake two major fasts one in Calcutta to make the people forget the past and live as brothers and the other in the national capital to impress on the Hindus and Sikhs to co-exist with the Muslims, whatever happened in Pakistan.

Gandhiji was averse to the trappings of office, just as today's politicians want more and more of them and are, therefore, the very opposite of Gandhiji. But it is one thing for Gandhi to remain away from the allurements of office and another for his followers to presume that he would never be interested and, therefore, not even formally ask him. Nehru moved into the Commander-in-Chief's house, now called Teen Murti Bhavan, in the name of security. Any number of cringing officials are always ready to suggest to the man in authority that he should remain protected and what better way to achieve protection than to live in a palatial house, occupied in the old days by the No. two man in the British hierarchy. The Viceroy, of course, lived in Government House, now called Rashtrapati Bhavan, and the Commander-in-Chief lived in the mansion closeby.

Contrast this with Gandhi's attitude. He was offered police protection and the searching of visitors to his prayer meetings since it was at one of these that Madanlal Pahwa had hurled a bomb a few days before he was killed. If Gandhiji had accepted only the search proposal Godse could not have carried his deadly pistol into the prayer grounds at the Birla House, now called Gandhi Smriti on Tees Janvari Marg in New Delhi. The present generation is used to seeing any damn fellow, who claims to be a VIP or VVIP, protected by a host of armed men. It is important that they know what kind of a man Gandhiji was. If only he had allowed the searching of the person of the visitors to the prayer meetings he could have lived much longer. He preferred death to security.

There was a different story in the eastern sector as compared with the travails of the western sector. Thanks to Gandhiji's efforts in the cause of communal harmony -- in fact, Mountbatten who had been chosen by the Congress leaders as the first Governor

General of free India for nearly a year had called him 'the one-man boundary force' in contrast with the 50,000 troops of the Boundary force in the western sector which failed to prevent the slaughter-- and other factors there was not much painful migration from or to India and East Pakistan. Some of those who wanted to make a fortune in the new country did migrate but in fact there was and has been a continuous flow of human beings from East Pakistan and later Bangladesh, first mostly Hindus but now mostly Muslims, and the number is as large as fifteen million illegal migrants from Bangladesh. In the first few years of independence more than six million Hindus migrated from East Pakistan to India.

The killings in West Pakistan, beginning in March 1947, as we have seen, had caused a big wave of retribution in the areas of East Punjab, including the present Haryana, Delhi and Western UP. The pent up anger of the Hindus and Sikhs in East Punjab burst at the seams on August 14 that year as the Muslim constabulary was disarmed and the British officers departed. Some killings were continuing in West Punjab and the Hindus and Sikhs, who had migrated earlier to Amritsar and other southern areas, now took it upon themselves to settle scores. The local population, many of them, joined the killers and looters and the Hindu-Sikh policemen, many with bitter memories of what they had endured in the pre-partition days, went on the rampage.

The chain reaction also started in West Pakistan and the Hindu-Sikh minority had a harrowing time as they tried to run for safety in India. In the specified areas of northern India also there was killing and plunder on a large scale. Muslim houses were broken into and forcibly occupied in many areas and the lawful occupants were either forced out or killed. While a number of Muslims had voluntarily left for Pakistan, even before partition, many others were now forced to do so. I was then in Delhi, working as a young journalist on the staff of the now defunct *Indian News Chronicle*, which later gave birth to the Delhi editions of the *Times of India* and *Indian Express*. I could see with my own eyes the devastation caused by Jinnah's partition and the lawlessness which caused untold hardship to the Hindus and Sikhs in West Pakistan, who were forced to flee, and to Muslims in parts of India who were the victims of retaliation. Ironically, the Muslims who were forced out of their homes and had to migrate to Pakistan remained Muhajirs by and large in that country, even till today, while some of them were lucky and got absorbed in the mainstream. Jinnah himself belonged to the later category but had no means to rescue his kith and kin, if he really looked upon the hapless people that way.

**Tragedy in Delhi**

I saw Muslim shops in Karol Bagh in Delhi, in what is now a fashionable shopping centre in Ajmal Khan road, being plundered by mobs, mostly of local Hindus and Sikhs, while the police looked on in apparent sympathy, as did many of the northern Indian army units. The houses of some Muslims were broken into in the large Karol Bagh area and the residents were compelled to seek refuge with relatives in Muslim mohallas or in the Jhandewalan refugee camp in the vast open ground. (Karol Bagh was a majority Hindu-Sikh area but there were many Muslims of the middle and lower middle class.) As the shops were looted, some of the looters did not care to pick up pairs of shoes and chappals in their hurry and later complained that they had "acquired" an odd pair. Among the victims of plunder and vandalism was a laundry owned by a genuinely nationalist Muslim who had the courage in those days to name his laundry as "Jai Hind" laundry. Not only a real lover of India was subjected to plunder by fellow Indians but the looters did not realise that the clothes and linen actually belonged to one another.

There was a curfew for long hours and days. The postal delivery was disorganised and many letters did not reach you for days together and some failed to arrive even then. The foresight and helpful attitude of the well known author, Nirad Chaudhuri, made him send across to me through his eldest son, then a boy of ten or so, a copy of my appointment letter in the News Services Division of All India Radio where he was working as Talks Officer, But for that gesture, I would perhaps have not joined AIR because the original addressed to me never reached me. Chaudhuri's house in Nicholson Road was close to my office and sometimes I and Dhruva Narayan, the emissary, recalled the event.

Order was gradually restored after a lot of people had enriched themselves at the cost of many Muslim shopkeepers in different parts of Delhi. The story is told of a prominent journalist of New Delhi whose family members had to make several trips to the shop being plundered in Cannaught Place. I particularly recall the touching sight of a little child hugging the cage of the family's pet parrot as the family was being evicted to be taken to the Jhandewalan refugee camp.

All this was part of the ghastly tragedy that was the partition of India. Millions of refugees were coming into India from West Pakistan and the Hindus and Sikhs in northern India were making the task of the harassed government of Nehru and Patel difficult by their retaliatory attacks. As two generations have grown up the memories of those terrible days have faded as these energetic people settled down to the hard realities of life and many in creative activities in different parts of India. The Punjabi refugees had some problems in being accepted by the generality of Indians but this is nothing when compared to the Muhajir problems in Pakistan. The progeny has forgiven the perpetrators of partition and some of them are in the forefront of the movement to befriend the people of Pakistan, largely a one-way activity, as the Nawaz Sharif government has not responded to Gujral's unilateral action on visas. Ironically, Gujral, who belongs to the category of people who were uprooted from West Pakistan, and some of his ilk crave nostalgically for the very homes from which they were forcibly evicted. His journalist and businessmen friends may offer from time to time one-way friendship to Pakistan but the latter remains untouched and does not care to respond. Pakistan keeps its doors shut and windows stuffed, or tries to do it.

Those who knew what was happening in West Punjab from March onwards would be living in a fools' paradise if they had led themselves and others to believe that after partition everything would be hunky dory and hereafter the two countries and their people would live in peace. The Congress leaders of Punjab and even Akalis like Master Tara Singh had been assuring the Hindus and Sikhs that no harm would come to them if they stayed on. Those who believed these assurances lived to see their houses being plundered and their own lives being endangered. Many of them lost their kith and kin as they fled leaving behind their well appointed houses.

**"Go To Gandhi"**

"Go to your Gandhi. Or go to Nehru and Patel," said some of the British officers in the Punjab districts in March 1947 when they were approached by helpless Hindus and Sikhs who were being robbed and attacked by Muslim mobs. As district officers and those under them it was their duty to protect and help the people entrusted to their care. But whether out of sympathy for the Muslims or because they were under the impression that they had finished their duty, as freedom was coming soon, these men did not lift their little finger. This is on the testimony, i.e. the lack of response and unwillingness to help, of Penderel Moon who was a British ICS officer in Punjab during the crucial days, as we have noted. He said:"... The charge of indifference may have more substance (than the one about stirring up trouble.) Of several British officers the story was told that when appealed to by panic-sticken Hindus for help and protection they referred the petitioners to Gandhi, Nehru or Patel."[3]

There was nothing to prevent the experienced and trained British officers to enforce order and ensure that the police carried out orders if they were intent on performing their duty and stopping the Muslim marauders. According to Moon, only in Multan district the law was enforced but elsewhere he had to record that either the officers were taking half-hearted measures or were reluctant to do anything. He said in defence of his British colleagues that the Muslim police, who, as we have seen, were in control of the province, had been affected by the rising tide of communalism.

Not only communalism was rising at an alarming pace but the human tragedy of the helpless Hindus and Sikhs, at the mercy of the British officers and their Muslim police, was forcing partition on the country. It was futile in the circumstances then prevailing to think of any other course and only those who did not know the ground realities could blame anyone for the partition of the country other than its high priest, Mohammad Ali Jinnah. The British officers were at best reluctant and at worst accomplices of the ravagers in West Punjab. It was the March riots which set the trend for the August and September 1947 killings in Punjab and adjoining Pakistani and Indian territories. Some half a million to a million people lost their lives in both countries and some five million

Hindus and Sikhs and an equal number or more of Muslims from India were made to flee their hearths and homes because the maker of Pakistan would not think of a "peaceful settlement" between brothers, as proposed by Gandhiji to him in the Gandhi-Jinnah negotiations, during the upheaval.

Clement Attlee, the Labour Prime Minister of Britain at that time, was a friend of India and a genuine believer in Indian independence. He was as committed to Indian freedom as his predecessor Tory leaders like Winston Churchill were opposed to it. While Churchill had the decency to say 'no' to Indian demand for freedom his colleagues were men of straw and indulged in rhetoric, untruthful pretensions and humbug. If they had not held endless round-table talks and instead had handed over genuine power to India in 1930 or thereabout the evil of partition could have been avoided. If Jinnah could be bewitched by mere ministerships in provincial governments he would have simply fallen for genuine power provided he shared it in the right proportions with the Congress, either in 1930 or even at the Cripps Mission's abortive efforts.

The British kept up the pretence that the princes of India were sovereign once their own paramount authority lapsed. But what Sardar Patel showed in 1947-49 could have been accomplished even in the thirties or in 1942. The question was were the British ready. They were never willing to handover power except, under Attlee, in 1946-47 when the inevitable was happening. If real power had been transferred to Indian hands during the Second World War, instead of the promise of control over defence canteens and a show of designations and bogus ministership-- power without portfolios--Indians could have been mobilised to save the country, instead of just providing cannon fodder to the British. What is more, a grateful India could have stood by Britain and the evil of partition could have been averted.

Perhaps the Muslims would still have walked away with more than their 25 per cent shares in the legislature in government jobs and in ministerships. But the likely drill about the transfer of power could perhaps have saved the country the massacres of 1947. But all this is wishful thinking because until Attlee arrived on the scene the British rulers were never genuinely interested in making the Indians the masters of their own destiny and in laying down sound principles which Jinnah or any recalcitrant Muslim leader would have jolly well got to accept.

Instead they allowed factional demands to be made and they pampered the divisionist Muslim leaders as though they thought that the Indians would not allow them to leave this country. Only Attlee was in a hurry to transfer power and he rightly chose Mountbatten to do a neat and quickfix job. The British in India were always imperialistic. The British in England often included men of vision and genuine concern for the welfare of India as a whole. The story may be related here of a good British army officer who, in the days of the second world war, was commanding a Gurkha unit in the British Indian Army. He was the chief guest at a Dusserah celebration of the unit. Those who know the Nepalis would tell you that Dusserah is their biggest festival. The Gurkha unit had done its duty and the CO gallantly responded, knowing that he must take interest in the activities of his unit, but being British he was ignorant of the basic facts of Indian history. He told the units while leaving "Iski tarah daka mat dalo". don't rob people like him. He was, of course, referring to the photo of Shivaji that had been hung in the Dusserah pandal, probably in recognition of the response of the Maratha Light Infantry unit men who had attended the celebrations by invitation. According to the little history that the British officer had learnt, Shivaji was a dacoit. There was a virtual revolt by the Gurkha and Maratha troops and the officer had to go back and apologise.[4]

The attitude of the British officers in India was always one of ignorance, prejudice and often one of partiality, and only in a few cases of understanding and sympathy. During the crucial days and weeks that followed the events of March 1947 their behaviour was a strange mixture of reluctance, abandonment of authority and deeprooted sympathy for the Muslims. The events of March were important as the pattern was being set and the disaster that followed in August and in subsequent weeks could not be averted. The Muslims of Punjab and the NWFP, now that the Pathans were even more volatile than ever and the control of Badshah Khan was weakening, and the Hindus and Sikhs of East Punjab and some in Delhi and adjoining areas, were taking it out on one another in the mohallas and villages.

**Women Worst Victims**

The women's agony can only be imagined. I was present in a group in Delhi soon after independence when an elderly Punjabi woman said, "Jananian bicharian mar gayian", the poor womenfolk had the worst of it. Many were the tales of the indignities on women, kidnapping, forcible conversion and rape or marriage, separation from near and dear ones, and some kindness and gentleness after forcible marriage to a member of another community.

The boundary force of 50,000 troops, both Indian and Pakistani, created by the departing British, struggled manfully to cope with the situation and escorted the refugees in crowded trains and, also for those with a clout, special vehicles, trucks, buses or private cars. We have it on the authority of Moon that the Boundary Force could not rise to the occasion as it was outnumbered and the violence and lawlessness were spreading much faster than envisaged.

"It was only after crossing the Indian border that we heaved a sigh of relief. We had survived. God had been very merciful". These are the words of Captain M. S. Kohli, retired officer of the Indian Navy and leader of the first successful Indian expedition to Mount Everest who recalled the harrowing experience of his migration from Haripur in the NWFP of Pakistan to India, in the company of his father. The elder Kohli was a petty shopkeeper in Haripur. They had migrated to India in March 1947 because of the March killings. Unfortunately neither the father could settle down in business nor the young Kohli could find a job. Assured by Nehru, Jinnah and Baldev Singh, in their acceptance of partition broadcast over ALL INDIA RADIO, on June 3, of their safety and well-being, the two of them went back to Haripur. The broadcast was to announce the acceptance of the Mountbatten plan (in reality the V.P. Menon plan) and the leaders appealed to the people to stay put.

But the reality was different. On August 15, M. S. Kohli was approached "by a Muslim friend of ours (who) rushed to our shop (the Kohlis had set up shop again) breathless and full of panic. He advised us to run immediately as a mob consisting of over a lakh Muslims from the surrounding villages had entered the town killing all Hindus and Sikhs". Kohli says they took shelter in a Gurdwara from the top of which he could see the entire town on fire. He managed to reach a nearby police station by jumping over the rooftops of houses, built close to one another, and finally making the last lap of fifty yards evading an attacking mob. The police officers, among whom there were some Hindus still, saved them and sent them to Wah, near Rawalpindi in Punjab, where a big camp of Hindus and Sikhs in distress, like the Kohlis, was under the care of troops, possibly of the boundary force.

From the Wah camp, they managed to get on to a goods train going to India, after making several unsuccessful attempts for days to enter trains for India. The overcrowding in trains could hardly be described. People travelled on rooftops couplings, footboard, dumped on one another if they could manage to get into a coach. Goods trains were converted into passenger coaches. On the way at Wazirabad, near Lahore, a Muslim mob wanted to kills all the occupants of that train on the strength of a rumour that a train full of bodies had reached that place from India the previous day.

Fortunately for the Kohlis, at that very moment when they were face to face with death, a train from India bringing a number of Muslim refugees alive drew up and it was under the command of no less a person than Col. Ayub Khan who later rose to be the first of three military dictators of Pakistan. Father and son knew him as he also belonged to Haripur and thus not only they but the other occupants of the goods train were spared their lives. From thereon there was a more or less uneventful journey to Amritsar. Not only was Capt. Kohli much indebted to Col. (later Field Marshal) Ayub Khan but the warmth and lavish hospitality (as only the Muslims are capable of) with which he was honoured on his later visits to Pakistan, when Kohli was well known as the first expedition leader, removed all the bitterness from his heart and the last vestiges of anger and rancour.

This phenomenon has to be understood. Kohli says his father and he were the only two Sikhs alive in Haripur on August 16 morning as the Hindu and Sikh houses were reduced to ashes and all the Sikhs had been killed. He escaped death by a whisker twice, once in Haripur and again in Wazirabad and managed to reach India in trains and buses packed like sardines in which getting in was itself a difficult proposition and required him to wait for days. Yet he has no bitterness in his heart and wants to go back to his town, the place where he was born and bred up, nourishing fond memories of his childhood.

**Cold Figures**

Coming to the cold statistics of the era, we have already said that half a million to a million could have been killed on the two sides of the border. Half a million is the estimate of Justice G. D. Khosla, retired High Court judge, writer and a really eminent person (not the kind whom the media nowadays call "eminent"). Some other calculations put the figure at 200,000 and some between this figure and half a million. There are those who put the figure of those killed at 5 or 6 million which is a clear exaggeration. The main killings were in the two Punjabs and the account given by Capt. Kohli would suggest that the NWFP did not escape the fury of the painful partition. Those Hindus and Sikhs, who could not escape while the going was good or who did not receive divine dispensation, as Kohli did, would certainly have faced extermination.

In Sind, there was not much by way of killing but the entire Hindu population, save a few in small pockets, had to migrate to India leaving behind vast properties on being completely uprooted from their homes as were the people of Punjab who also faced, in addition, the certainty of death if they did not manage to escape. In the princely states of Patiala and some others, close to East Punjab in India, things were equally terrible. There were, indeed, some attacks on persons in and around Delhi and life was not safe. But largely, the problem was one of forcible eviction and dispossession of property which naturally was a matter of grave concern to the Muslims of Delhi and until Gandhiji fasted to restore a sense of confidence in January 1948 the issue was not settled in a peaceful manner.

Some innocent people were done to death in western UP and Rajasthan. But what happened in Pakistan was simply unbeatable. Pakistan was denuded of its entire population of Hindus and Sikhs. A miniscule minority remained back and now leads a fearful existence. Until the last days of British rule, many members of the Hindu community in what is now Pakistan had a thriving business, many were in the professions and in government service. Likewise the Sikhs, hardy farmers as many of them are, were rich agriculturists in the colony areas of West Punjab and were also otherwise wealthy farmers, besides those in urban occupations. The Sikh peasantry has been well known for its enterprise, innovativeness and amenability to modern farming practices. The terai region in UP, near Pilibhit and elsewhere, has been colonised by these hardy men.

**Jinnah's Crocodile Tears**

Jinnah knew little of the Muslims in areas other than Punjab and less of the Punjabi Muslims. He was glibly talking of the safety of the minorities on August 11, 1947, just three days before he became the first Governor General of the country he had created. In an address to the Constituent Assembly of Pakistan in Karachi, which was to become the new nation's capital and remain so until the military dictator Ayub Khan built Islamabad, in the sixties, Jinnah said: "...there is no discrimination, no distinction between one community and another, no discrimination between one caste or creed and another".[6]

Yet even at that stage and in a couple of days later mass migrations of Hindus and Sikhs from his Pakistan and of the Muslims from some areas in India was going on. The continuing discrimination which is the fate of the small Christian minority in Pakistan, doing mostly menial jobs like street and house cleaning, the same as the unfortunate lot of many dalits in India, belies Jinnah's fond and largely hollow hopes. The case of the boy Masih, who was about to be hanged for alleged blasphemy in Pakistan, until rescued by the intrepid woman lawyer, Asma Jahangir, and in whose cause the United States put pressure on its close ally, Pakistan, is an instance in point.

The superstructure of the new nation is built on discrimination. It is declared an Islamic state, only a Muslim can become the head of state, and large numbers of Ahmediya Muslims are declared non-Muslims, suffer persecution and cannot pray in their own mosques. If Sir Mohammad Zafrullah Khan had lived today, he would be spending his days in a remote corner of the country or in a Pakistani jail instead of defending Pakistani aggression in Kashmir in the United Nations which he did when he was Foreign Minister of the new country. He was after all an Ahmediya. Jinnah had talked through his hat when he claimed there would be no discrimination in Pakistan. He had so far been talking of two nations, Hindus and Muslims. The bogus claim of separate identity being abolished could only convince the *Times of India* which reproduced his address to the Constituent Assembly to show how concerned it was about secularism.

Jinnah said in that address: "...you will find in the course of time Hindus would cease to be Hindus and Muslims would cease to be Muslims, not in the religious sense, because that is the personal faith of each individual, but in the political sense as citizens of the state..." Note that now Jinnah had begun to talk of religion being the personal faith of an individual which is the sane thing to do. But, only a few years earlier, in February 1940, in a press statement designed to prepare the minds of the Muslims for Pakistan, for which he had a resolution adopted only a month later in the Lahore session of the Muslim League, he had said: "The Hindus and Muslims belong to two different religious philosophies, social customs, literature. They neither intermarry nor interdine together...Their aspect on life and of life are different...To yoke two such nations under a single state, one as a numerical minority and the other as a majority, must lead to growing discontent and final destruction of any fabric that may be so built up for the government of such a state".[8]

The newspaper which printed the text, in the fiftieth year of India's freedom and Pakistan's creation, thought it would prove its secular credentials thereby. But it tried to conceal the poison that Jinnah had spread in the few years preceding and his attempt to sweep it under a carpet now. The man had brought undescribable destruction to large parts of Pakistan and even India at the very moment he was laying claim to such fine sentiments. There is an Indian proverb: "Sau chuhe mar kar billi haj ko jati hai", the cat is off to the Haj pilgrimage after finishing off a hundred rats. But the people of Pakistan were no hypocrites and needed no hypocritical advice from Jinnah. They swung into action even before Pakistan was proclaimed and unfortunately many in the adjoining Indian territories behaved in like fashion.

Even an ardent opponent of Hindutva had to admit that Jinnah had spewed poison against the Hindus in his campaign to attain his goal of Pakistan. He said: "The only parallel was another man born in Karachi, M.A. Jinnah. He too generated hatred and violence against an entire community, just to secure political power".[9]

Every year the United States brings out a "Report on Religious Freedom" around the world, an echo of the time when its concern to protect the Christians all over the world was highly pronounced (and it is only slightly less now.) On July 22, 1997 it brought out its report for 1996-97 and it had this to say about its close ally and beneficiary of its largesse: "Pakistan's constitution establishes Islam as the state religion. Since 1986 section 295(c) of the Penal Code has stipulated the death penalty for blaspheming Prophet Mohammad. According to the Human Rights Commission of Pakistan, police opened one case against a Christian, Ayub Masih, under section 295(c) in 1996. The blasphemy provision contributes to inter-religious tension, intimidation, fear and violence...Islamic extremists have assaulted, raped and even murdered members of religious minorities...In February 1997, Muslim mobs destroyed houses and churches belonging to Christians in the Khanewal area...Discriminatory legislation has led to acts of violence directed at Ahmadis, Christians, Hindus and Zakris".[10]

Jinnah's crocodile tears are of little avail to the hapless people of the minorities in Pakistan who might not know that the father of Pakistan ever uttered these words which were never practised and were never meant to be. According to writer Arun Shourie, former editor of the *Indian Express*, there are some 3,000 sectarian killings in Pakistan in a year. "Pakistan remains in its mind an Islamic state. The Gujral doctrine is trying to defang an exclusivist ideology through concessions."[11] Quoting Winston Churchill on the politics of concessions Shourie said: "It means feeding one's relatives to the crocodile in the hope that it might eat you last".

## NOTES

1. Quoted by Ram Gopal, *Ibid*.

2. "Raj Karega Khalsa", the pure (meaning Sikhs) would rule, he said, following the dictum by the tenth and last Guru of the Sikhs, Guru Gobind Singh, an undoubtedly great man, who converted a religious sect into a fighting force.
3. Penderel Moon, *Divide and Quit. Ibid.* Moon also cites the instance of the District Magistrate of Amritsar, who used a company of British soldiers, at his disposal, the Inniskilling Fusiliers, to stage a flag march, instead of using them to put down rioting. He contrasts this with the massacre of Jallianwalla Bagh in the same city in April 1919, when with only fifty men armed with rifles, (Brig. Gen.) Dyer killed hundreds of people. Moon says: "The Amritsar district was to be the scene of fearful bloodshed later in the year. The complete breakdown of authority in the city at this time (March 1947) prepared the way for it". At another place, he calls the killings of March "a foretaste of the blessings of Pakistan".
4. As narrated to the author by an MLI JCO.
5. *Hindustan Times*, Delhi, Sept. 14, 1997.
6. Text reproduced by the *Times of India*, Delhi, August 12, 1997.
7. *Ibid*.
8. Quoted in *Indian Muslims A Political History, Ibid*.
9. J.S. Bandukwala, *Times of India*, letter to the editor, Sept. 24, 1997.
10. US State Department Report on Religious Freedom, July 22, 1997.
11. *Indian Express*, Delhi, July 26, 1997.

*Chapter 7*

# PAKISTAN DIVIDED

It was the winter of 1956 and Delhi was getting colder by the day. As Information Officer attached to the then Ministry of Commerce and Industry, I was made a member of the Indian delegation to the trade negotiations with Pakistan. A large delegation of Ministers, mostly Bengalis from East Pakistan, and officials, mostly Punjabis from Pakistan's Punjab province, who had already acquired domination over the country, and some Muhajirs, descended on the Indian capital. The ministers were as determined to revive the border trade between East Pakistan and the adjoining Indian state of West Bengal and generally restore the trade tries between the two countries as the officials were to prevent it. Partition had cut off the trade ties between the two close neighbours and rudely deprived the toiling East Pakistanis of their livelihood as fishermen and farmers because they could not sell fish and eggs to the Bengalis in India across the border. It was well known then as now that partition had created a wall in the middle of several villages and separated the sources of fish and poultry from their buyers right across the Indo-Pakistan border. The Punjabi and Muhajir officials were, on the other hand, convinced that there should be no trade contacts or contacts of any kind, very much like their successors today.

This was the only time when the majority living in the eastern wing[1] was in effective control in Karachi, the political capital of Pakistan then. Even now, after military dictator Ayub Khan, the first of three, took away the capital of the country to Islamabad in the extreme north of the country, Karachi is still the largest city of Pakistan and despite the abounding ethnic, and lately even the sectarian killings, one of the finest cities in the world. Suhrawardy, who had stayed back in India for a few months after partition and fraternised with Gandhiji to prevent the communal killings in Calcutta, was now the Prime Minister of Pakistan and a number of other ministers from East Pakistan held important portfolios. Among them was Abul Mansoor Ahmed, Minister of Commerce, who led the delegation from Pakistan, while the official wing was headed by the redoubtable Aziz Ahmed, who was then Commerce Secretary. Later he rose to be Foreign Secretary and even Minister of Foreign Affairs, being a highly competent man and sky was the limit for such men in Pakistan. He had been schooled in the hawkish style of Pakistani bureaucrats. It was senior civil servants like him who had divided the Central Secretariat in Delhi in the crucial years, 1946 and 1947, into India and Pakistan and made the Indian leaders realise that if India was to be saved there was no option but partition or else the country could go to the dogs as the forces of destruction were holding it to ransom.

Aziz Ahmed was for many years the leader of the anti-Indian establishment in his country and did everything possible to prevent an Indo-Pakistan trade agreement being reached. He would just walk out of the official level talks when he found the going tough and the next day sheepishly walk back into the meeting because his Bengali minister wanted him to continue the dialogue. An agreement was finally reached and provided for the resumption of border trade between the two Bengals so that fish, staple diet of the people, could be brought in from East Pakistan as headloads now permitted under the agreement.

The important point is that along with the delegation came in a whole lot of Bengali ministers and officials from Dhaka (then still spelt Dacca). The Karachi crowd consisted of only one Bengali minister and the rest of them hawkish Pakistanis. Among the youthful ministers who had trooped in from Dacca was Sheikh Mujibur Rahman later to become Bangbandhu and Father of the Nation of Bangladesh. He was killed by some Bengali army officers, acting on instructions from Pakistan, after Bangladesh was created and Mujib had been in power for nearly four years.

All the Bengali ministers and their entourage of private secretaries were full of bitternesses against the Punjabi establishment in the western wing of Pakistan and full of friendship and admiration for India. Later when I spent nine months in the United States, under a joint Indo-US training and familiarisation programme in mass communication, I was to find that there was no love lost between the West Pakistani students, who were quite numerous in the United States, and those from East Pakistan, who were equally numerous. Not only that. The Bengalis from East Pakistan mixed freely with the Indian student community and some even shared rented accommodation with their Indian counterparts. There was indeed some togetherness between Indian and Pakistani students from the western wing also but the friendship between the Indian students and the Bengalis had to be seen to be believed. Not merely among the Bengalis on both sides but generally between the student community from India and the East Pakistani students.

**India Looked Upto**

In their struggle against the unjust rule from Karachi (and later Islamabad) the Bengalis from the eastern part of Pakistan naturally looked upon India and the Indians as their reliable and true friends and allies. When Bengali staffers and ministers in the trade delegation from Pakistan told us that they looked up to Delhi and Calcutta, not to Karachi and Lahore, they meant what they said. This spirit of friendship and camaraderie was to manifest itself in a strong way when during the bulk of 1971 the Bangladeshi freedom movement worked together with Indians which really ensured the success of the struggle to free Bangladesh of the West Pakistani oppression.

The real break had come much earlier when the Bengalis could not feel emotionally at home with their fellow citizens from West Pakistan. Jinnah had created a new state of Pakistan and handed it over to the Punjabis and regional feelings ruled the heart of Pakistan, rather than the Islamic spirit under which the nation had been carved out of India. Along with the Punjabis there were still a few Muhajirs from India, who shared the power, but they have been gradually driven to a corner in what is left of

Pakistan. If the Bengali component of the trade delegation from Pakistan felt at home with the Indians and the East Pakistani students in the United States preferred to live with the Indians, rather than their fellow (west) Pakistanis, it was because the realisation that they had thrown in their lot with strangers at the time of partition had come to them much earlier. The raw deal was being felt by the Bengalis from the first day.

"The movement for Bengali separatism did not develop in a short period. It has deep roots in the history of Pakistan. Several attempts at national integration were made by various governments but the process of nation building was hampered by different factors..."[2] This is what a Pakistani writer, Safdar Mahmood, has to say in his book *Pakistan Divided*. Jinnah broke up India, into India and Pakistan, in 1947. Mujib broke up Pakistan into two in 1971. Mujib thus played Jinnah to Pakistan. Britain had acted the midwife at the first partition. It was left to India to perform the role at the second. If Jinnah's Pakistan plan was vague, Mujibs famous six points were vaguer still. There was, however, a basic difference between the two. Mujib was a mass leader who had come through fire. Jinnah was a lawyer who always argued to the brief held by him for the time being.

There was yet another dramatic personae in 1971. Zulfiqar Ali Bhutto called himself the sole representative of West Pakistan just as Jinnah called himself the sole representative of the Indian Muslims. Bhutto was as dictatorial as Jinnah. Bhutto held 81 seats in the first ever elected National Assembly of Pakistan whereas Mujib held 162, out of a total of 300, in fact, all the seats from East Pakistan, whereas Bhutto only had a bare majority of the West Pakistani seats. Yet he had so much clout that the second military dictator of Pakistan, General Yahya Khan, dared not convene the assembly and allow Mujib to take over as Prime Minister. After all Jinnah had always claimed a "parity" with the Hindus in undivided India where the Muslims were 25 per cent of the total population. Bhutto claimed the right to rule the whole of Pakistan. There were thus two Jinnahs in the Pakistan of 1971. When you hold a pistol to someone's head, it is not necessary for you to be logical, much less reasonable.

Jinnah's Muslim League had only 108 seats, in all Indian

provinces put together in 1937, against 741 seats won by the Indian National Congress. The Congress had managed to win 26 Muslim seats when the electorate was communally divided while the League had secured 108 seats out of a total of 492. The League had suffered a crushing defeat in the Muslim majority provinces of the Punjab and in the North-West and in Bengal, and its successes were only in the Hindu majority provinces, like the Bombay and Madras presidencies. The separate electorates had come down from 1909 when the British created two blocks of Hindus and Muslims. Of course, Jinnah improved his position vastly in 1946. The appeal of Muslim separatism was so strong that most eligible Muslims cast their votes for Jinnah's Pakistan, although many regretted it bitterly later, as did the Bengalis of East Pakistan.

They not only nursed a feeling of hurt from the outset but they also had a real grievance. Pakistan was, in fact, a monstrosity. There were two wings separated from each other by more than a thousand miles (over 1,600 kilometres) of Indian territory which Pakistan regarded as hostile territory. The circumstances attending partition and the happenings which preceded it were both terrible. There was an absurd demand for a corridor across the length and breadth of India but neither the British could concede it nor was Jinnah in a position to press it as part of the partition settlement. The question of India agreeing to it did not arise.

**A Unique Country**

That the Bengalis, who constituted a majority of Pakistan but who were ruled by the dominant Punjabis, with the Muhajirs gradually fading away, felt bitter from the beginning is illustrated by Abul Mansoor Ahmed's speech in the Constituent Assembly of Pakistan. He said: "Pakistan is a unique country, having two wings which are separated by a distance of more than a thousand miles...Religion and common struggle are the factors...With the exception of these two things, all other factors, viz. the language, the culture...practically everything is different. There is nothing common in the two wings, particularly in respect of those which are the *sine qua non* "to form a nation".[3]

The "common" struggle which Ahmed talked of was largely a mythical one since it was a struggle for power not against a foreign ruler for the freedom of India as we understand the word "struggle". Pakistan was created not on the basis of a struggle but of religion and Jinnah's two nation theory. Not only the Bengalis realised soon after partition that they were different from the Punjabis, dominating Pakistan, but even in West Pakistan the ethnic minorities like the Pathans, Sindhis, Baluchis and the Muhajirs are held together by the Punjabi army in the name of Islam and they have no way of getting out.

Pakistan has always presented a picture of ethnic and linguistic diversity and the bond of Islam is proving too weak to hold the nation together. In any case, the Bengalis soon fell out with the dominating Punjabis and discontent grew because of the neglect and exploitation they were subject to. Then, as now, the elite was mainly constituted by big landlords. There were 28 landlords in West Pakistan's 40 members in the Constituent Assembly of Pakistan. By contrast the East Pakistani members were all lawyers and other professionals, not landlords. There was, indeed, more cohesion among the East Pakistan members who shared the Bengali language with one another. They had, in fact, more in common with the Bengalis of West Bengal in India, including the Bengali language which they loved deeply. The West Pakistan members, on the other hand, spoke many languages—Punjabi, Pushto, Sindhi, Baluchi and so on—although Urdu was forced on them, as well as on the Bengalis of East Pakistan, as the common language. Urdu, a beautiful language, has always been the special language of the Muslims, whether in Pakistan or India.

In India, Punjabi has grown into a major language thanks to the special attachment of the Sikhs to their mother tongue and the care and attention lavished on it by successive Punjab governments in Indian Punjab. *Ajit*, a Punjabi daily of Jalandhar, has become one of the leading Indian papers. A large number of books is published in Punjabi in India and a number of well subscribed magazines are also being brought out. Thus while Punjabi has a well deserved status in India, it is nowhere being a major language in Pakistan although the dominant Punjabis, who occupy all the important positions in the Pakistani army and in many civil services, apart from politics (Mian Nawaz Sharif, the present Prime Minister is a Punjabi) speak Punjabi the language has no status and no major newspaper is published in Punjabi in Pakistan. All the leading papers of Pakistan are either in Urdu or English.

**Language a Divider**

It was over language that the first open conflict between the two wings of Pakistan surfaced. The view that East Pakistan was a colony of West Pakistan was expressed as early as 1948, the very first year or Pakistan's independent existence. The attempt to foist Urdu on the Bengalis of East Pakistan was now strongly resisted. Demands were voiced by influential people from that region that Bengali should enjoy the status of an official language, along with Urdu and English. Bengali was actually the language of the whole of East Pakistan whereas Urdu was only spoken by the Muhajirs from India. The first Prime Minister of Pakistan, Liaquat Ali Khan, like Jinnah was also from India and was a big landlord of Uttar Pradesh. The language of the migrants from India was being forced down the throats of Pakistanis, including the Bengalis, although it was only the language of the Indian Muhajirs.

When Jinnah visited East Pakistan in March 1948, the only time he condescended to go to the far away part of his country before he died of tuberculosis in September that year, he encountered protest demonstrations by the Bengali students. He did his best to pacify them. As ill-luck would have it, Iskandar Mirza had imposed virtual military rule in the region. Mirza had banned the Communist party (the Communists were among the first political parties in India to support the demand for Pakistan), placed the newspapers under rigid censorship, arrested a number of popular people and dismissed the provincial government. Fazlul Huq's government was accused of fostering secessionism. Fazlul Huq had moved the Pakistan resolution at the Lahore session of the Muslim League and although he had on occasions betrayed signs of opportunism it was a kind of poetic justice that he was now being accused of seeking to break up Pakistan by a man (Mirza) who had done nothing to popularise the demand.

The people of East Pakistan rightly felt that they had been robbed of their government by the West Pakistanis. The latter frequently used the phrase "in the national interest", little realising that they were laying the foundations of an independent and sovereign Bangladesh. But Bangladesh was far off yet. A division cannot be effected overnight. The factors which contribute to the growth of a separate nation were present. After all, Pakistan had been carved out of undivided India and a new nation could very well be created out of the new country. But the world prefers *status quo* and the people themselves have to work for their freedom. These conditions did not yet obtain in East Pakistan.

But things were moving in that direction slowly but surely. The imposition of military rule in Pakistan, first with Ayub Khan, in October 1958 and later when Gen. Yahya Khan seized that power from an ageing Ayub in 1969, meant that the eastern wing had to bear the brunt of it. Military rule was, in essence, rule by West Pakistan over the whole of Pakistan because the provincial assemblies and governments were out of question. The autonomy demand had also gathered strength in the eastern wing. In fact, the provincial assembly had adopted a resolution in April 1957 declaring that all subjects be brought under the control of the provinces except foreign affairs, defence and currency.

Suhrawardy, as we saw, had become Prime Minister of Pakistan in 1956. He tried to play down the resolution, although his own partymen had passed it in the provincial assembly, and he was not successful. He had himself been eased out of the Prime Ministership in October 1957. There was a kind of free for all atmosphere in both the eastern as well as the western wings. The army clamped down in 1958. It was a disaster for East Pakistan.

**Foreign Exchange**

East Pakistan earned 60 to 80 per cent of the country's foreign exchange[4] through the export of jute; West Pakistan appropriated a large part of it. The Pakistan government spent much more on West Pakistan than it did for the people of East Pakistan. Between 1948 and 1960, the Pakistan government's development outlay was Rs. 8,017 million for West Pakistan; it was only Rs. 2,750 million in the eastern wing although a majority of the population of Pakistan lived in the eastern part. There was even a net transfer of resources from the east to the west.[5]

The principle of parity, something very dear to the Muslim Leaguers, was accepted by the Constituent Assembly of Pakistan in 1955. This, of course, meant that the rulers of Pakistan did not want to give the Bengalis their due. They found solace for this attitude of putting down the eastern wing in the fact that more than ten per cent of the population of East Pakistan was Hindu and there could be no greater sin in the eyes of the West Pakistanis than having 10 per cent Hindus in their midst. Many enterprising and hard working Bengalis came from the eastern part but they had all migrated to the Indian state of West Bengal, even before partition, and many even later. There were pogroms from time to time, mostly at the instance of the West Pakistanis, against the Hindus of the eastern part of the country and some elements from East Pakistan also took part in it. During the 1971 crisis which finally led to the creation of a separate Bangladesh, as many as ten million Hindus had to migrate to India as refugees.

The West Pakistanis perpetrated yet another emotionally divisive measure. Pakistan was yet not a republic and it had a Governor General as the head of the state. The convention was that if the Governor General was from West Pakistan the Prime Minister was a Bengali from East Pakistan and vice versa. But in the game of musical chairs that was being played in Pakistan, before the army takeover in 1958, even this convention was violated. The Governor General, Ghulam Mohammad, who was a Punjabi, appointed another Punjabi, Chaudhury Muhammad Ali, a former civil servant with a reputation for efficiency and integrity but one who felt like fish out of water in the game of politics. In any case, the Bengalis, who looked upon West Pakistan as an alien land, were now further alienated.

Then came martial law under Ayub Khan. The people of East Pakistan felt that this was a West Pakistani ploy to perpetuate their colonial rule over East Pakistan. If democratic principles were followed military rule would have become unnecessary in Pakistan. But that required that the Bengalis were given what was due to them. The rule by the army commanders was, in fact, a rule to ensure that power was vested in the West Pakistani hands. The institutions of government were to be used as mere tools to achieve this purpose. Although the army, navy and air force of India and Pakistan are descended from the British Indian armed forces of undivided India, they have gone their different way. Not only there have been three military coups and during their rule the military officers have fully wielded civilian authority, but even during the days and years that the country has known democratic regime the army is an important, often the dominant, element in the affairs of Pakistan.

In India, the President, a civilian who is elected for a five year term, is called the Supreme Commander of the armed forces. No such term is used in the Constitution which only mentions that the Supreme Command of the armed forces vests in the President. This only means that the armed forces are subject to civilian control, the President's authority being used by the Prime Minister and his Cabinet. India is yet to have its first military coup, the armed forces being completely depoliticised. People do not realise that there is a vital difference between India and Pakistan. Even in Bangladesh there have been two military coups in its 26 years of existence. Military rule has thus something to do with Islam. People often ask why the United States must support Pakistan vis-a-vis India when one is an unadulterated democracy and the other has had military rule, open and unalloyed, for half its existence and for the other half the army is ever present at the political table. The answer is: the world's only superpower is interested in getting stooges not in fostering democracy.

The Bengalis of East Pakistan were not far removed from the truth when they thought that the army rule was only a device to perpetuate West Pakistani domination over them. Ayub Khan represented the landlords of Punjab, the anti-Indian establishment, now predominantly Punjabi since the Muhajirs were being pushed out of the key positions, and, of course, the army which was, in any case, a predominantly Punjabi body. The Bengalis' share of the military plumes was very small. Even when Bangladesh was created in 1971, not a single Bengali had ever headed the any of the three wings of the armed forces and there was not a single Lt. General in the army who came from East Pakistan.

As it was the Bengalis' share in the civilian and military top brass was extremely small and even in the middle rung positions they were numerically much smaller as compared with the West Pakistanis. Add to this the loss of political power in their own home and in the nation. Ayub Khan had neither the vision nor the wisdom to bind all Pakistanis together. He went on hammering the idea of Islamic unity. Curiously, however, he said, in his address, to the Dacca university in January 1960 that "we are basically similar". He was referring to the people of Pakistan, the Bengalis of the Eastern wing and the mixed population of Punjabis, Sindhis, Pathans and Baluchs of the west. No longer he was claiming that they were all *one* or the *same*. Maybe his choice of words was not marked by a sense of sophistication. He was devoid of wisdom but he indirectly conceded that the Bengalis were only similar, being otherwise different and separate from the West Pakistanis. But neither he nor anyone else in his martial law regime had the courage to follow up the cardinal fact. If that had been done, perhaps the Bengalis would not have been compelled to seek total separation.

**Mujib Emerges as Voice of Eastern Wing**

Mujibur Rahman, popularly called only Mujib, was coming up in a big way as the voice of the suppressed Bengalis. He was boldly expressing the feelings of the people who constituted a majority of the total population of Pakistan. He was fully aware of that basic fact. Once when he was asked whether East Pakistan would secede from Pakistan he replied: "Why should we secede? Let them secede. We are the majority". These were brave words in a society which was under martial law and the Punjabi army could deploy its unlimited power over the hapless people of East Pakistan any time as they did when the chips were down.

A military regime also needs to convince itself that it is popular with the people and has their support. Ayub Khan made quite a few concessions to Bengali sentiments but that was in the nature of too little too late. Some Bengali politicians were inducted into his government but Mujib was twice imprisoned during Ayub's eleven-year rule. He knew that Mujib was a prominent popular leader who voiced the feelings of the Bengalis for greater autonomy but he could somehow not bring himself to concede it. More to the point, he had no such intention.

Time was running out. The Bengalis were feeling more and more humiliated. It was galling to them that while they were as good Muslims as the people who ruled over them from West

Pakistan the name of Islam was being used for keeping them under the jackboot of the Punjabi army. They knew that they were cheated by the formation of Pakistan on the basis of religion but like many Indian Muslims who belatedly realise that Jinnah divided the Muslims of the sub-continent and left them in the lurch, the people of the eastern wing of Pakistan found themselves unable to do much to redress the position.

Even in 1964, six years after Ayub Khan's military rule and 17 years after the formation of Pakistan, only two Bengalis were found fit to hold the rank of permanent secretary to the Pakistan government. Their position too was that of "acting" secretaries. Although the people of East Pakistan constituted a majority, 54 per cent of the population of Pakistan, only 58 Bengali ministers had enjoyed the privileged position out of the 138 who had held the coveted office before the first military dictatorship of Ayub Khan came on the scene in 1958. Ayub claimed to have restored the imbalance but actually there were 22 Bengalis in his four cabinets out of a total of 58 ministers. Yahya Khan, the army chief who ousted Ayub in 1969, made some amends: there were five Bengalis in his eleven-member government.[5]

Mujib came out with his famous six points in 1966. There was a parallel, as we have noted, with Jinnah who had first propounded his 14 points followed by his two-nation theory and the Pakistan resolution which he got the Lahore Muslim League session to adopt in 1940. Mujib's six points were also to take the same course as he pronounced a sovereign Bangladesh in 1971. His six points were amended in 1970 at a time when the future of Pakistan was being hotly debated and Yahya had declared that elections would be held to the National Assembly, the first and last in an undivided Pakistan. Yahya Khan had also said that he would hand over the military dictator's powers to the elected government. But the Assembly never met, even after being elected, and Z. A. Bhutto who proclaimed himself the leader of West Pakistan, although he had secured only 81 of the 138 seats from West Pakistan whereas Mujib had won all the 162 seats from his East Pakistan, which was also a majority of the total strength of 300 in the Assembly, was acting in concert with Yahya. The two conspired to keep Mujib out of power and deprived him of his right to rule the whole of

Pakistan. All that is recorded history, although a number of Pakistani writers try to put a different and more favourable interpretation on the developments.

They, like Safdar Mahmood, accuse Mujib of nursing ambitions of forming a sovereign state of Bangladesh, although Mahmood recognises that Mujib was robbed of his right to form a government. But when the events show that Yahya and Bhutto were hell bent on keeping Mujib out of power he cannot be accused of nursing ambitions of sovereignty. He was driven to it because even after his massive electoral victory he was not trusted to head a Pakistan government. Mujib was naturally concerned about his people but he was driven to secession by the duo of Yahya and Bhutto. Since the proud Bengalis could not go on providing the West Pakistan leadership with more quislings they chose the only honourable course of fighting for their independence and getting it.

**Six Points**

The six points of Mujib were somewhat vague in the sense that to his Pathan and Baluch colleagues from the west he said that these were designed to extract the maximum from the Pakistani leadership and in the circumstances in which he was placed he did not wish to declare the virtual separation of East Pakistan from the west. This was implicit in his programme.

As it was, the six points spelt out the Bengali demand for the maximum autonomy. He wanted a federation with a unicameral assembly. Mujib knew that the Pakistani leaders were capable of manipulating their continued domination through the upper house if this was agreed to. He wanted that the assembly be elected on a population basis (a principle which was virtually conceded by Yahya in the 1970 elections). The federal government would only handle defence and foreign affairs and there were to be two separate currencies for East and West Pakistan. The two wings (that is, the provinces) would have fiscal powers and the duty to provide the federation with the money it would need to look after defence and foreign affairs. Foreign trade and communication, along with international aid, were to be the responsibility of the provinces.

On the face of it, the six points provided the basis for a new federal system which would satisfy the people of East Pakistan and keep them in this unnatural country. But the West Pakistani leadership, which was controlling the destiny of the entire nation, was bent upon keeping the Bengalis under its thumb as in the past two decades and more. They could never bring themselves to see the Bengalis sitting as equals in the national assembly.

There have been all manner of federations in the world, some loose and some well-knit. The system in Pakistan had proved unequal to the task and could never meet the aspirations of the East Pakistanis although they were the majority. The real problem was that the West Pakistanis wanted to call all the shots and wanted the reluctant Bengalis to live under the banner of the green and white crescent Pakistani flag. They now called Mujib's plan secessionist and thus forced the Bengalis, already estranged, to fight for their sovereignty.

Although the Bengalis were openly dubbed as secessionists they enthusiastically participated in the 1970 elections. Mujib's Awami League (the people's league) not only swept the polls and took all the 162 seats it also won 75 per cent of the popular vote in East Pakistan. Bhutto, on the other hand, only made claims which were not borne out by the elections results. Although he called himself the sole spokesman of West Pakistan, he won for his PPP, Pakistan People's Party, 81 of the 138 seats in West Pakistan. As to the percentage of popular vote Bhutto secured 41.6 per cent of the votes in Punjab, the biggest and most important province of the western wing, 44.9 in his native Sind, only 14.2 per cent in the North-West Frontier Province and a paltry 2.3 per cent in Baluchistan.[6] The NWFP and Baluchistan normally do not enter the calculations of the Pakistani rulers. Yahya tried to get some seats for his faction of the Muslim League but in vain. The old horses of the party, which had created Pakistan, got only a few seats.

### Mujib Denied His Right

Mujib was now perfectly entitled to form a government and become the Prime Minister of Pakistan. That he was denied that right goes to prove that he was not a secessionist but the bosses, like Yahya and Bhutto, were driving him to the wall and wear the mantle of a nation maker. Yahya hailed him as a leader of Pakistan but his manouevres with Bhutto were all calculated to rob Mujib of his right and deny the Awami League the fruits of its absolute majority. Yahya and Bhutto had hoped that while Mujib would get a majority of the East Pakistan seats there would be quislings and stooges who could be easily manipulated with promises of ministerial berths and other allurements. To their utter surprise, Mujib had emerged as the sole and supreme leader of the Bengalis.

It was not for lack of trying. For example, the two factions of the Muslim League, the Convention Muslim League and the other faction known as the Council Muslim League, had together more candidates in East Pakistan than in the western wing. They failed to win a single seat. There were others in the field too. The Jamaat-e-Islami, the extremely fundamentalist body which is able to impose its will on many Muslims in India, Pakistan and Bangladesh but cannot win their votes in an open election, fared no better. So did the National Awami Party of Maulana Bhashani, a rabid East Pakistani who was even more radical in his demand for autonomy than Mujib, because the people would not trust him with their votes.[7]

Even the Qayyum Muslim League, which had the special backing of Yahya Khan, had put up as many as 65 candidates in East Pakistan, only two less than in the west. Needless to say that this faction also drew a blank. Bhutto's PPP, a party inherited by his daughter, steeped in corruption and misuse of power now being exposed by Nawaz Sharif, after she was badly beaten in the February 1997 polls, could not find a single candidate to fight the elections from East Pakistan. Mujib, who took the whole lot of 162 seats in his East Pakistan, could put up seven candidates in West Pakistan but none was successful. This only shows that the two most successful leaders were pronouncedly based in their respective regions, Mujib one hundred per cent in the east and Bhutto only emerging as a majority leader in the west.

Yahya ran from pillar to post, from Islamabad to Dacca, with Bhutto in tow. The purpose of the entire exercise was to ensure that Mujib would be rendered harmless and ineffective even if he had to be given the Prime Minister's post. At one stage, Bhutto even proposed that there should be two Prime Ministers which was an indirect admission of the separation of the two wings. The

Assembly was never convened. Is there another instance in history of elections being held but the house not being constituted? Mujibur Rahman, instead of being sworn in as Prime Minister, had ultimately to go to jail. He was imprisoned on March 26, 1971, three days after he had proclaimed Bangladesh as he was denied his rightful claim to the Prime Ministership of Pakistan.

Before his arrest, Mujib had agreed to the postponement of the first session of the Assembly. Yahya had actually called the Assembly to meet in Dacca on March 3, 1971. While agreeing to the postponement Majib had said a new date should be set. It was never done. Bhutto had even threatened to boycott the Dacca session saying his members could not make the "arrangements" for going to Dacca. As though the Bengali members would not be required to make "arrangements".

His men in West Pakistan attacked the Awami League office in Lahore, burnt its flag and broke the nameboard. Mujib had slightly modified his six points to allow the Federal government, called the Centre as in India, to have its currency along with defence and foreign affairs, and lay down that the centre would levy revenue from the provinces. According to his formula, Punjab's share was to be the highest, followed by that of Bangladesh (the new name of the East Pakistan province). The least share of seven per cent was to be paid by Pakhtoonistan, the new Mujib name of the NWFP.

Although the Pakistani leaders did not consider Mujib's modifications it showed that he was prepared to go to any possible limit to remain part and parcel of Pakistan. If the Pakistani intentions of Mujib had been tested and then he was pronounced a secessionist it could have stood to reason. The Assembly was never convened and Mujib was not allowed to take the oath of office as Prime Minister. The Pakistani leaders had no intention to share power with the East Pakistanis and give them an equal share in the governance of the country even after they had proved their solidarity and their faith in Pakistan.

Yahya and Bhutto flew back from Dacca to Islamabad only to outlaw the Awami League party on March 26, impose press censorship on East Pakistan and put Mujib in jail from where he was released only after Bangladesh had become a reality and the Pakistani forces had been defeated on the battlefield by the Indian troops and the Mukti Bahini of Bangladesh. Bhutto revealed his complete collusion with Yahya and called for total cooperation with the military rulers. He declared: "Pakistan has been saved". He could instead have said, more truthfully: "I have destroyed Pakistan". They were to see the results of their folly in less than nine months. The military in a fell swoop came down heavily on the hapless people of the eastern wing.

But there was equally strong resistance and it grew in intensity as India lent powerful support. Elements which had left the Pakistan army formed the nucleus of the Mukti Bahini (army of liberation) and many other young men and women of East Pakistan joined its ranks. Those Awami League leaders who escaped the Pakistan army dragnet now provided the political backbone of the Bangladesh struggle.

**The War of Liberation**

As terrible repression was let loose by the armed men from West Pakistan, Bengali refugees began to flee their homes and take shelter in India just across the border. It is so porous that people often walk across into each other's territory which enables millions of Bangladeshis to migrate to India in large numbers (now said to be 15 million) and some even going to Pakistan across India. Eventually the numbers of the refugees from the eastern wing of Pakistan in India rose to be ten million, many of them Hindus who were feeling unsafe in East Pakistan. The world media saw their plight and this created an impact which helped the Bangladeshi cause to flourish.

The Pakistanis questioned the number of refugees but even they had to admit that there were three million of them. That is a high figure and that is also the number of Afghan refugees in Pakistan, mostly invited by Pakistan to enable it to claim more and more aid from an obliging United States. That this generous aid has created the Kalashnikov culture in Pakistan and has led to widespread gun running is dealt with in another chapter. Not only the gun culture but the heroin and drug evil in a large way is eating into the vitals of Pakistan.

World sympathy for the cause of Bangladeshi freedom and for the refugees swarming in India was mounting as Mrs Gandhi, the then Prime Minister of India, ceaselessly appealed to the governments and peoples of the world to extend their help. The groundswell of sympathy for a freedom loving people was becoming evident as Mrs Gandhi toured several world capitals to arouse official and popular interest. Her emphasis was on the cause of the refugees but it was obvious that India had now taken up the cause of an independent Bangladesh as her own. Overflights of Pakistani civilian and military planes across Indian territory were banned adding to Pakistan's difficulties of maintaining its administration and control over its far-flung eastern wing. This was in retaliation of the burning of a hijacked Indian civilian aircraft at the Lahore airport in January 1971 when Bhutto is believed to have personally instigated his supporters to resort to his preposterous action.

India had realised that the Pakistani establishment had stepped up its hostility towards India and in India's view, this was an opportunity to settle scores and help the Bengalis of East Pakistan to throw off the West Pakistani yoke. A big confrontation with Islamabad was inevitable. The men there were never inclined to see reason and now that they had let loose terror on the Bengalis they considered anyone who dared to come across their path as enemies to be destroyed instantly. There had been two regular wars over Kashmir and now a third war was in the offing over Bangladesh. In the first war, soon after independence, Pakistan had unleashed thousands of raiders in Kashmir, later to be identified as and reinforced by its regular troops. The Indian army had saved the capital city of Srinagar and cleared much of the state when Jawaharlal Nehru agreed to a ceasefire in Kashmir against the advice of the army generals in 1949.

Later in 1965, the military dictator, Ayub Khan, invaded Kashmir but India took retaliatory action in the mainland of Pakistan. This 22-day war resulted in a kind of draw in India's favour but Pakistan celebrates the events as a "victory". So an opportunity was needed to settle the issue and this Pakistan was providing by its ruthlessness in the eastern wing. India realised that a military confrontation could not be avoided if the refugees had to go back to their homes with honour and if the freedom struggle of the Bengalis of East Pakistan was to be crowned with success. That this could result in a division of Pakistan and the

Americans and some other friends of Pakistan would not be too happy about it had to be taken into account.

Mrs Gandhi knew that India's task was an arduous one. The plus points were the widespread sympathy for the freedom loving people and the refugees who had already migrated to India and those who were still coming in. But the chanceries of the world consist of hard headed men and women who are not easily swayed by revolutionary struggles and generally opt for the status quo. Where somebody's sovereignty was involved they would naturally side with the supposed "victim" rather than with the real victims. Pakistan had two major allies, the United States and China. The latter was still hostile to this country although the 1962 adventure was nine years old.

The United States had so far behaved as though People's China did not exist. The island of Taiwan was given the United Nations seat of mighty China who had also forgotten that India was the first country to raise its voice against this injustice. The rulers in Peking (now Beijing) were now close allies of Pakistan and the latter played a big role in facilitating the task of the Nixon administration now in power in Washington, in its policy of fraternising with China. Secretary of State Henry Kissinger first visited Peking with Pakistani help and then Nixon himself as a prelude to the United States ending its ostrich-like pose towards this big country. It was all to the good but the Chinese, who are said to have long memories, did not recall the years in which Nehru and his men struggled in the UN and outside to make China acceptable to the world.

Yahya Khan himself had visited China in 1971 and although that visit did not go as well as Islamabad expected, it was expecting that both China and the United States, with which Pakistan had military and political ties from the days of John Foster Dulles, would rise to the occasion and defend it in case the Indians acted in concert with the freedom fighters of Bangladesh. As explained, the United States' policy-makers were more interested in having military allies and stooges than in fostering freedom in the world. The latter attitude declined with the death of President Roosevelt and now the ruling doctrine was "those who are not with us are against us".

Still Mrs Gandhi tried to enlist the sympathy of Nixon in the cause of Bangladesh's freedom and the humanitarian help needed by the ten million Bengali refugees in India. Public opinion even in the United States was more and more friendly to these causes. But Mrs Gandhi knew that the only country who could boldly stand by India in a crisis and counter the threat from both China and the United States, in the event of a conflict with Pakistan, was the Soviet Union. India had excellent relations with it and the hostility between the two communist giants was making the Soviets even more friendly to India. But India had to give up her inhibitions against having treaty relations and military ties with another country, specially a big power. What would happen to non-alignment was the fear of some mandarins of South Block, the headquarters of the Foreign Office in Delhi.

**Indo-Soviet Treaty**

The compulsions of the impending armed conflict with Pakistan made India shed those inhibitions and on August 9, 1971 India entered into a treaty of peace and friendship with the regime in Moscow. The Soviet Foreign Minister, Mr Andrew Gromyko, specially flew to India to sign the treaty with Swaran Singh, one of the ablest and wisest Foreign Ministers that India had in a long time. Non-aligned India had entered into treaty relations with Nepal in July 1950[7] but that was more to keep the Indian sphere of influence inviolate. Now a specific treaty was being concluded with one of the big powers to buttress India's strength in the event of an armed conflict with Pakistan, or to put it more plainly, in case India had to fight the Pakistani armed forces over Bangladesh. A new interpretation was placed on non-alignment, virtually giving up the pretence that India stood equidistant from the two military blocs. National interest is what any foreign policy has to subserve.

Clause nine of the Indo-Soviet treaty of peace and friendship reads: "In the event of either party being subjected to an attack or threat thereof, the high contracting parties shall immediately enter into mutual consultations in order to remove such a threat and to take appropriate effective measures to ensure peace and the security of their countries". The Soviet Union with its successor, the Russian government, has always been friendly with India except in the first few years of independence when the Soviet dictator Joseph Stalin had suspicions about India being really non-aligned and not an "imperialist stooge", as alleged by Indian and world communists. In the war of Bangladesh's liberation, which began on December 3 and ended on December 16, 1971, the Soviet Union stood by India like a rock. Not only it carried out its commitments about arms supply, but also in terms of propaganda and diplomatic moves as well as in its role in the UN Security Council, where it exercised its veto in favour of India, it proved what a good friend could be in the murky world of international diplomacy.

Pakistan's army and the government of Yahya Khan had high hopes that its two closest allies, the United States and China, would rush to their aid with arms and other supplies and when the occasion arose also intervene on its side. There were fierce air and land skirmishes even before the actual hostilities began but the excuse for the war was provided by Pakistan which launched surprise attacks on December 3 on Indian airfields in the western sectors in the hope of destroying IAF planes in their hangars. Pakistan found that not only the Indian armed forces were completely prepared to meet the challenge but the entire people of Bangladesh were hostile to it and friendly to India. The West Pakistan army hated the Bengalis and had done everything possible to alienate their sympathy and the fact that there were Hindus in their midst irritated the West Pakistanis even more. This hostility was now repaid in full.

Pakistan waited in vain for the expected help from China and the United States. It was like waiting for manna to fall from heaven. Neither the Americans nor the Chinese intervened. The Soviet bulwark to India, under the August 1971 treaty, was too important for them to ignore. President Nixon did send his Seventh Fleet and the Chinese issued a number of "strong" warnings to India and the Soviet Union, but they did not jump into the fray. It was quite easy for the Chinese to open a front against India and the American ships were already in the Bay of Bengal and their marines could land on the coast. But why should they burn their fingers in the Bangladesh fire and risk not only fighting India but also provoke the Soviet Union to counter their actions, possibly with nuclear retaliation.

The December 3 aggression by Pakistan proved a godsend for India. New Delhi now launched a fullscale attack on the Pakistani forces in East Pakistan and defended its western border. The western fighting was carried on in the bravest of traditions of the Indian armed forces but the real action lay in the eastern sector where the entire Bengali population backed the Indian troops while they routed the Pakistanis. In both sectors the Indian Air Force and Navy played a glorious role and the Bangladesh Mukti Bahini fought bravely to liberate their motherland. Indian troops reached Dacca on December 16.

**India Fortunate**

India was extremely fortunate in having at the helm, in both the military formations and in civilian high positions, not only wise men and women but mature political leadership as well. Mrs Gandhi was indeed insecure and vindictive in dealing with her political adversaries at home and often arbitrary in her administrative decisions. But she displayed real guts and a high degree of maturity in handling the Bangladesh crisis. She was assisted by Jagjivan Ram as Defence Minister and he had an enviable reputation for political wisdom, coolness and administrative experience of a superior kind. He, in turn, was assisted by K. B. Lall as Defence Secretary. Lall was deservedly reputed for his ability and sagacity and as an old I.C.S. officer he was widely respected. In dealing with the sensitive military officers as well as his political bosses and the media Lall showed a rare brand of administrative ability not easily found even in highly rated officers.

Exceptional ability not found among senior army and air force as well as naval officers was displayed by the military commanders. They were headed by a highly pragmatic and commanding if somewhat egoistic, army officer, General Sam Manekshaw, one of the ablest generals the Indian army had. He was rewarded with the rank of Field Marshal after the war for his distinguished services. (The much loved first Indian Chief of the Army, General Cariappa, who had retired long ago was created a Field Marshal afterwards). In the eastern sector which was the most vital, the troops were commanded by the able Lt. Gen. Jagjit Singh Aurora and he had under him some able corps commanders one of whom, Lt. Gen. Raina, soon rose to be the Chief of Army Staff. Gallantry was the watchword of the three wings of the armed forces of India and within 13 days, Gen. Aurora proceeded from his Fort William headquarters of the Eastern Command in Calcutta to Dacca to take the surrender of the Pakistani General, Lt. Gen. A.A.K. Niazi, as more than 90,000 Pakistani troops surrendered to the Indian army.

That was a surrender without any precedent. The hopes of Niazi and his officers that the Americans and Chinese would come to their rescue were dashed to the ground and they had neither the gumption nor the capacity to withstand the onslaught of the Indian Army and Air Force and the brave and patriotic Mukti Bahini. The people of Bangladesh rose as one man to help the Indian army without which the Indian troops could not have achieved this swift and complete victory. The people knew that they were fighting for the freedom of Bangladesh and the Indian troops were actually doing their job.

Events followed quickly thereafter and Bangladesh, which was a dream so far, became now a reality. It was recognised by most world powers one by one, India being the first. Even Pakistan, under the wily and egoistic Z. A. Bhutto, followed suit somewhat later and after much hewing and hawing. Indo-Bangladesh relations could not remain as friendly in the years that followed although the ties were on an even keel as long as Mujib was alive. He was assassinated on August 15, 1975, along with almost all his family members, except his daughter Sheikh Hasina Wajed who escaped the slaughter as she was out of the country. She eventually came back to lead the Awami League party and after two decades succeeded in capturing power in a democratic election. This event helped the relations with India also to improve and a number of steps were taken to remove the irritants but India will have to walk warily as the Pakistani influence among a number of important politicians and in the administrative and military circles in Bangladesh is a great danger to India.

But while there were lessons for India from the developments in Bangladesh those for Pakistan were vital indeed. Pakistan has lost more than 50 per cent of its population and its previous glory as a great Islamic nation has suffered crucial diminution. Despite the ISI's big presence in Bangladesh and the political manipulations of its political leaders in Bangladesh, the country would not ever become an ally of Pakistan. Pakistan has, however, not learnt one important lesson. It remains unreconciled to its inferior status vis-a-vis India and the fact that it suffered a major setback by the emergence of Bangladesh. It regards India responsible for the happening and is doing everything possible to seek revenge. The proxy war it has unsuccessfully fought in Kashmir and the failed experiment of sponsoring terrorism in Punjab are only some examples of this attitude. Its urge to equal and outstrip India in the nuclear field is another. India can neglect this attitude of the rulers of Islamabad at its peril.

It cannot, however, be denied that Jinnah's two-nation theory signally failed in Bangladesh. The West Pakistani leaders have, of course, not been able to reconcile themselves to this cardinal truth. The Punjabi Muslims dominate the army, the civil and diplomatic establishment and all other aspects of the life of Pakistan. They find it hard to face the truth that venality was responsible for the loss of Bangladesh. They lack the vision that religion cannot force ethnic groups to come together under one roof and unity is possible only if diversity is recognised.

But it is too much to expect that Pakistan will be run on rational lines and it is certain that its basic approach will remain anti-Indian despite what the do-gooders in India and the votaries of the failed Gujral doctrine may say or do. India could and would do little to harm it, although the RAW would play its destructive role as long the Pakistani ISI plays its dirty role in India and in the countries surrounding India. Pakistan's ethnic problems with its large minorities among the Sindhis, the Muhajirs, and the Pakhtoons would only aggravate since the Punjabis who dominate its life cannot bring themselves to behave justly with these groups. But an unstable and weak Pakistan would also be a threat to India and many Indian Muslims would always continue to look upon Pakistan as a kind of dreamland, knowing full well its many and cruel failings.

## NOTES

1. In 1951 the eastern wing of Pakistan had a population of 42.15 million as against 34.08 million in West Pakistan.
2. *Pakistan Divided*, Safdar Mahmood, Alpha Bravo, New Delhi. Dr Mahmood is an officer of the Central Superior Services of Pakistan and a visiting professor at the Quiad-e-Azam University, Islamabad.
3. *Ibid.*
4. *Ibid.*
5. These figures are given by Safdar Mahmood, an ardent Pakistani, who had to admit that "the Bengalis felt that they had insufficient representation in the structure of the state (of Pakistan). This contributed substantially to the growth of Bengali alienation".
6. *Pakistan Divided, op. cit.*
7. See *The Triangle— India-Nepal-China* by the author, Gyan Publishing House, New Delhi.

*Chapter 8*

# SECULARISM IN ACTION

To Indians secularism comes naturally. Secularism is tolerance and tolerance is at the core of the life of the people 82 per cent of whom are Hindus. It is part of history that when Islam first came to India, not through the invaders but through the Arab merchants on the south-west coast, and they were able to convert quite a few people to their religion, some of the Hindu kings in Kerala and Gujarat punished their own Hindu subjects, mainly their officials, for objecting to the proselytizing activities of the migrant Muslims.[1] So jealous were they of their reputation as upholders of tolerance that they would go to the extent of penalizing their own subjects so that the foreigners whom they had sheltered would have free access to the large body of indigenous Hindus for conversion.

Despite the cataclysmic events of the country's partition, the Hindus have by and large adhered to secularism and nobody has proposed that India should be a Hindu state just as Pakistan has proclaimed itself an Islamic state. The head of state in that country has to be a Muslim and, in fact, the entire government machinery is Islam-oriented. Even much gentler Bangladesh, which still has a ten per cent Hindu population, makes Islam the state religion and has proclaimed the country an Islamic state. The Indian Constitution is nothing if not secular and there is no state religion, although the word secular was all-pervasive and was not used in the Constitution as it was originally framed. The word was added in the preamble to the Constitution during the emergency rule of Mrs. Gandhi, but the original format makes India one of the few really secular states.

There are multi-religious societies in the world. Indonesia, a predominantly Muslim country and one which has more Muslims than India and even more than Pakistan, which wears the Islamic label all over its person, is known for its tolerance. Its language, Bahasa Indonesia, which is almost the same as the Malay language of Malaysia, Bahasa, Malayu, draws on the rich vocabulary of Sanskrit. In that language even the word for Islam, as a religion, is "Agama", which any Sanskrit scholar would tell you is the word for the Vedic religion. Agama is something which has come down, obviously from the Supreme Being, or God, as opposed to "Nigama" which is man-made like the Manusmriti and other Smritis. It goes without saying that in Bahasa Malayu also the word for Islam is "Agama". I was made to realise that when the Imam in the mosque outside my house in Lewis Road, off Bukit Timah, in Singapore, used to refer to Agama again and again in his Friday discourse. Most of the worshippers were Malays of Singapore, and some Indian Muslims. In the island republic's population the Chinese are 75 per cent, Malays are about 15 per cent and the Indians, that is people of Indian origin, who are citizens of Singapore or those allowed to live there, are about eight per cent.

Indonesia's religion is Islam and the people are devout Muslims but their culture is based on the Ramayana and Mahabharata, although they have somewhat different versions of the two epics. The first Indonesian President, who was ultimately ousted in 1966 by the present President, Gen. Suharto, was a great scholar of the epics, both the Indonesian versions and the Indian original. Soekarno, as his name was, had even named the villa in which he was detained until his death, as "Bheema Shakti". He enjoyed flooring successive Indian ambassadors by his prolific knowledge of the epics and the poor ambassadors had only a small inkling of the epics, mostly what they had seen in the Ramlila performances during the ten days of the Dusserah festival. Only Apasaheb Pant, a scion of the small principality of Aundh in Maharashtra, was able to stand up to him. Many houses in Jakarta, Indonesia's capital and other cities of the country, are named after the Ramayana and even hotels are named after Ramayana. The popular mode of commuting, the cycle-rickshaws, called trishaws, are often named Ramayana, not like the vogue in Delhi where the autorickshaws are often called "Babloo te Nita di gaddi (vehicle of Babloo and Nita, obviously the children of the owner or rickshaw driver.[2])

**"Perdana Mantri"**

Malaysia is again a significantly tolerant country, although the Malays, who are all Muslims, are about 50 per cent of the country's population and tightly hold the reins of power. The Chinese, who have much economic power, are about 40 per cent and the Indians, again meaning the people of Indian origin who have become citizens of Malaysia, ten per cent. The Chinese and Indians have to play second fiddle to the Malays to share in the power structure as collaborators of the Malays. The tolerance of the Malays can be seen from the fact that some of the Malay sultans, who are the heads of the states of West Malaysia and elect by rotation the head of state of Malaysia, make grants for Hindu temples, as does the Malaysian government. The Malaysian Prime Minister, who wields the real authority in the country's parliamentary system, is called "Perdana Mantri", the same as Pradhan Mantri in India, and the Malaysian Queen, the wife of the head of state, is called "Raja Parameshwari".

In India, on the other hand, under the Gujral dispensation, the Urdu bulletins of the Radio and TV have stopped using the Pradhan Mantri designation for the Prime Minister and instead use the expression "Wazir-e-Azam". After all Pradhan Mantri would sound Hindu, although the Malaysians, who are also Muslims, prefer to call their Prime Minister "Perdana Mantri". These bulletins have discarded using the honorific Shri and instead use 'Janab'. Perhaps Gujral likes to be called 'Janab', not 'Shri'. The point is not what Gujral likes but about the separatist mentality of the Urduwallahs, among whom the chairman of the minorities commission of the Indian government is one. A language grows by absorption and even Urdu has adopted a number of English words without acknowledgement because there are no Arabic equivalents but it is *infra dig* for the Urduwallahs to borrow from Sanskrit. It matters little to them that Sanskrit is Indian and many foreigners learn it and become proficient in the language. When, however, there are people like Gujral to cater to their ego and encourage separatism why should they care?

Despite many claims made on behalf of Urdu, it remains only a status symbol for the Muslims. I know of Muslims who cannot read or write the language but are proud that they speak it. In several parts of India, the Muslims speak only the language of the area, miscalled regional language, and in Kerala, Gujarat and some other states the Muslims have made useful contributions to the respective languages. In Gujarati, one of the best produced dailies is the Muslim-edited and controlled *Gujarat Today*[3] of Ahmedabad and likewise there are Muslim dailies in Kerala and other parts. Yet the Muslims must hug Urdu. There are, of course, Urdu papers in Tamil Nadu, Karnataka and Maharashtra and some other states and there is no restriction of any kind and both the central DAVP and the respective states are placing advertisements in those papers lavishly. Both AIR and DD have a number of Urdu bulletins and there are no restrictions but even the uniformity in the designations of the President and the Prime Minister has been rudely shaken by Gujral's dispensation and the separatist attitude of some people.

When I had visited the United States and met some of the elder and younger Pakistan students they indicated that they listened to the AIR Urdu bulletins and found nothing objectionable in the language. If they had found the usage of Pradhan Mantri and Rashtrapati (under the Gujral dispensation the word is now rendered as Sadar) they could have told me about it. They, in fact, said the language was easy (as compared with the artificially high flown Urdu used in the Pakistani official media). Perhaps they wanted to get an inkling of India and learn about their own country through our bulletins since the official media in that country were then and now are utterly propagandistic, more so than AIR or DD.

It would be a shock to many Hindi and Urdu experts that when I was in Ahmedabad (1961-63) I received an invitation from a Muslim-owned laundry shop addressed to me and all the invitees as 'tum' instead of the customary "ap". In Gujarati, 'tum' is fine, although some hailing from the old princely states even now use 'ap' which is not correct. A UP Muslim I met in Ahmedabad was bitter that he was being addressed as 'tum' instead of the usual 'ap' by many of his fellow Muslims. These instances are being quoted to underline the point that Urdu is not the language of the Muslims in most parts of the country, although the separatists only echo what the Muslim League did before independence when all Muslims everywhere were being asked to state Urdu was their mother tongue in the Census enumeration.

The point sought to be made here is that even among the multi-religious nations India stands out as one which has endeavoured to ensure for its minorities a place under the sun. They are assured of a future as good as the one ordained for the generality of the population, absolute equality for all the citizens, irrespective of their religious faith. The votebank politicians promise the Muslims even better things than for the others but, in effect, they do not care to keep their promises once the votes are cast, whether it is the Congress party or the Samajwadi party of Mulayam Singh Yadav, the new messiah for some Muslims. But treating all citizens as equal, no matter what his religion is, is the essence of secularism. The word secular and secularism came into vogue in Europe when Roman Catholicism or its reformed version, the Protestant denomination with all its variants, dominated the work of the governments and even the life of the citizens in general. Separating religion from the activities of the state and its instruments was then taken as secularism.

India has striven not to allow religion to dominate life and the activities of the state ever since freedom. Secularism also has a positive aspect which is as important as the other aspect of the state being insulated against religion. There should be no disability suffered by any Indian because of his religion. It is possible that this situation does not obtain a hundred per cent at several places but aberrations always occur even in the best of societies.

Under Gandhiji's influence and the outlook of the other leaders the Indian approach was one of pluralism, opposed to exclusiveness, and allowing all citizens equal opportunity for the development of his personality. Gandhiji has often been misunderstood and the Jinnah apologists cite his religiosity as a provocation for the communal minded leader to strike out his own path. The truth was the exact opposite because Gandhiji's religion was all inclusive. He did not worship any image nor went to any temple. His daily prayer meetings were devoted to religion and God as he saw them, not to any particular way of approaching God. The sacred words and verses from different religions, including Islam, were regularly recited at these prayer meetings. Unlike the 'netas' of today, he spent no time in 'puja', Gandhiji had said: "The deeper I study Hinduism the stronger becomes the belief in me that Hinduism is as broad as the universe. Something within me tells me that, for all the deep veneration I show to several religions, I am all the more a Hindu, none the less for it". He had told Dr S. Radhakrishnan, then only a professor, when he was seeking to bring out a commemorative volume on Gandhiji's 70th birthday: "My religion is Hinduism which, for me, is the religion of humanity and includes the best of all religions known to me".

**Gandhiji's Humanism**

Gandhiji knew of the various observances of the traditionalist Hindus, like fasting (for half a day) on Mondays or Tuesdays, on Ekadasi or Shivaratri (eleventh or fourteenth day in a fortnight of the moon's bright or dark cycle) or visiting a temple on these days. But he did not practise it. He had no gurus, although many looked upon him as a spiritual guide. All his life was spent in the service of humanity but he found time to remember his Maker and whatever he did was ultimately placed at His feet. If he used religious imagery he knew that the people would understand him better and because of his conviction, not because he was more a Hindu than a fiercely patriotic Indian who ultimately laid down his life in the cause of Hindu-Muslim unity. It was his ambition to go to Pakistan to carry on his mission if the assassin had not ended his life's journey on January 30, 1948.

Marxist ideogists and others keep on attacking him while the apologists for Jinnah accuse him, out of ignorance, for his alleged love of Hinduism. For the Marxists, religion is the opium of the masses and while he was living they could not close their eyes to his mass following the intellectuals steeped in Marx, rather drunk on Marx, unleash their fusillades from time to time, now that he is dead for well nigh fifty years.

In an article on Gandhiji's 128th birth anniversary[3] Jagmohan, former governor of Kashmir, said: "...Hinduism, as viewed by

Gandhiji, is nothing but spiritual secularism and a service-oriented way of life based upon the highest principles of ethics and morality." Surprisingly, Nani A Palkhiwala, an eminent jurist and a former Indian Ambassador to the United States, and what is more, himself a Parsi, from the smallest Indian minority of Zoroastrians, wrote to the paper[4] which had published Jagmohan's article on Gandhiji, endorsing Jagmohan's article which, he said, was something "every Indian should wholeheartedly agree with irrespective of whether he is a Hindu or a Muslim, a Christian or a Jew, Zoroastrian or a Buddhist. "Palkhiwala said: "Hinduism is the only religion in the world which was not founded by any identifiable person. It is a universal, eternal religion and the credit for having evolved that religion goes to India".

Palkhiwala was so much impressed by Jagmohan's article on Gandhiji as a Hindu that he undertook to defray the expenses of making the article widely read by students in all colleges and schools. In the concluding part of his article Jagmohan has this to say: "Hinduism, as made clear by Gandhi, sees all human beings as 'sparks of truth/divinity'. It doesn't go against any other religion. Nor is it incompatible with the constitutional goals of equality, fraternity, liberty and justice. If the same divinity constitutes the core of all individuals they cannot but be equal. And divinity in one person cannot be unjust to the same divinity in another person". Not surprisingly, a Muslim reader of the daily, Arif-ul-Islam of Aligarh, fired off a letter to the paper in which he linked Mahatma Gandhi with the demolition of the Babari mosque.[5]

This somewhat elaborate exposition was called for because a distinguished citizen and a Parsi indirectly answered some of the carping criticism of Hinduism by the so-called secularists. They condone and even uphold Islamic orthodoxy and even fundamentalism while attacking Hinduism, under various pretexts, when, for example, they attack the Bharatiya Janata Party or the so-called Sangh Parivar (meaning the BJP, the RSS and Vishwa Hindu Parishad), finding loopholes in the Indian system, which they do not like. Forgetting that India, alone of the three nations which have sprung from the womb of the former rulers of united India, is secular and makes no distinction between citizen and citizen on grounds of religion, they are only strengthening the separatist outlook which created Pakistan. The communalists are not in favour of the modernisation process in the Muslim community because they know that thereby orthodoxy and fundamentalism would come to an end as a new generation of men and women is emerging as free citizens. They call the Muslims a minority when it suits their argument but at times claim that the Muslims are about 200 million and, therefore, cannot be dismissed as a minority.

The 1991 census says that there are 82 per cent Hindus in India, the Muslims are 12.1 per cent, Christians 2.3 per cent, Sikhs 1.94 per cent, Buddhists 0.76 per cent, and Jains 0.4 per cent. Now that the Indian population is more than 900 million the Muslim population should be around 108 million, nearly half of the figure of 200 million claimed by some Muslim separatists.[6] The target of some of these fringe fundamentalists could be that at a future date they can claim a separate status for themselves. If eighty or ninety million Muslims could come out of India, under the British, why cannot the assumed figure of 200 million, runs the logic of this section.[7] The Muslim population in India is rising faster than the general growth which is bad enough as it eats up many of the advantages of development. These and other fundamentalists, and even the Muslim writers in the media, keep on attacking anything which is vaguely "Hindutva". They ignore the fact that the Supreme Court has in its judgment on Hindutva said that the term cannot be considered as derogatory or illegal.

**Equal Rights**

In the chapter on Fundamental Rights, the Indian Constitution has provisions which confer equality on all citizens, the right to practise and propagate one's religion, and the right to maintain educational and other institutions of the minorities. These are at the core of the Constitution, which in the opinion of the Supreme Court, are unalterable and unamendable, and can be enforced by a citizen or citizens going to one of the High Courts or the apex court. The basic freedoms are guaranteed by these articles of the Constitution, like the right to life and liberty, freedom of speech and expression, and, what is relevant here, the right to equality, without any distinction of religion, sex or caste.

Article 13 states: "The state shall not discriminate against any citizen on grounds only of religion, race, caste, sex, place of birth or any of them. "The state is required to ensure, under article 16, equality of opportunity to all citizens in matters relating to employment or appointment to any office under the state and not to allow any discrimination to be practised "only on grounds of religion, race, caste, sex, descent, place of birth, residence or any of them".

Nothing could be more specific and categorical. Non-discrimination is further elaborated in article 15 which states that no citizen shall be subject to "any disability, liability, restriction or condition with regard to access to shops, public restaurants, hotels and places of public entertainment" or in the "use of wells, tanks, bathing ghats, roads and places of public resort maintained wholly or partly out of state funds". Article 25 confers on all citizens the right to freedom of religion, including the right to propagate one's religion. This is, of course, subject to "public order, morality, and health and other provisions of this part" of the Constitution. Mass conversion in a mela-like situation, as in Meenakshipuram in Tamil Nadu, over which a Tamil Nadu Congress leader presided, is not entitled to such freedom and would really speaking be a misuse of the freedom conferred by this article. Alas, there are elements which continue to dream of making India a *Darul Islam*, a majority Muslim state like Pakistan. They are the fringe elements but they are not disowned by the others.

How has secularism worked in practice, the secularism of the real kind which affects the average Indian, Muslim or others, not the one which the interested parties want, their secularism meaning being pro-Muslim. The Congress and the Left and other parties in the 13, 15 or 17 party United Front dub all those who boldly proclaim themselves in favour of the Hindus as communal. Nothing prevents them from speaking about the protection of the minorities nor does it make them communal, although their intention is to exploit the Muslims as voters. They close their eyes to the fact that the BJP has an effective alliance with the Shiromani Akali Dal which is in power with the BJP in Punjab state since February 1997. The Akali Dal is almost solely a Sikh party. But, according to these people, the Sikhs are not a minority because they continue to refer to the BJP, by name or otherwise, as a communal party. For these people only the Muslims are a minority.

Coming to opportunities for all on an equal basis, let us take the case of the President of India, the head of state. He is, no doubt; a constitutional head and the governance of the country is the responsibility of the Prime Minister and his cabinet, who are both answerable to the Lok Sabha, the lower house of Parliament. But there are some delicate situations when the President comes into his own, as for example, when the Lok Sabha is a hung house and there is no majority for a single party. The President has, in any case, to appoint the Prime Minister who has to go before the Lok Sabha and prove his majority there.

So the head of state also has a crucial role to play in the making and running of India. Of the twelve eminent men who have adorned the office there have been two Muslims, Dr Zakir Husain and Fakhruddin Ali Ahmed, and one a Sikh, Giani Zail Singh. (The Sikhs are also a minority, let us remind the "secularists"). The incumbent President, who took over on July 25, 1997, K. R. Narayanan, is a member of the former untouchable or scheduled castes or dalits. Can any nation in the world boast of such a record? Even in Malaysia, one of the tolerant nations, as we have seen, the headship of the country is filled by rotation and only one of the Sultans, who are Malays and Muslims, can aspire to occupy the position. In Indonesia, although there are Christians and Buddhists, among the Chinese in the population, and there are of course, the Bali Hindus, only the Muslims have been heads of state. In fact, Dr Soekarno was forced out and now Gen. Suharto is the head in the nearly fifty years of free Indonesia. The United States, said to be the leading nation in many respects, is yet to have its first black President. Most of its Presidents have, indeed, been WASPish, White, Anglo-Saxon and Protestant.

Besides Zakir Husain and Fakhruddin Ali Ahmed, Justice Mohammad Hidayatullah, acted as President from July 20, 1969 to August 24, 1969 when the incumbent, V. V. Giri, had stepped down to be able to fight for a second term. Giri, who won the second term in a nail-biting finish against Neelam Sanjiva Reddy, whom Mrs Gandhi's Congress party had nominated for the presidency but went back on the nomination and called for a "conscience" vote, a euphemism for backtracking. Hidayatullah was one of the most respected Chief Justices of India, one of the three Muslims to occupy the position, the other two being Justice M. H. Beg and Justice A. M. Ahmadi. Hidayatullah was also elected to the high office of Vice President of India. But for the fact that he had an excellent rapport with the Janata party, the first non-Congress party to form a government at the centre, he would have been an elected President but Mrs Gandhi, who had again come back to power, instead chose Giani Zail Singh, a Sikh.

Many other Muslims, besides the three to be the Chief Justice of India, have been Supreme Court judges or judges of the various High Courts and some have indeed been Chief Justices of the High Courts.

Both Hidayatullah and Zakir Husain worked for a full term as Vice President of India. Any number of Muslims, some eminent persons and others political appointees, have occupied the high positions of governors of states. Presently, Mrs Fatima Beevi, a retired Supreme Court judge, has been working as governor of Tamil Nadu, besides such people as Mohammad Shafi Quereshi and Dr A. R. Kidwai, governors of Madhya Pradesh and Bihar respectively.

There is no dearth of Muslims who have held important portfolios at the Centre and four Muslims have been Chief Ministers in states, Abdul Ghafoor in Bihar, Barkatullah in Rajasthan, Alimuddin in Manipur and Koya in Kerala, besides Dr Farooq Abdullah in Jammu and Kashmir where only Muslims have been Chief Ministers from the time of Dr Farooq's father, the legendary Sheikh Abdullah. Because Kashmir is a Muslim majority state, only Muslims are chosen as Chief Minister, although the four others adorned the office in states which are not majority Muslim states, Kashmir being the only one. Interestingly, both Hidayatullah and Barakatullah had Hindu wives.

The great M.C. Chagla was External Affairs Minister and held the Education portfolio and before that he was Chief Justice of the Bombay High Court. One of the most successful External Affairs ministers was Sardar Swaran Singh, a Sikh, like Giani Zail Singh, who was Home Minister before he rose to the presidency.

Fakhruddin Ali Ahmed was minister of Industries before he rose to be President by election. Maulana Azad, by common consent the greatest Indian Muslim, was free India's first Education Minister for more than ten years. We have had occasion to recall the services of Rafi Ahmed Kidwai, one of the truly great administrators India has known, who was Minister of Communications and Food and Agriculture, besides being Jawaharlal Nehru's right hand man advising him on such matters as Kashmir.

Even H.D. Deve Gowda, who was only Prime Minister for ten months in 1996-97 before he was overthrown when I. K. Gujral succeeded him had in C. M. Ibrahim his Man Friday with two major portfolios, Information and Broadcasting and Civil Aviation. When Gujral became Prime Minister he had to strip Ibrahim of the Information and Broadcasting portfolio and give it to his loyalist, S. Jaipal Reddy, although Gujral was known for his partiality for the Muslims. Secularism has its limits after all. Ibrahim had to pay for his loyalty to Deve Gowda.

This land belongs to all its citizens and anyone who is a member of either house of Parliament or can get elected within six months of his appointment to either house can become a Minister and enjoy the powers and perks of the high office. The difficulty arises when the holder of the position gives expression to undesirable sentiments, as for example, did Ibrahim when he attributed some of the media criticism of his tenure to his being a Muslim.[8] He did not realise that his proximity to Deve Gowda was creating many enemies for him and some of the criticism could be on that account, apart from his own failings.

It is true that there are not enough Muslims in Parliament, not in proportion to their population, but it is not a product of any prejudice. In a way it is the result of the peculiar political system and the votebank politics of some parties which seeks the votes of the Muslims but do not put up sufficient number of candidates from among the community. If there are Muslims coming forward to participate in public activities at the Panchayat, municipal and state as well as national levels, there is no reason why their efforts should not be rewarded with success. This was proved beyond doubt by the success of Begum Zeenat Naaz who was elected chairperson of a nagar panchayat in the stronghold of Islamic orthodoxy of Deoband in Uttar Pradesh and worked as efficiently as anyone else. There are other instances like those of Ghulam Nabi Azad whom the Congress party brought to either the Lok Sabha or Rajya Sabha from states other than his own Kashmir, from where he could hardly get elected. For two consecutive terms he was elected from Maharashtra until Maharashtra refused to be a stronghold of the Congress.

Unfortunately, there are many Muslim "leaders" who cannot abandon their communal standpoint in public affairs and fail to identify themselves with the affairs of the mainstream of which the Muslims are as much part as anybody else. There is a constant harping on the theme of Muslim interests, as though they were separate from the interests of the general body of people and on Muslims being subjected to hardships, suffering and discrimination. Many of the political parties ever alert to the opportunities of votebank politics help to nurse the grievances, often imaginary, and blown out of proportion. The media also help to exaggerate the issues and help in the process of separatism by constantly referring to 'Muslims resist this' and 'Muslims oppose that', as though the Muslims always react in a mass. Many in the media have a pronounced tendency to sensationalise things and indirectly help in the process of separatism. This is true of several newspapers and some TV channels which would play up any incident, however petty it might be and forgotten after a few days.

**The Missile Man**

When you speak of the civil servants and technologists, the name that comes to mind, above all else, is that of the technocrat and scientist, Dr A. P. J. Abdul Kalam, Scientific Adviser to the Defence Minister and head of the DRDO, Defence Research and Development Organisation. As the man who has put India on the missile map of the world, he was rightly honoured with the nation's highest award of Bharat Ratna in December 1997. Being the only scientist, after the great C. V. Raman who was created a Bharat Ratna way back in 1954 when the awards were first instituted, to be so honoured, Abdul Kalam has carved out a niche for himself in the gallery of great men of India by developing short and long range missiles. Only a pusillanimous government could stop him from developing the Agni missile because the Americans objected to it. Narasimha Rao first succumbed to the US pressure and then it was the turn of Gowda and Gujral to cowtow to the world policeman.

Any way it is not the fault of scientist Abdul Kalam that Agni is not yet a reality. In Dr Abdul Kalam we have the typical and shining example of India's secularism which allows talent to develop to its full form and encourages devotion and commitment to scale great heights in the pursuit of one's goals. There are Muslims in the top echelons of the armed[9] forces, several Lt. General and Major Generals in the Indian Army and top officers in the Air Force and Navy, including a former Air Force Chief, Air Marshal I. H. Latif who was, on retirement, appointed governor of Maharashtra.

As we saw, there are other minorities in India—the Christians, Parsis, Sikhs and even the Anglo-Indians, who have produced great soldiers, airmen and naval officers. One of the first Field Marshals, actually one of the two, is Sam Manekshaw, who was also the Chief of the Indian Army during the Bangladesh liberation war. He is, of course, a Parsi, one of the smallest minorities in India, which also gave the nation an Air Force Chief, A. M. Engineer, and a Naval Chief, Admiral Cursetji. The Anglo-Indians perhaps as small a community as the Parsis, have given India all three services chiefs, Gen. S. F. Rodrigues, who headed the Indian Army, Admiral O. S. Dawson, Naval Chief, and Air Chief Marshal D. A. la Fontaine, Air Force Chief. The Sikhs are often referred to as the sword arm of India and have contributed great soldiers, airmen and naval officers. Lt. Gen. Jagjit Singh Aurora was the commander of the Eastern Command in 1971 and took the surrender of the Pakistani general, Lt. Gen. A. A. K. Niazi, and more than 90,000 of his troops in Dhaka in December 1971 which created the sovereign nation of Bangladesh. Two Air Force chiefs, Air Chief Marshal Arjan Singh and Air Chief Marshal Dilbagh Singh, came from the Sikh community.

If the minorities have played a notable role in providing officers of the highest ranks in the three services, those whose duty it is to fight for the nation have also produced well known heroes and brave men. Along with the Hindus, the Muslims, Sikhs, Parsis and other communities have given their best in the service and the defence of the Motherland and earned for themselves the highest gallantry awards. Among them one comes across such names as Lance Naik Karam Singh, one of the early winners of the highest gallantry award of Param Vir Chakra, Subedar Joginder Singh, who died in the cause of the nation fighting the Chinese invaders in 1962, Havildar Abdul Hamid, who laid down his life in the 1965 war against Pakistan, Lt. Col. A. B. Tarapore (a Parsi) who also died in the same war, Flying Officer Nirmal Jit Singh Sekhon, who attained martyrdom in the 1971 war against Pakistan, and Lance Naik Albert Ekka, a tribal Christian, who died in the 1972 war. All of them received the award of Param Vir Chakra.

There is no monopoly in heroism and the concept of martial races has long been given up as wrong. The important point is that the Indian system and its pursuit of secularism enable men of all communities to rise to the highest positions of responsibility and earn for themselves the highest awards of gallantry by being the first and foremost in the defence of the nation. There is no prejudice based on religion and community, except the residual one of personal prejudice which sometimes could be based on religion also. There is ample scope for men of ability and performance to rise to the best of their ability and prowess and virtually the sky is the limit for men of talent and hard work. What you need is ability, strength of character and hard work.

The nation also benefits by the great contribution that the men and women of the minorities have to make. Imagine an India, following in the footsteps of Pakistan, shutting its doors to Muslims and, indeed, to the other minorities also. You will have on your hands not only a lot of disgruntled people but you will be denying yourself the contribution that these people have to make. Can you imagine the success of the missile programme without an Abdul Kalam making a signal contribution to it. Likewise, the bravery of the Sikhs, the dash of the Anglo-Indians, the quiet skill of the Parsis and the heroism of the Muslims make this nation great. If you follow a closed door policy you are without the notable contribution of the minorities. Secularism thus enriches the nation while it opens up immense opportunities for the individuals.

In the administrative and police services there are men and women of all communities. The Election Commission of India is now headed by a Sikh, M.S. Gill, and one of its two other Election Commissioners is J. M. Lyngdoh, a Christian from the tribal areas of Meghalaya which has also given the nation one of its ablest Speakers, P. A. Sangma. A Muslim officer rose to the highest position of Cabinet Secretary although there were doubts about his suitability. Men of the other communities have also adorned some high offices, like Dr P. C. Alexander who rose to the office of the Principal Secretary to the Prime Minister before he was made governor of Maharashtra. Dr Monetek Singh Ahluwalia, a Sikh, is Finance Secretary and, indeed, the man who presented six budgets of India in a row, was Dr Manmohan Singh, the Sikh Finance Minister under Narasimha Rao. Whether one agrees with his policies or not, one has to admire his ability and devotion to duty.

A number of Muslims have occupied the office of Chief Secretary to a state government and several of them have distinguished themselves in the diplomatic field. Salman Hyder rose to the office of Foreign Secretary and although Gujral bent over backwards to buttress him there is no denying his worth and ability. The question is not that Muslims have distinguished themselves in the administrative, police and diplomatic services; the question is that several have taken the difficult competitive examination which gives them the opportunity to rise to the highest offices. If the Muslims would refuse to listen to the advice of their "leaders" and attend the right schools, instead of attending Madrassas and religious schools, they could rise to great heights. It is as simple as that. You have to take the competitive examination as there are no nominations as in the British days. The votebank politics of many hues, from the Congress to the Samajwadi party and the leftists, who would keep the Muslims backward, prevents them from taking the right course to success.

These leaders often fail in their designs and Muslim boys and girls opt for the secular path and take the hard road to success by attending classes and schools like the rest of Indians. The Muslims are often held back by their leaders, the votebank politicians, their own poverty and ignorance, the perverted and sensation loving media, both of the Urdu press variety and some English dailies;

still despite these handicaps men and women are coming forward in large numbers to try their skills and face the test of ability and hard work.

**Indian System is Secular**

So far we have dealt with the functioning of the public services in democratic India to show that secularism is part and parcel of the Indian system. But what do we find at the level of life where the laws and the Constitution do not come into the picture? In reality, the Indian system, despite its drawbacks and several inequities, is thoroughly secular in the sense that religious or communal considerations do not find any application. If you have the talent and the capacity for hard work, enterprise and some luck you can go forward and capture the world.

One should not forget that High Court judges are largely selected from the ranks of practising advocates, apart from those picked up from among suitable district and session judges. To be a successful advocate one has to have a good reputation for knowledge of the law, ability to put forward forcefully your point of view in the court, an analytical mind and the ability to win the confidence of clients or litigants. Upto a point a Muslim lawyer can carry on with only Muslim clients, but to be a good lawyer of civil cases, or what is called a "criminal" lawyer, you have to have all-round clientele which is not confined to your own community. There are other factors in the selection and appointment of High Court judges but we need not spend more time on it here.

What is important to note is that the Indian system holds no bars to a talented person, who is also capable of hard work, to forge ahead in life, the kind of barriers which prevent the minorities from pulling their weight in some Islamic countries. What to speak of Pakistan, even in Bangladesh no Hindu has risen to any senior military or bureaucratic position nor in the realm of sports. In India, any number of Muslims can be found being selected to represent India, besides those selected for representation at the state and district level, and in school and college competitions. If you speak of the most popular of the team games, cricket, you find that four Muslims captained India in the years since independence. Of them Mohammad Azharuddin had the longest tenure, the other three being Ghulam Ahmed, the off spinner, batsmen like Abbas Ali Baig and Mansoor Ali Khan Pataudi, wrongly called a Nawab because Pataudi is only a small tehsil town in Haryana. His cinema actor son bombastically calls himself "Chhote Nawab". The age of Rajas and Nawabs is gone and dead like the proverbial dodo, but this is not to deny the batting prowess of Mansoor Ali Khan, often called the tiger.

The Indian cricket team which beat Pakistan in the second Sahara cup in Toronto in September 1997 had two Muslims, Saba Karim the wicket-keeper besides Azharuddin, then no longer carrying the burdens of captaincy, and two from the other minorities, Abey Kuruvilla, a Christian, and Harvinder Singh, a Sikh. Kuruvilla is often referred to as a Mumbai player, which he is, but it is not generally known that he is the first test and one-day player from his native Kerala which has a sizable number of Christians. Besides captains, there have been several Muslim players like the greatly loved Mushtaq Ali, happily still alive, Salim Durani, who like Baig, Mansoor Ali Khan and Azharuddin has a Hindu wife, perhaps all of them converted to Islam, Abid Ali, a member of the successful Wadekar team which won in 1971 two test series, one in the West Indies and the other against England, and several others. There have been several Parsi players, two of whom we must mention here, Polly Umrigar and Farokh Engineer, besides Christians like the great Vijay Hazare.

The Indian secular system is often carried to ridiculous limits. In 1991-92 the Indian cricket team, led by Azharuddin, was in Australia for a test series with Australia and for the world cup staged partly by Australia and partly by New Zealand. He failed to get India a berth in the semi-finals of the world cup, far from winning the cup, nor did he win the rubber against Australia. Still, the trio of the captain, the coach, Abbas Ali Baig, and the medio, Dr Ali Irani, were invited to continue in that respective capacity. Only Baig declined the honour but the other two carried on. There was nothing unusual in three Muslims holding the key positions, although nobody noted the truly secular character of it and none bothered that the failed trio should be still asked to continue.

This is despite the fact that sometimes Muslim cricket fans support the Pakistani team as against the Indian team when the two are involved in contest at Sharjah, Toronto, and lately in India and Pakistan. The fans forget that their own sons and nephews, if they have the talent and ability, have to play as members of the Indian team. The Pakistanis would not allow them to set foot on the Pak (sacred) soil, much less let them play for them. This is a deplorable phenomenon which some "secular" writers connive at and even try to justify when the Muslim sport lovers openly back Pakistan against India.

Even as late as 1997 when a Pakistani cricket team, under Rameez Raja, sacked by the Pakistani selectors after the debacle against India in Toronto, visited India many Muslims in Hyderabad, where one of the matches was played, plumped for the Pakistani team. One of the fans held up a placard "Afridi the Hiter". Regardless of the spelling mistake the placard revealed the joy of the holder at Afridi's undoubted hitting ability. There could not and should not be any objection in an Indian, Muslim or any other, applauding in a sporting manner Shaheed Afridi's hitting and strokeplay but there is a difference between that and backing him to the hilt against one's own country. You have to make a distinction between pure sporting appreciation and the enthusiastic display of partisanship based on Pan-Islamic considerations. The issue cannot be brushed under the carpet because it shows the separatist Muslim attitude in action. That India alone is not a victim of this communal display, which throws the Indian spirit to the winds, was proved when a Srilankan Muslim minister had to appeal to his fellow Srilankan Muslims not to back the Pakistani team against "their own" Srilankan team. That was on the occasion of the Asian Cup staged by Sri Lanka in which the Pakistanis failed to reach the final.

It is not cricket alone where the Indian Muslims have proved their ability and have found an honourable place in the national team. In popular games like football and the national sport of hockey there are any number of Muslims and other minorities. Whether it is the individual items like athletics or individual-cum-team games like tennis all Indians, irrespective of religion, find a place in the national squad and indeed bring laurels to the country. The nation is as proud of Leander Paes's glorious achievements in tennis as he is proud as an Indian to have achieved them. He is an Anglo-Indian but when the fans, mostly Hindus, egg him on at the

DLTA in Delhi or the South Club in Calcutta "Go Leander Go" they are not at all conscious of his religion or community. This is as it should be but does it make any impact on the minds of those who find excuses for the separatist feelings of many Muslims?

Half or even more than half of the Junior Hockey team which scaled great heights at Milton Keys in England in 1997 and were runners up in the tournament were non-Hindus—Sikhs, Muslims and Christians besides Hindu players. Likewise the Indian Football team, which won the SAARC tournament in Kathmandu, had a number of non-Hindus in it. Ironically the Nepali crowd, which normally should have cheered the Indian team, supported the rivals throughout the tournament, although they came in large numbers to see the matches. That the Nepalis are mostly Hindus, more than even the Indians, should have made them plump for the Indians but it is some indication of the Hindu spirit that the Nepali crowds did not back the Indians on religious grounds, although it should be a matter of concern to lovers of Indo-Nepali good relations that the crowds were not backing the Indian team.

**Cinema Muslims**

What goes for sports goes for the cinema and TV serials. The Muslims, in fact, dominate the cinema scene in Bollywood. The Hindi film industry is now almost entirely concentrated in Mumbai which was earlier known as Bombay and the home of Hindi films came to be known by the imitation name of Bollywood, not taking into account the imitation of the Hollywood films which many successful Hindi film producers have indulged in. In the old days, some memorable Hindi films used to be made in Calcutta and Madras, now called Chennai. For historical and other reasons there are a number of Muslims among actors and actresses, directors, song writers, miscalled lyricists and even poets, editors, cameramen, and, of course, the humble and indispensable spot boys, not forgetting the cinema writers in film magazines, called mags, and even in leading dailies like the *Times of India*. There is, alas, nobody of the calibre and outstanding ability of Mehboob Khan, who made immortal films like *Mother India*, rated by many as the best movie made in India, but that does not prevent any number of secondrateres and even thirdraters to pass off as directors.

With substantial funds for the Indian film industry coming from the Mumbai mafia dons, most of them in Dubai or in Pakistan, and almost all of them pronouncedly Islamic in their approach, some of the Muslims in the entertainment industry have a psychological and emotional backup, although it would be unfair to see any general linkage. Interestingly, a number of actresses and actors and singers come from Pakistan under the onesided exchange, more after Gujral came on the scene, and this naturally is an image building exercise.

There were great actors and actresses from the Parsi and Muslim communities coming down from the pre-partition days, among them Nurjahan, Sohrab Modi, and Anglo-Indians like Sulochana. Nurjahan later migrated to Pakistan and became a byword for excellent singing of light songs. She had acted in memorable films like *Anmol Ghadi* in Bombay. Although Lahore was even then a secondary centre for Hindi and Urdu films, she perhaps thought it proper to come down to Bombay. Zubeda was another actress of the pre-independence days and the entire family of a small nawab in an area near Surat in Gujarat was in the film business. Mehboob Khan himself came from Billimora, a small town in south Gujarat. He was rooted in the soil of Gujarat and could, therefore, make films related to the problems of the people. Two great Parsi actors, D. and E. Billimoria, first in the silent era and then mostly in stunt films of the picture with voice period, came from the same town.

Some pseudo-secularists have tried to read an anti-Muslim sentiment in the fact that great cinema actors and actresses of the past, like the immortal Madhubala and Meena Kumari, and the one who is happily with us, Dilip Kumar, had to adopt Hindu screen names to avoid prejudice among the spectators, although they were Muslims. These "secularists" display not only their utter ignorance but also their own bias in doing so. Two of the authors of this pernicious theory—Prof. J. S. Bandukwala and Bhikhu Parekh—are from the M. S. Unversity at Baroda (Vadodara) which came into existence at my alma mater, the century old Baroda college. If I did not know that many Gujaratis, whether Hindu, Muslim or Parsi, adopted their ancestral profession as surname, I would have been frightened by a name like

Bandukwala. That does not mean the theory is frightening. In fact, it is flimsy and baseless.

**Baseless Theory**

Their argument is that these three all time greats had to take Hindu names to become acceptable to largely Hindu audiences but now there is less of this prejudice as actors like Shahrukh Khan, Aamir Khan and Salman Khan are able to win the hearts of the viewers even with their Muslim names. This is absurd for reasons, given below, but what is regrettable some impressionable "scholars" are quoting the argument even now. If it were not regrettable it would amount to being prejudicial because they do not know the ABC of Hindi films.

They do not know that it is customary for actors and actresses to adopt filmi names. Even a great actor, often called an actors' actor, Sanjeev Kumar, had to discard his own name, Hari Jariwala, for this filmish name. He may have been told by some producer that his name, Hari, was prosaic and the element Kumar was a must for any aspiring actor, like Raj Kumar, Rajendra Kumar, Manoj Kumar and even Dilip Kumar. The practice continues to this day. The real name of the popular actor, Akshay Kumar, is Rajeev Bhatia. What is wrong with a name like Rajeev Bhatia but Akshay Kumar does sound a little romantic. Likewise, the real name of Manoj Kumar was Hari Goswami. Subhash Ghai gave his new actress of the film *Pardes* the screen name of Mahima.

If the Bandukwala-Parekh theory were correct why did not Nargis and Waheeda Rehman, almost the equals of Madhubala and Meena Kumari, adopt Hindu names? There were many like Rahman, Mumtaz, a highly popular actress of the sixties and seventies, who kept their names much before the tribe of Khans was born in the Hindi films. The naming of an actor or actress is purely coincidental, like most names given by parents which one has to bear like a cross all one's life. Some are strong enough not to accept any suggestion for a change, some are never asked and some meekly accept the change.

In the case of the much loved Madhubala and Meena Kumari many of the cinema audiences knew that they were Muslims. Dilip Kumar makes it very obvious that he is Yusuf Khan and his pro-Muslim approach gives away the man, although the Muslim mafia have not spared him either. Yet the cinema audiences love them, no matter what their names and religion are, whether it is Dilip Kumar or Shahrukh Khan, irrespective of whether he and Aamir Khan are both married to Hindu girls. The cinema industry is highly commercial and profit is the main motive, although they give themselves the title of a creative industry. The choice of heroes and heroines is generally dictated by this motive, even when the mafia dons of Dubai and Karachi lay down who should be the heroes and heroines of the pictures financed by them.

Surprisingly the Bandukwalas and Parekhs and the "scholars" who imitate the argument have nothing to say about the bomb attacks on the house of Maniratnam, the producer-director who made the film *Bombay* in which a Muslim girl marries a Hindu. Although the film was largely against the Hindus in portraying the riots in Mumbai, it did not have a smooth run as all kinds of problems had to be encountered and the release was also held up in several cities by resort to legal action or just hooliganism. The so-called leaders cooked up all kind of excuses, like the Muslim girl running away with some religious book and objecting to the film on that account. The fundamentalists did not bother that the music of the film was scored by a man called Rahman who was a recent convert from Hinduism to Islam. They care little that in TV serials and even in the cinema some Muslim male character is shown as loving and marrying a Hindu girl and the author of the script is also a Muslim.

The Bandukwala-Parekh duo perhaps knows that a Hindu artist like Sujata Jhaveri has assumed a Muslim-sounding name, Alisha Chinai, and the fact that music lovers of the pop variety adore her should disprove any theory based on assumed names. The truth is that by and large the Hindus are tolerant and there are fanatical elements among the Muslims who have the tacit support of the generality. The insistence of these people, and the writers and "leaders", on a Hindu girl marrying a Muslim man getting converted to Islam has been dealt with in another chapter.

How is a Muslim portrayed in Hindi films and serials? We are not referring to the classical movies of Mehboob Khan and memorable Saigal movies from Calcutta's New Theaters but the films of the present age, which incidentally, are of great commercial value because the Muslim audiences in Pakistan, which see them in videos or on the cable and satellite TV channels, also view them. The Pakistan government has banned all Indian movies from their theatres, something which Gujral never took up with his friend Nawaz Sharif of Pakistan. The Indian Hindi films are immensely popular with the Pakistani audiences at home or in the Gulf and the U.K., and naturally their producers are careful not to offend the audiences, besides the Muslims in India.

This approach is not without its merits and there should be no unjustified offence given to anyone. But then the film-makers take every possible liberty with Hindu sentiments. For example, it is customary for a hero to denounce the god in the temple or in the mother's puja room and in the end he would make amends for his behaviour but no Muslim is ever portrayed denouncing Allah in a mosque or an equivalent place. There is nothing inherently wrong in agnosticism or even non-belief being portrayed but you have to remember that the Hindi film producers are extremely careful about not offending Muslim sentiments, for fear of legal action, pure hooliganism or audience rejection.

The portrayal of the Muslim in the films and many of the TV serials is interesting. The Muslim is generally shown as a good man, helpful and trustworthy, free from prejudice and always praying. You may have Muslim friends who never visit a mosque but in our films and serials they are particular about the five time prayers and the dialogue writers are keen to point it out. In fact, while the Indian films make the Muslim character often swearing by Allah (Hi Allah, Subhan Allah) the Pakistani cinema and serials take Allah for granted. There is no mention of God or He is given His due place. The Pakistani programmes are more secular than the Indian counterparts where even a smuggler and mafia don, who kills without any compunction, is shown as praying. Of course, in most cases the Hindus only are shown as smugglers or dons. The Muslim is always loyal and ready to give his life and makes no bones about his Muslim character.

No people are essentially bad or good and goondas or mafia can be found in all communities but the preponderance of the Muslim mafia in Mumbai, now hiding in Dubai and Karachi, cannot be gainsaid. What is important the Hindi film-makers, and following them the producers of serials, have their stereotypes of a "Madrasi" (Madras may have changed its name, there are four southern states, apart from Pondicherry, and there is no such thing as 'a Madrasi' but our films have to have the stock character), a Parsi, a Christian, a Marwadi, a Gujarati, a Bengali, a Bombaywallah meaning a Maharashtrian, and sometimes even a Punjabi, although many of the producers are themselves Punjabis, more often a Sikh. What are the stereotypes? A Christian is a drunkard, although priests because of their apparel are always respectfully portrayed and churches come handy for their photogenic presence, a Parsi is always funny and converses in Gujarati (something which some of the westernised Parsis would object to), a Madrasi speaks Hindi in a funny way, a Marwadi is money-minded, (who is not) and a miser, and so on.

In the cinema's world of make believe there are stereotypes of Muslims. If there is what is called a Muslim social, there would be superficial affluence, kotha going young and middle-aged men, *mushairas*, women in purdah, men at prayer, an altogether idealised portrayal of a largely non-existence society. The cinema makers forget that a Muslim has the same aspirations and urges for betterment as any other Indian but the cinema makers must make him appear as somewhat different from others, somewhat different from the reality and not touch his problems of unemployment and backwardness in education at all.

To make themselves more acceptable commercially the films and serials have characters which would show that the Muslims and Hindus are close to one another. Alas the social contacts between the two communities are not so close as portrayed by the films, which, one must emphasise, have great mass appeal and are seen by a very large number of people. There are some films in which an attempt is made to touch the communal issue but except for homilies, usually delivered by Nana Patekar, the real issue is always skirted or avoided for fear of offending the Muslim audiences.

Secularism consists of equal rights to all citizens irrespective of their religion and without regard to majority or minority character of the people. India is one of the few countries which have achieved the goal they set out to reach. Not only in the sphere of the governmental activity but even in areas and aspects of life where the government's long arm does not reach, the Indian spirit of fairness and tolerance pervades the scene. There are unfortunately departures from the objective and there are instances where the secular ideal is violated and injustice is done to several people. But only the unthinking and ungrateful generalise from such instances and accuse the nation.

**Danger to Secularism**

The danger to secularism and to a proper relationship of the Muslim minority to the generality of Indians arises from the ever present threat of separatism. Almost continuously attacks are made on Indian secularism by prominent Muslims. They take offence at small things and promptly generalise from the specific to the basic and larger issue. A leading Muslim, who now adorns the Minorities Commission chairmanship under the Indian government, Dr Tahir Mahmood, once raised a storm in a tea cup over the delightful practice of breaking a coconut as an auspicious start to any undertaking. Many were shocked by his objections on the supposed ground of secularism and some people angrily reacted and refuted his criticism, including some Muslims, because they saw nothing religious in the practice. It is certainly not a violation of secularism.

I was reminded then of the breaking of a coconut by the Muslim wife of the editor of the Bombay (Mumbai) afternoon daily, *The Afternoon Despatch and Courier*, at the opening of the Delhi office of the paper. I was present because I was lending a helping hand from Delhi in the growth of the paper. The gracious lady was under no compulsion to break a coconut and, indeed, no puja was performed. No puja is performed at the launching of a naval ship at which the coconut is broken. Yet it occurred to her to include this charming ceremony in the inauguration.

The umbrage of the learned doctor is the kind of sensitiveness betrayed by some prominent Muslims whose intolerance irritates others. If a large number of retired military officers choose, without any expectation of reward, to join the BJP, including some Sikhs and Christians and a Jew, it is because they feel there is need to strengthen the Indian spirit and save it from this kind of ultra-separatism which would cavil at the mention of the word "votebank" politics, to which also some Muslims have objected. When such people object to harmless things there are always sensation loving news media ready to publicise the views and create an impression that some violation of secularism has taken place. If there is a counter-reaction it would be termed as Hindu communalism, without realising that in the first place they have encouraged it.

Hindu communalism is largely a reaction to Muslim separatism and a direct consequence of the feeling of separateness nursed by men like the chairman of the Minorities Commission. It is these "learned" men who quote some text as some people quote the Oxford dictionary or Nesfield's grammar who ultimately spawn communalism of one kind and provoke counter-communalism. When their separatist views are played up by some media and the Urdu press they feel elated and think they have voiced an important point of view. When their words produce a counter-reaction they think Indian secularism has declined. Fortunately, there is a growing number of young men and women among the Muslims who wish to rise above these feelings.

## NOTES

1. "King Jayasimha Siddharaja of Gujarat (1094-1143) punished some of his subjects for interfering with the worship of the Muslims". *History and Culture of the Indian People*, Vol. V, Bharatiya Vidya Bhavan, Bombay. The same history books says in Vol. V: "Sarangadeva (1294-1297) of Gujarat gave a grant for a masjid to the local Muslim Community of Prabhas Pattana with the blessings of the high priest of Somanatha". The same temple was sacked by Mahmud of Ghazni.
2. Indonesian, Malaysian and Singaporean references are based on the author's personal information collected during his stay and visits to these countries.
3. *Indian Express*, Delhi, October 2, 1997.
4. *Indian Express*, Delhi, October 6, 1997.
5. *Indian Express*, Delhi, letter to the editor, October 16, 1997.
6. *Times of India*, Delhi, December 29, 1994, letter to the editor, by Shah Rukh Kirmani, Aligarh, in which he said that the Muslim Community in India is 20-crore strong. Actually, the Shahi Imam of

Delhi's Jama Masjid, Syed Abdullah Bukhari, propounded the theory that the Indian Muslims were 200 million. This perhaps caught on. If the Muslims were 200 million the Indian population should be about 1,600 million right now, in 1997, a dismal prospect for an overpopulated country. In ten years, between 1981 and 1991, the population of Muslims has gone up from 11.4 per cent to 12.1 per cent.

7. See 6 above. The Indian Muslims, contrary to a popular misconception are numerically somewhat less than the Muslims in Pakistan. The total population of Pakistan, in 1994, was 131.5 million, according to the *Statesman's year book, 1997*. The Muslims were 96.68 per cent of this figure, so the Muslim population would be around 127 million. The Shias are 15 to 20 per cent of the Muslim population, Christians are stated to be 1.55 per cent and Hindus are said to be 1.51 per cent.
8. Interview in the *Times of India*, Delhi, August 5, 1996, in which he accused the Indian media of being against the Muslims, although he was himself Minister of Information and Broadcasting.
9. For details on Chiefs of Staff of the three armed services and gallantry award winners see *India 1996, a Reference Annual*, Publications Division, Delhi.

*Chapter 9*

# LEADERS AND THE LED

In some of the previous chapters we have seen how Muslims in important positions, some of them holding offices in political parties and others noted as writers and commentators, keep on harping on separatist issues. They are joined by religious leaders to whom a pure form of Darul Islam alone is acceptable, something which they cannot achieve in a multi-religious society unless the Hindus one day become a minority and the Muslims a majority. They think that the media attention they get is proof of the validity of their assumptions. Often the media are blamed for one ill of the Indian society or another, and often they are guilty of overplaying something in the interest of sensationalism, but they are mostly performing their main task of presenting different points of view. Several do it purely out of that consideration but some do it because they think that sensationalism generates more circulation which in turn leads to more advertisement revenue.

All newspapers love controversy, and conflict, as a rule, makes better news than mere goody goody things. While there is truth in that, there is such a thing as responsibility which all good newspapers have to bear in mind. There are few legal curbs on the press which enjoys freedom of expression, guaranteed by the Constitution, and the courts jealously guard it, apart from what the Press Council of India does. We need not enter the controversial area of whose freedom it is anyway, but let us not forget that media attention is not proof of the validity of an argument. Unfortunately, the Urdu press thinks it has to bear the cross of safeguarding Muslim interests which once more disproves that Urdu is the common property of many Indians, irrespective of their religion. It often goes all out to preach separatism and, therefore, relishes such articles and statements. Needless to add that when we speak of the media we speak of a section and that applies as well to the Urdu press which also has several dailies and magazines upholding and supporting the Indian system.

Like some political parties which fight elections to Parliament and the state assemblies but believe in an ideology hostile to democracy, there are Muslim writers who buttress separatism in the name of secularism. Some writers have the free run of leading papers but what they preach is not what the enlightened sections of the Muslims should do but only their softness for some evil practices in the name of an ancient system. When there is a movement for women to enter mosques, considered a male preserve, these writers would quote ancient practices which allowed it. Why then these good practices fell into disuse? They do not condemn the evil practices now prevailing because that would put them opposite what they think is the main current of Muslim society.

What is needed is that such scholars come out openly in support of reforms so that the Muslim society is rid of ills like instant or triple 'talak', divorce, which continues in India while a number of Muslim countries have abolished it. This is not something for the Muslims only to think about, because the Indian Constitution confers equality on men and women and if some women, in the present case, Muslim women, are subjected to inequality that has to be ended. Even in Pakistan which has such evils as the testimony of a woman only regarded as half as valid as that of a male, the triple 'talak' is curbed. Again the evil practice of polygamy continues in India while many Islamic countries have banned it or made it difficult.

Unfortunately, the writers, referred to above, would not lead a campaign, or even support it, for the abolition of polygamy or instant divorce. This would be 'unpopular' to do and some of the sources for the institution for which one may be working would dry up. They would at best say how the evil has crept in and sometimes even blame the Hindus for it. Some of them link it with the demand for a common civil code and point out how harmful is the proposal to national unity, although the Supreme Court has lent its powerful support to it and it is provided in the Constitution. But why can't the Muslim law itself be codified, at least in regard to the two evils, so that monogamy is prescribed for the Muslims males, as much as for the other communities, and the practice of triple 'talak' is abolished. It is true that polygamy is not widely practised by the Muslims but that should be a reason for banning it altogether, not for skirting the issue in a fashionable manner.

It is equally true that among some Hindus, mainly the cinema crowd, two marriages by the actors and producers and some others, is tolerated by the suffering first wives. This is an argument for strengthening the provisions of the Hindu code so that legal action can be taken, not for justification of the practices in Islamic society. Whether it is practised by the Hindus or Muslims, polygamy or bigamy is bad and should be ended as soon as possible. The Hindu code of 1955 outlawed bigamy altogether but loopholes still exist which means the law has to be tightened.

Many Muslim writers look the other way when they have to condemn the two evils because like most political parties they would not like to offend the Muslims in general. The politicians, with some exceptions, would like to let sleeping dogs lie, not caring for the poor women who may have to suffer many indignities and injustices whereas the Constitution provides for complete equality. But neither the politicians nor the writers are aware, or pretend they do not know, that at once the main plank of Hindu separatism would be removed if the system of polygamy is abolished. Now the Muslim is widely believed to be enjoying a privilege which the Hindus do not have.

The writers, like Asghar Ali Engineer, would refer to some ancient practice but would not run down a patently unjust system. Religion is not what is written down in some text or the ideal system that could have been in existence at some period of time but what is actually practised by the people and what is believed by them, underwritten by "men of learning" whose writ runs for the time being. Fortunately, a reform movement has sprung up among the thinking Muslims while the Ulema continue to harp on separatism and the writers connive at the evil practices and exercise their skills on issues which the media would enjoy to highlight because of the alleged injustice to the Muslims.

**Women in Mosques**

The Imam of the big Palayam mosque in Thiruvananthapuram, capital of Kerala, a state in which the Muslims are in substantial numbers, decided that women could and should go to the mosque for prayers just like men. That was in January 1997. He triggered a reformist movement throughout the length and breadth of the country driving the hardliners to man the barricades against the women who had taken up cudgels against them. Until then, barring some areas in the country, mosques were a 'no entry' area for Muslim women who had to pray in the solitude of their homes. Contrast this with the thronging of boisterous Hindu women in temples and religious congregations.

Some Muslim writers point their fingers at the 'Ghunghat' (partial covering of the face) and the 'Chunni' (head and breast cover) to justify the 'purdah' (veil) among Muslim women. They fail to realise that no religious ceremony among the Hindus could be complete without the wife being seated along with the husband. Rama who had abandoned his wife, Sita, had a gold image of his wife made for the big 'yajna (sacrifice)' he was performing. He was a strict monogamist despite the prevailing tradition of having more than one wife.

The movement for the entry of women to the male preserve of going to the mosque, started by P. K. K. Ahmed Kutti, the Imam of the Palayam mosque, set off a nationwide wave in favour of mosque going, leaving the writers far behind. Women everywhere are ill-treated but if they cannot go to a place of worship, while the male could flaunt his religiosity, is certainly a great inequity which has to be set right soon. The argument against women going to mosques is that their presence distracts the men who would otherwise seek communion with God. Are the men not distracted by the presence of women in the homes and other social occasions where at least they can appear in public in the company of relatives. God is, in any case, omnipresent.

The Thiruvanathapuram Imam's bold action unleashed a nationwide debate in which both the opponents and protagonists of women's rights participated. The well-entrenched males came out with 'fatwas' against women's entry to mosques—even at the time of the Friday congregational prayers, not from day to day—but facts also came to light that in several towns in Andhra Pradesh the practice of women attending Friday prayers was in vogue for some fifty years. This was prevalent in the coastal towns of the state, like Vijayawada, Visakhapatnam and some others, not in the hardcore orthodox places in the old Nizam's territory in the Telegana area near Hyderabad.

The practice stood to reason on all possible grounds of equality, decency, morality and the right to follow one's religion. It was found that in the heartland of Islam, in Mecca and Medina, in Saudi Arabia, where more than two million Muslims from many countries in the world go for the Haj pilgrimage, during the holy month of Ramazan every year, women routinely go to the mosque, apart from their presence at the time of the Haj pilgrimage. But not in north India and many other parts of the country where the menfolk succeeded in keeping the women out of the mosques. Nobody raised the question of equality and the right to practise one's religion guaranteed by the Constitution. So much is the fear of Muslim orthodoxy that everyone kept quiet, including the champions of 'human rights' who jump up when a terrorist is involved. The terrorist himself is no respector of other's rights.

The flame lit by Ahmed Kutty had, however, reached some of these bastions of orthodoxy. Lucknow is the home of the Shia faith. The Shias are one of the main sects of Islam, the major sect being the Sunnis who look down upon the Shias and in Pakistan, where also the Sunnis are much more numerous than the Shias, the men of the two sects sometimes kill off the others, specially at prayers in mosques, not, of course, the women who cannot enter the shrines of God. In this domain of the Shias, an eighteen year old college girl, Sadaf Rizvi, took up the challenge on behalf of other women. She led about 100 women into the ancient Asafi Imambara on the auspicious day of August 15 which was also a Friday. By next Friday, the number of women ready to enter the mosques had risen to 150 and some venerable Maulanas also came out in support of Sadaf's campaign, citing, as usual, some ancient authority. After all, Asghar Ali Engineer does the same and forgets about the matter thereafter.

Here again nobody raised the question of Constitutional rights being violated by refusing women entry into mosques. Some antiquated authorities were cited in support but not equality for the women. Constitutional rights are only for the males among Muslims, it would appear, specially when Hindu brides married to Muslims are to be converted to Islam. They are almost always converted. But it was left to Ahmed Kutty and Sadaf Rizvi to blaze a new trail.[1]

"The Muslim woman in India is generally illiterate", said Uzma Naheed, writing in the *National Herald*, Delhi, on August 14, 1997. She blamed the conservative attitude of parents, in many parts of India, for their backwardness because they would not send their daughters to school on the logic, as Naheed says, "they don't have to go for a job...why should they go to school". But said Uzma Naheed: "Women are more vulnerable to exploitation and illiteracy; lack of religious knowledge results in the misuse of 'talaq', non-payment of 'mehr' (a kind of alimony which the divorcing husband must pay to his ex-wife but often does not) and alimony to children until they are grown up. In this way her miseries multiply". The males do not show enough concern about these practices and the "leaders" connive at it. The votebank politicians look the other way and the Muslim writers and journalists, who shout the loudest against the Hindus, are generally silent on the issue.

Qamarunnisa Anwar, a former chairperson of the Kerala Social Welfare Board, was among the prominent Muslim women who supported the Ahmed Kutty initiative for women's admission to mosques. In an article in the *National Herald* on September 12, 1997 she lamented that the 'fatwas' of the Mullahs and their influence on society in general was one of the reasons for the community's backwardness. According to her, the Muslim population in Kerala was 21.5 per cent. In other words every fifth Malayalee (as the Kerala people are known) is a Muslim and the percentage is considerably higher than the average of 12 per cent in India. She noted with natural pride that despite the low entry of Muslim girls in the schools and the high rate of their dropout, Muslim women had made much progress in the state.

Fatima Beevi from Kerala was the first woman from the Muslim community, in fact the first woman, to be elevated to the Supreme

Court bench and later to be the governor of Tamil Nadu on retirement. Qamarunnisa told her readers with much pride that another Muslim woman from her state, Mrs Fatima Rehman, was a judge of the Kerala High Court. Mrs Anwar asked: "Why is it that in our country alone Muslim women are lagging behind? We have to rectify our mistakes. We have deviated from the fundamentals of Islam."

There is thus a continuing conflict between the advocates of modernity and change and the protagonists of status quo. The government, the Hindu community and the Constitution are generally blamed for the ills of the Muslims. If some media also harp on it and if the votebank politicians also talk of it with approval what is the need for looking at one's faults? But the sad fact is that women are the worst victims of this wrongheadedness, the calculated hypocrisy of the politicians, the "leaders" of the community and the writers who enjoy advocating separatism rather than turn the searchlight inward.

**Shabban's Fatwa**

The indignities of the Muslim women seem to know no end. In Hyderabad, an organisation suddenly appeared and it called itself "Tehrik Muslim Shabban", with a leader known as Mustaq Malik. It announced that it would stop burqa-clad Muslim women from seeing Hindi films in cinemas in the city and in other parts of Andhra Pradesh also, specially cities and towns with a sizable Muslim population. Malik clarified that his volunteers would "peacefully" prevent the women from entering the places if they were wearing burqas. Neither the Andhra Pradesh government, nor the ruling Telugu Desam Party, which was a constituent of the United Front, whose government was thrown out twice by the outside supporter, the Congress, tried to resist the blatantly anti-constitutional movement. Nobody has the right to prevent women or any other citizen from entering a public place which a cinema is. If the person has a valid ticket issued by the theatre owner even the owner cannot enforce such a ban. If the movie has been approved by the CBFC, Central Board of Film Certification, popularly known as the Film Censor Board, nobody has the right to prevent anybody's entry. Only the Board can say whether a movie is fit for universal exhibition, for adults only or fit neither for adults or others. This is, of course, subject to law.

No Shabban or anyone else has the right to lay down what is good or bad in terms of movies and prescribe any dress code for cinema goers. The Constitution of India and the law are involved but neither the media nor the government of India nor the ruling party in Andhra Pradesh raised their little finger against the totally illegal movement of the Muslim outfit. So much is the fear of orthodoxy in the country. Many were concerned about the religious rights. But this is an issue in which the constitutional right is very much in the picture and others have as much a say in the matter as the Muslims. Fortunately, the Shabban could not ultimately cause much of a problem but the media gave it and Mr Malik a lot of publicity.

Political parties prefer to keep silent when the issue is perceived as affecting Muslims without realising the larger implications of an anti-constitutional action. If women's rights are affected, the mere propagation of the action to enforce a ban is an offence. If the women against whom the ban is sought to be enforced protest against it and challenge it in a court of law it would be treated as a violation of their rights. If the affected women are prevented by social inhibitions from coming forward to fight the ban, there are women's organisations to take up their cause. But if they are also under the spell of a political party, which in turn is bothered by considerations of votebank politics, the constitutional action would become the responsibility of some voluntary body, the NGO.

A mature and forward looking writer, Rashid Talib, had this to say about the undercurrents in the Muslim community in the later part of 1997, when India celebrated the 50th anniversary of her independence: "In the wake of the trauma suffered by the Muslims in the early 1990's, the community seems to have developed a split personality. One part of its body politic is willing to move forward through an adaptation of its outdated laws and practices so that they are in better accord with the cherished human values of our times. The other part of it would like the community to respond to the Hindutva challenge with a militant assertion of its Islamic identity, lest a more reasonable stance be mistaken for weakness".[2]

Talib thus recognised that there are some Islamic laws and practices which are outdated and not in accord with the human values. What, we may ask, is the Hindutva challenge? Despite the Supreme Court's judgment of December 11, 1995, it has been a regular feature of Muslim writing and some writings by other intellectuals to ascribe communalism to Hindutva. What the apex court said should be recalled: "Considering the term 'Hinduism' or 'Hindutva' *per se* as depicting hostility or intolerance towards the other religious faiths or professing communalism proceeds from an improper appreciation and perception of the true meaning of these expressions emerging from the detailed discussion in earlier authorities of this court. Misuse of these expressions to promote communalism cannot alter the true meaning of these terms".[3]

To presume hostility towards the Muslims and Islam among the Hindus is a common failing of even liberal writers, what to talk of the fundamentalists and the commentators who cannot be classified as liberals. It is doubly unfortunate since Talib is not only a liberal writer but also a lawyer. The demolition of the Babari mosque in Ayodhya in UP in December 1992 by overenthusiastic bands of 'kar sevaks'[4] was a deplorable action. The Congress party suffered in election after election because its Prime Minister, P. V. Narasimha Rao, sat unaffected in Delhi, while the alleged kar sevaks went about their task of demolition, and never deployed the massive paramilitary forces, assembled in nearby Faizabad the district headquarters of Ayodhya. The Muslim electorate, which is presumed to vote *en bloc*, but often individuals vote according to their light, also voted against the BJP in the UP assembly elections in 1993. The BJP lost its majority in UP in that election which shows that many Hindus also did not like the demolition job, however controversial the monument may be. (It is even now referred to in official parlance, as the "controversial structure".)

**History Can't be Rectified**

Across the length and breadth of this vast country thousands of temples were destroyed by Islamic zealots, the fundamentalist rulers and their agents, during the hundreds of years of Muslim rule in different parts of the country. Nobody can bring back to life those temples nor is it desirable (and even possible) to demolish the mosques built over their ruins. History cannot be rewritten or "rectified", as the first President of free India, Dr Rajendra Prasad said, while blessing the restoration of the Somnath temple in Gujarat in 1951. He had then said:

"It is, no doubt, possible to turn back but it is not given to man to return to the moment that has passed away...Today our attempt is not to rectify history.". Rajendra Prasad, who was endearingly called Rajen Babu, affirmed his catholicity thus: "Even though I am a Sanatanist Hindu by faith and daily practice, yet, I believe that man can reach God by worshipping Him according to the dictates of his own faith...Whenever there is an opportunity I go to the 'durgah' and 'masjid', the church and the Gurdwara, with the same feeling of respect with which I go to the temple of my faith."[5]

The above extract has been reproduced here to show that the first head of state of India had a truly liberal outlook and was thoroughly secular while being a devout Hindu. The idea is also to counter the argument of some ignorant people who have attacked Rajendra Prasad because he had honest differences with Prime Minister Nehru. He did not, however, allow his differences to come in the way of the discharge of his duties. He was so scrupulous that when he conferred the 'Bharat Ratna' award on Nehru in 1955 he said he was breaking for the first time the rule that the President always acted on the advice of the Prime Minister.

The demolition of the Babari mosque was not justified from any account and has to be deplored. From a practical point of view also it was a highly anti-Hindu act because its demolition was the cause of the destruction of hundreds of temples, according to one calculation, 600 shrines in India, Pakistan, Bangladesh, UAE and in London in the U.K. When the Islamic writers and "leaders" recall the Babari mosque destruction they never mention the demolition of these temples. The BJP recovered its position to a considerable extent in the 1996 election to the Lok Sabha but not to the extent where it could win a majority or sufficient strength to form a government and remain in power for a full five year term. It, however, impelled the party to remove Muslim fears and doubts about its attitude towards the minorities in general and the Muslims in particular.

The demolition of the shrine in Ayodhya was reprehensible but it does not absolve the Muslim "leaders" of their responsibility to provide a solution to the thorny issue since the matter has been agitating the minds of many people for decades. The Ayodhya controversy has come down to us from British days and legal battles have been fought since 1885. Much before the BJP made the shrine an issue, the Congress party had made attempts to create a vote-catching wave in its favour over the Ayodhya problem.

Why did Rajiv Gandhi, then Prime Minister and president of the Congress party, launch his election campaign from Ayodhya in 1989? He was, of course, defeated in the ensuing election and ceased to be Prime Minister but this does not explain the launch of the campaign from Ayodhya of all places. There are other holy Hindu places, like Kashi and Hardwar, if he was seeking the blessings of mother Ganga and Lord Vishwanath. But his action was of a piece with the Congress government in UP, under the orders of his close associate, Arun Nehru, opening the locks of the shrine in 1986, which had been illegally occupied by some people in December 1949. Sardar Patel, often unjustly accused by many Muslims of anti-Muslim bias, was the first person from the government of India, as Home Minister, to ask the UP Chief Minister, Govind Ballabh Pant, to take action against the people who had installed idols in the shrine.

**Sea-change**

Although many Muslim "leaders" and writers find it convenient to keep on harping on the Babari demolition, there are fortunately quite a few writers who say fearlessly that after the unhappy incident of December 6, 1992, there has been a sea-change in the thinking of the Muslims all over the country. Writer Sultan Shahin would have us believe that the traditional leadership of the Muslims, holding them back and obstructing their progress, has suffered a decline after the Babari episode. He said: "They (the Muslims) simply want to forget the Babari nightmare and move forward. Their preoccupation now is simply *taleem*, *tarbiat* and *tijarat* (education, training and trade)".[6] He voiced the objections raised by several individuals about the utilisation of the funds collected in the name of fighting for the rights of the Muslims. The danger arising from the vacuum in the Muslim leadership and the possibility of it being filled by obscurantists and fundamentalists was pointedly raised by the writer.

The error in the thinking is that the nation owes it to the Muslims to prevent the leadership passing into the hands of such undesirable people. If the forward looking people, like him, assume command of the leadership, the Muslims in general would follow them and reject the leaders who are curbing their urge for progress in the name of some "ideology", whether it is the one-man "Milli" parliament, the Students Islamic Movement, under the umbrella of the Jamaat-e-Islami, or the Jamiat-ul-Ulama-e-Hind seeking a Pakistan-like ban on the Ahmediyas or any other.

In another article, the same author,[7] regretted the paranoia and lack of gratitude for Indian secularism cultivated by the Muslim "leaders" who are preventing the Muslim citizens from feeling grateful for the benefits conferred by the positive aspects of our secular and democratic way of life. Perhaps in their hearts, the Muslims realise that but for secularism and the tolerance generally practised by the Hindus they would have faced many difficulties. Shahin is convinced that the separatist leaders like Sultan Salahuddin Owaisi from Hyderabad, the Shahi Imam of Delhi's Jama Masjid, and Syed Shahabuddin are being rejected by the Muslim masses. "It is not Owaisi's, Shahi Imam's or Syed Shaib's kith and kin who get hurt or killed. The Indian Muslim too has gradually come to realise the fruitless exercise. Precisely the reason why Syed Shahabuddin, along with the other leaders of the same fervour, are fast losing their base among the Muslim masses."

There is no doubt that as the *Asian Age*, edited by a Muslim who was once a camp follower of Rajiv Gandhi, editorially remarked! "A new generation has grown up in post-independence India and it is not prepared to accept the old bogey and the resultant shackles imposed by the fanatical group (of Muslims). It has seen the world change around it, it is proud of being Indian. It is keen to compete on equal footing and has realised that it can make a mark by moving forward... The impetus for the change came with the demolition of the Babari Masjid which exposed the opportunism of Muslim politics as practised by the supposed saviours of the community in this country."[8]

The so-called leaders of the Muslims are being lambasted by other thinking Muslims also. Wahiduddin Khan, who has emerged as a reasonable and mature advocate of the cause of the Muslims, said in an article: "It is common for Muslim writers and speakers to lay the blame for this (their political deprivation) at the door of the Hindus. But this view is entirely without foundation... If the truth be told it is the incompetence of the Muslim leaders which has given rise to this unfortunate situation".[9] Wahiduddin Khan regretted the tendency of Muslim writers and speakers to harp only on issues affecting the Muslims. He said he had attended innumerable meetings since 1947 "without coming across any notable Muslim gathering which had been convened specifically to discuss the problems of the Indian nation. National issues simply do not figure on (the) Muslim agenda. At Muslim meetings, communal issues, or more often communal grudges, are the favourite subjects of discussion... This makes it abundantly obvious that the Muslims have in no way identified themselves with the political mainstream". If one talks of separatism one is not far behind the truth.

**Mainstream What**

There are some Muslim writers who do not recognise the mainstream at all. But there are a number of Muslim writers, journalists and others, who are wittingly or unwittingly encouraging separatism. "Babari apology fails to impress Muslims",[10] says a report in a English daily by Aisha Khan. The presumption here, as always, is that Muslims think and act as a community. This was a report which followed up the Congress party's statement at its annual session in Calcutta, indirectly acknowledging its connivance in the demolition of the mosque in Ayodhya. Yet another Muslim journalist, Rasheed Kidwai, tells us in his report in the *Telegraph* of Calcutta: "Muslims plan front to lobby for demands".[11] Among the "distinguished" Muslim leaders mentioned by him were G. M. Banatawala and E. Ahmed, both confirmed Muslim Leaguers, Ibrahim Suleman Sait, formerly a Leaguer now leader of the Indian National League, and the veteran from Hydrabad, Owaisi. The last named told the eleventh Lok Sabha of which he was a member, that the Muslim ratio in the government services was 30 per cent (when, he did not specify) and this should be restored. This report would like us to believe that the Muslims think alike and some of the discredited leaders are also important.

Then we have Abid Shah in the *Statesman*[12] Delhi, who writes of the BJP's efforts to face the future without its President, L. K. Advani, and calls him a "firebrand President". Is Advani a firebrand? He can be accused of several things but not of being a firebrand, that is one who pours venom on the Muslims and others whom he hates. Umabharati could perhaps be called that and Sadhvi Ritambhara is definitely entitled to that honour but not Advani who is suave and refined in his manners. It is not our concern that leading papers tolerate this brand of writing. In one case, however, the continuous pointing out to the powers that be in a leading paper of the capital, based in Mumbai, led to some taming of a talented Muslim writer who had displayed communal proclivities.

These stray quotations raise some important points but there is a distinctly positive one. These are only samples or stray quotations out of many in the form of columns, reports and interpretations (there is no distinction left between a factual report and an interpretative one, full of adjectives and prejudices, miscalled 'news analysis'.) The positive point is that talented Muslim men and women have come up in a big way in the journalistic profession, mostly by the dint of their competence and hard work, except for a few who might be there for 'other considerations'. This would also disprove the argument of many Muslim "leaders" that the Muslims are a suppressed and depressed lot, often discriminated against, also backward and neglected, who must be rescued by the votebank politicians before the BJP eats them up.

That these men and women have come up the hard way is a tribute to them as to the Indian system which, by and large, does not believe in religious distinctions, encourages talent, and recognises the worth of an individual irrespective of other factors. Nobody has conferred any favours on them but it would not be too much to expect from them that they would feel grateful for the secular society in which they live. Unfortunately, many of these people directly or indirectly advocate separatism and do not mind insulting the Hindu community in season and out of season. They, of course, presume that the Muslims act and think as a group, a community, a conglomerate, separate and apart. If that is not separatism what is?

This brings us to the sensitive question of the conversion of Hindu girls marrying Muslims. The traffic in the reverse direction is a trickle. Often Hindu men who marry Muslim girls are "persuaded" to convert themselves to the wife's faith; at least that makes it somewhat easy for the girl's parents to accept the marriage. This explains the absurdity of a man having a Hindu surname and a Muslim name. No blame should come to the boy but he must thank his strong Muslim mother and weak Hindu father for the situation. The persuasion is nothing but emotional blackmail but there are some Hindu brides who withstand it.

A mixed marriage should really speaking be regarded as a natural thing in a mixed society like ours. The Constitution also provides, among the fundamental rights, the right to practise one's faith and also the rights to convert another person to it. But we have on the authority of a noted Muslim journalist, Sultan Shahin, that "Muslims suffer from a kind of mania for conversion. The conversion mania is virtually a part of the Indian Muslim psyche."[13]

**Refusal to Convert**

Shahin speaks of his own experience: "My next experience was even more personally embarrassing and shameful. As some newspaper readers would recall, I was sacked from the editorship of a magazine on my refusal to force my Hindu wife to convert to Islam. The people running this magazine are considered the most enlightened secular elite of the Indian Muslim community. The Chairman of the Board of Directors is the renowned Islamic scholar, Maulana Ali Mian Nadvi. My successor as chief editor of the magazine is a retired IAS officer and former Vice Chancellor of the Aligarh Muslim University, Syed Hamid". After reeling off more names of prominent Muslims, Shahin said: "None of them could resist the temptation of buying a cheap berth in heaven". This refers to the popular belief among Indian (and Pakistani) Muslims that converting a Hindu, as a non-believer, to Islam earns one a passage to heaven. This, according to Shahin, is reducing God "to a supplier of wine and women for the Muslim residents of heaven". But, says the author, Islam specifically forbide forcible conversion. If that is so, how does the world hold as much as 20 per cent Muslims in its population? Not all of them could have voluntarily accepted Islam. There are only a small number of conversions, whether to Islam, Christianity or any other religion, by conviction.

Hindu women being more advanced and less susceptible to parental influence, than their Muslim counterparts, contract a marriage with a Muslim male more often than a Muslim girl from a more conservative and tradition-bound background. If one is convinced of the virtues of Islam as a religion, conversion should not be objected to. In that case, it should take place much before the marriage. Some Hindu men used to conveniently convert themselves to Islam since bigamy is banned for the Hindus and lawyers, who are notorious for getting even hardened criminals on bail, so that they can abscond and commit more crimes, advise such clients to convert to Islam which in India is polygamous. Such conversions of convenience were banned by the Supreme Court when the case of the first (Hindu) wife of a male who had conveniently become a Muslim came up before the court.

But the conversion of a Hindu bride of a Muslim or a Hindu man marrying a Muslim girl cannot be struck down, under the Constitution, because it is said to be "voluntary". There is, no doubt, pressure and emotional blackmail in most of these conversions but as long as the individual affected by it keeps mum the law cannot intervene. The Muslim "leaders" and even many of the writers are firmly against polygamy being banned and the votebank politicians would let "sleeping dogs" lie.

The number of Hindu girls marrying Muslims and being usually converted to Islam is not too large but neither it is so small as to be ignored from the point of view of "forcible" conversion. From the late Vice President, the highly respected and fine gentleman, Mohammad Hidayatullah, to any number of cinema actors, technicians, sportsmen, hairdressers, journalists and others are in the list of Muslims who took Hindu brides and got them usually converted to Islam. One does not know whether Mrs Hidayatullah had also changed her religion, but there is little doubt about the conversion of Hindi film actress Sharmila Tagore when she married former Test cricketer, Mansoor Ali Khan, miscalled 'nawab" of Pataudi. She was given the name Ayesha on marriage and was considerably embarrassed when voters in Bhopal asked her about it as she campaigned for her husband who unsuccessfully contested a parliamentary election on Congress nomination. Their son, Saif Ali Khan, a cinema actor, got his bride, Amrita Singh, also a cinema artist but ten years his senior, a Muslim name on marriage. When popular cricketer, Mohammad Azharuddin, divorced his Muslim wife, Naureen, and married a Hindu woman, Sangeeta Bijlani, a cinema starlet, she went through the Nikah ceremony and was given a Muslim name.

**Misrepresentation**

In Jammu a Hindu boy became a Muslim and assumed the name Rafiq Khan in order to quieten the storm being raised by Muslim fanatics, who are the real trouble makers in the state, when the boy was in love with a Muslim girl Ruby Naz, and both wanted to marry. They went through the Nikah ceremony. The matter came to the Supreme Court in Delhi because even though the boy had changed his religion the secessionists in Jammu and Kashmir were after the blood of the couple and the apex court gave them protection. This was played up by the *Times of India*, Delhi, which proclaimed in a frontpage banner: "Inter-religious marriage gets SC protection".

It was left to the author to correct the impression that it was an inter-religious marriage since the boy had already converted himself to Islam and the marriage was performed as Nikah. I said in my letter to the paper: "The fact that in spite of conversion, the couple faces a threat from Islamic fundamentalists is a poor commentary on them and the faith they profess. Also it shows that those who uphold the secessionist movement in Jammu and Kashmir as secular do not know what they are talking about. It is also not correct to say that the Supreme Court has given protection to an inter-religious marriage... The court has only protected the rights of two individuals to choose their life partners..."[14]

An inter-religious marriage cannot be objected to on any ground whatsoever, but the forcible conversion to Islam (or

Hinduism, Catholic Christianity or any other faith) can be objected to, whether there is emotional blackmail, lack of religious conviction or any other force involved in it. In some exceptional cases, that are within the author's knowledge, there is no conversion as neither the Muslim husband nor his immediate family has raised that question. But one has to contend with the husband's right to polygamy, as long as the law is not amended, and his right to divorce the wife in instant 'talak', if the marriage is performed under the Nikah system. (Nikah can be performed only between two Muslims, so the wife has to undergo conversion). In cases of inter-religious marriages in the enlightened society cases of resort to polygamy or instance 'talak' have not come to notice. But there are stray cases as that of a cinema producer who specialises in marrying Hindu women, three of them one after the other, the first two having been divorced or separated.

Some people say what does it matter if the girl follows her Hindu faith or becomes a Muslim for the sake of her love and marriage. If religion can be changed like a shirt or blouse one can only say that it is not worth changing. If it matters little the religious label is not worth having. A Muslim by convinience is not a Muslim at all; but then there is the question of the cheap passport to heaven and the question of numbers as many Muslims insist that they are not a minority but a second majority in India. The early cases of inter-religious marriages, like those of Aruna Asaf Ali and Shanti Sadiq Ali, were in a special category. Aruna was revered by many of her countrymen because she was a great freedom fighter and was posthumously awarded the Bharat Ratna also. Nobody could object to her marriage, as indeed, nobody ever did. We must also record that several of the inter-religious marriages are happy, as happy as any other marriage.

**Lahore Judgment**

In March 1997, the Lahore High Court in Pakistan upheld the right of a young woman called Saima Waheed to marry a person of her choice and the credit for getting Saima her freedom to love and marry went to that gallant woman, lawyer and upholder of human rights, Asma Jahangir. Although Saima was abducted soon afterwards, the case and the judgement created quite a sensation in Pakistan and also in India, where these things are watched with much interest, specially by the Muslims. Some people wrote to the papers pointing out that the bride's consent was being obtained by the marriage-performing Maulvi, a mere formality and one in which the bride herself hardly ever utters the acceptance, but there were others who were frank enough to say that the Nikah was not based on consent. "Unfortunately, the Nikah in the Indian sub-continent has been reduced to a mere formality. The very idea of the necessity of a girl's consent is being reduced to a symbolic gesture. It is time the Muslims introspect(ed) and stopped flouting the Islamic spirit".[15]

Reference has been made to Supreme Court rulings affecting both Hindus and Muslims. In August 1997 the apex court also decided that a Muslim male was liable to pay maintenance to his children, independent of providing for his divorced wife. This was welcomed by several people as a step in the evolution of a uniform civil code.[16] But the court had also ruled more than ten years earlier that a Muslim husband was as much liable to pay maintenance to his divorced wife, under Section 25 of the Criminal Procedure Code, as anyone else. There was a bitter controversy and the Congress party's Prime Minister, Rajiv Gandhi, set aside the court judgment by passing fresh legislation, euphemistically called the Protection of Muslim Women's Rights on Divorce Acts. This was done to maintain the hold of the Congress party on the Muslim voters but, alas, Rajiv Gandhi lost in the 1989 election, but the Shahbano legislation remained on the statute book to create difficulties for divorced Muslim women. The Supreme Court's August 1997 ruling was also objected to by several Muslim "leaders".

How do the two things match—the propaganda about the Muslims being a suppressed and depressed lot and some Hindu girls marrying Muslims and being subjected to conversion. If they are not going to join the ranks of the "suppressed" the propaganda is hollow.

In June 1997, 92-year-old Janak Kumari Jalil Asghar died in Lahore (Pakistan) in utter penury. She was a close relative of Jawaharlal Nehru and married Dr Jalil Ahmed, who was in the ICS, and went over to Pakistan with her husband. Everything went off well for the couple until Dr Jalil retired (as Defence

Secretary of Pakistan) and died. Even before the death the couple had to sell some movable property to meet the cost of his medical treatment. The real travails of Janak Kumari began after the husband's death. She had worked for years for the Children's Aid Society and recognition for her voluntary service had come even from the dictator, Ayub Khan, who had decorated her with "Sitara-e-Khidmat".

But she had committed a crime in the eyes of her husband's relatives. She had never converted herself to Islam. So nobody was ready to help her in her old days and she was even persecuted with litigation about property. She had no money of her own and charity did not make life even bearable, much less enjoyable. If you give up your ancestral faith by conversion, your soul suffers agony. If you do not suffer any qualms of conscience and convert for the sake of your marriage, you are neither a good Hindu nor a good Muslim, a mere pleasure seeker. According to the Pakistani journalist who reported Janak Kumari's death, "Janak never converted to Islam...While society never minded this, it was her relatives who chose to make it a point of conflict".[17] You are damned if you do, and damned if you don't.

The Pakistani journalist who reported the incident also said that "on her side (meaning apparently the side of the family in which she was born) apart from her immediate family and Indira Gandhi, no one really forgave her for marrying a Muslim". If by the immediate family you mean the parents, brothers and sisters, and if they accept the marriage that should be taken as a plus point. The marriage does not have to be acclaimed and applauded by society in general. It is no doubt true that by and large the Hindus are tolerant but they also feel offended by such happenings. The suffering of Janak Kumari would only help to strengthen the feeling of revulsion against such marriages which involve forced conversion.

Often parents lodge complaints of abduction and forcible marriage if the girl is of tender age and there are court cases and sometimes there are also riots. There are also cases in which the Nikah is performed by the Maulavi, more than willing, when the girl is not of marriageable age. Take another instance from the same Nehru family which was noted for its catholic outlook. But also because of its involvement in politics it was keenly aware of the adverse implications of a girl of the family making off with or being abducted by a Muslim boy known to the family.

**Syud Hussain**

This is what happened to the late Vijaya Lakshmi Pandit, Jawaharlal Nehru's sister. Syud Hussain was editor of Motilal Nehru's paper, the *Independent*. He was young and of an aristocratic background, being the son of Nawab Syud Mohammad of Dacca and Calcutta. "...late 1919, when Motilal and Jawaharlal Nehru were involved in the Punjab trials, (he) is said to have eloped with Motilal's eldest daughter, to have been married according to Muslim rites by Maulana Fakhir of Allahabad and on the news coming to light to have been compelled by the Nehrus to perform a Muslim divorce; Syud Hussain was sent to England with the Khilafat deputation, allegedly with a large payoff, and then went to America".[18]

The quotation is from a British writer who worked as a teacher in the University of London and who has carefully and painstakingly researched the facts in his book. The youthful affair was fairly known among the media and political circles. As a young journalist I met Syud Hussain in Delhi in the years before India's independence, when he had returned from the United States, and Mrs Pandit was happily married to Ranjit Pandit, but I was not aware of the details of the elopement until I read Robinson's book.

The case of Farah Mohammad is a tragic one. She married a Jawaharlal Nehru University teacher from Orissa, a Hindu. She also probably belonged to Orissa. The parents did not approve of the marriage, forcibly took her away from her husband, then whisked her off to Pakistan there to die under rather mysterious circumstances, while the poor husband searched for her high and low and sent frantic letters to the Indian diplomatic mission in Pakistan.

Muslim society is far too conservative and opposed tooth and nail to their daughters marrying the *Kafirs* but would do anything to prevent any young Hindu girl going back to her parents if some Nikah has been performed. The Indian media, among them sections of the English press ready to sensationise the event and keen to display their liberalism, and the communal sections of the Urdu press, blow up the event and, as we noted, there are sometimes riots.

The fundamentalists, who know they have popular sentiment with them, would even prevent the screening of *Bombay* showing a Muslim girl marrying a Hindu boy and even bomb the residence of Maniratnam, the maker of the film. If Sultan Shahin is to be believed—and he has not even been contradicted—eminent Muslims have sought to punish him for not forcing his Hindu wife to become a Muslim.

The great divide we talked of in the beginning of this book comes in here. The effort to bridge the gulf is too weak, if there is any at all. This is despite the preaching of modernity, the impact of consumerism and the licentiousness preached by sections of the media. The latter go sometimes out to dub insistence on the values of one's religion as of no consequence, meaning, of course, only Hinduism.

Rashid Talib has observed that there are two, contrary and opposite, trends among the Muslims, one looking forward and the other backward. It is the backward looking section which is at present much larger than the other one and the votebank politicians are naturally more concerned about them in fact they are not the least bothered about the other. The votebank politicians are of different hues, from the status quoist Congress, to the casteist Samajwadi party which now banks on its Muslim support, and God-knows-where-they-stand Marxist Communists. They would like to exploit and manipulate the Muslim vote and the community's large body of journalistic writers do not think they have a duty to perform except to ventilate grievances, grouses as Wahiduddin calls them. Fortunately, there are also forward looking people among the Muslims although their number at present is not big enough.

We have the prospect of the Jamiat-ul-Ulama-e-Hind president, Maulana Asad Madani, threatening to launch a nationwide agitation to get the Ahmediyas declared non-Muslims following the example set by Pakistan. He was joined in this unholy task by another divine, Maulana Marghbour-ur-Rahman, Vice Chancellor of Darul Uloom of Deoband in Uttar Pradesh, the nursery of conservatism. Several individual Muslims and some Muslim-edited newspapers condemned the move and the government has not come out to uphold and accept the demand of the venerable Maulanas that it declare the Ahmediyas non-Muslims. That, of course, would be against the Constitution of India. That Pakistan has done it and is harrassing the Qadiyanis, as the Ahmediyas are also known, should actually be an argument for India not accepting the demand.

The Ahmediyas believe that Mirza Ghulam Ahmed of Qadiyan, in India's Punjab province, was a prophet. They do not accept the finality of Prophet Mohammad, much like the Bahais of Iran who have a worldwide movement based on the philosophy that there was another prophet, Salamatullah. The Qadiyanis are not so widespread or apparently affluent but they also seem to be determined in their belief. The action of the Islamic government of Pakistan to declare them non-Muslims has not deterred them, although they are not allowed to hold prayers in their mosques.

**Ahmediyas**

Religions which believe in a prophet would not relish that another source of parallel authority should emerge and outsiders have no right to interfere but to go the extent of declaring the Ahmediyas non-Muslims on the pattern of Pakistan would amount to muzzling religious freedom. You cannot have it both ways: religious freedom for yourself, including the crucial power to convert others to your faith, and no religious freedom to others. What Pakistan has done to restrict polygamy and instant divorce is not to be emulated but its reactionary practices are being recommended for India to follow. It is some measure of the thinking of the large body of Indians, including many Muslims, that this totally unacceptable demand has been completely cold-shouldered.

The learned Maulana said that the Ahmediyas were getting foreign money.[19] But are not the conservative Muslims being flooded with funds, from Saudi Arabia, the fountainhead of Muslim fundamentalism, and some other sources. Some like the secessionist Hurriyat leaders in Kashmir are said to be guilty of diverting the foreign funds they receive for their personal aggrandisment. The government has enough information about the funds and their misuse in its files and enough powers to come down on the guilty but nothing is apparently being done. The dubious foreign funds received by the Congress party are still being probed by the government's investigating agencies under court pressure.

If the Maulana's charge of the Ahmediyas misguiding innocent people are true, as stated by the Jamiat president, there is a clear case for criminal action, not for banning the movement or declaring them non-Muslims. There is nothing to prevent the Maulana and his friends to launch a peaceful agitation to convince the Muslim masses that the Ahmediyas are wrong and keep on the right side of religion but if you prize your own freedom you cannot deny it to others.

The political parties keep quiet on such issues for fear that their votebanks would be in jeopardy. The Congress had, at one time, the KHAM concept to win elections. Victory in the elections is the be-all and end-all of political parties. They have in the process split up Hindu society into different groups and profess they are out to cater to the requirements of these groups rather than serve society as a whole. K in this syllogism stands for Kshatriyas, or Rajputs who were at one time the fighting class, H for the Harijans, now called the Dalits, A for the Adivasis or tribals, and M for the Muslims. All of these sections are vulnerable to this type of propaganda. The Dalits are, without doubt, the most suppressed and exploited section of Indian society, but most people who speak in their name are only interested in exploiting them rather than make life easier for them.

The discredited former Chief Minister of Bihar has a different formula, MY, Muslims and Yadavs, a section of the Hindus. He believes that all you need to do is to have a formula like that and not do anything else, like serve them and remove their poverty, so that you can remain in power for long. The Samajwadi party leader, Mulayam Singh Yadav, would have a slogan, 'jawan, kisan, Musalman'. How exploitative these politicians can become! All you have to do is to coin some slogan to mislead the people, then sit back and enjoy the fruits of power. If the people go to hell, law and order is destroyed and there is no development worth the name, as in Bihar, so let it be.

The formulas of winning power are stolen from one political party by another. The Congress played on the fears of the Muslims for decades and told them it alone could protect them. The Muslims put their faith in the party and suffered a rude shock when its lethargic Prime Minister, P. V. Narasimha Rao, just looked on as bands of alleged Kar sevaks were demolishing the Babari mosque. But he woke up in good time to dismiss the BJP's governments in four states, UP, Madhya Pradesh, Himachal Pradesh and Rajasthan. The all powerful Central government thereby had nearly half of India at its direct disposal. Doing the right thing and leaving the consequences to take care of themselves is not the cup of tea of today's politicians. The film and TV serial makers avoid taking the right course because they want to lengthen their films and serials. Our politicians would rather allow festering sores to multiply while they address a rally and the media play up the "bigness" of the gathering. Competition in bigness is encouraged by the media which have a wrong yardstick.

The media, particularly the Muslim journalists, lambast the BJP and Shiv Sena, its somewhat vulgar version, and dub them communal but ignore the fact that when the BJP or Shiv Sena are in power there are practically no communal riots. These riots are engineered, as has been convincingly proved, when the Congress was in power, in Bihar, Gujarat, Maharashtra and elsewhere. Horrendous riots took place in some of these states under Congress rule. Yet the Congress calls itself secular and the media use the label. Labelling itself is a wrongheaded action but putting a wrong label on someone is even worse.

The BJP has also to learn to eliminate the fears of the Muslims. It has won the confidence of the minorities like the Sikhs but this has to be extended to the Muslims in particular. They ought to be convinced that there is nothing anti-Muslim in its agenda. If there is something to which Muslim opinion objects the people concerned should be taken into confidence and a time will come when they will come round. The fear exists, even though it may be more psychological than real. Much of it is due to the demolition of the Babari mosque. Much of it was due to the failure of the Congress government when it was in power at the Centre and in UP, to address the problem in its proper perspective and find a solution acceptable to all. Although the issue is complicated and opinions are sharply divided, it is not a hopeless case that a solution cannot be found. Specially in 1991 and 1992 there was ample opportunity to bring the two sides together and hammer out a solution. But Rao depended on his friend, Chandraswami, to find a way out and kept the Hindu and Muslim groups separately instead of letting them confront each other and force them to agree to something. The truth that if you do the right thing the votes will automatically come to you has never dawned on our politicians.

**Iftar Parties**

The fractionalisation of India must be countered at all costs. Indira Gandhi, who had many good qualities, lacked self-confidence and, in her desire to woo the minorities, introduced the deplorable practice of throwing Iftar parties during the Muslim month of fasting. Now the practice has come to stay and everyone imitates it. The bill is ultimately paid by the Indian taxpayer, among whose ranks are also the Muslims. No minister, not even the Prime Minister or the President, pays a paisa out of his pocket. Similar parties are not held for the Hindus observing a fast on Mahashivaratri or Janmashtami or a similar occasion. This Iftar practice is clearly non-secular but the champions of secularism would not be able to point it out. People like Tahir Mahmood who cavil at what they consider a departure from secularism and flay the government and the Hindu community, would not be able to utter a word against it.

Iftar is a religious observance where a devout Muslim shares his food with the poor and his friends as he breaks his Ramzan fast. The same crowd of Muslim and non-Muslim politicians, hangers-on, and, of course, the media, many of whom kept no fast, are the round-robin guests at the various Iftar parties. The dominant theme of conversation is politics and the media are naturally interested in who attends and who skips whose party. At one of the parties in 1997, the Railway Minister, Ram Vilas Paswan, who specialises in factional politics and his Bihari brand of Hindi oratory, ran up a bill of Rs five lakhs. Considering that the Northern Railway, which must have done the catering, would charge him no more than Rs. 200 per individual guest, there could be no less than 2,000 guests at Mr Paswan's Iftar party! Even politicians, who do not have a government department at their disposal to pick up the hefty bill, ask their parties to do it. There could not be a more blatant misuse of funds than hosting such parties. This is not merely a denial of secularism but a denial of Islam too. The Iftar food must be pure, not procured out of public funds or the funds of a political party.

The hope for a truly secular society lies in, what some journalists, like Firoz Bakht Ahmed, say, in the enlightened class of Muslim youth. "Today, a new class of enlightened and liberal Muslims is emerging, blooming with enthusiasm and a will to challenge the orthodox traditions and norms, unreasonable and irrational".[20]

## NOTES

1. For Sadaf Rizvi see report in the *Telegraph* of Calcutta, August 25, 1997 on which the *Times of India* editorial, September 5, is based, without acknowledgement. For Ahmed Kutty's bold initiative see *Indian Express, Hindu* and *Times of India*, all of Delhi, January 1997. For the prevalent practice in Vijayawada and other coastal Andhra cities and towns, see *Indian Express*, Delhi, September 12, 1997.
2. Talib's article, *Asian Age*, Delhi, August 12, 1997.
3. See extracts from the judgment reproduced in the appendices.
4. A term derived mainly from Sikh religious tradition, of doing voluntary religious service, like construction work, cleaning or guarding worshippers' shoes as an act of piety.
5. *Speeches of President Rajendra Prasad*, Publications Division, Delhi, 1955.
6. See article in *Asian Age*, Delhi, December 7, 1996.
7. *Pioneer*, Delhi, January 31, 1997.
8. *Asian Age*, Delhi, July 4, 1997.
9. *National Herald*, Delhi, February 7, 1997.
10. *Asian Age*, Delhi, September 1, 1997.
11. *Telegraph*, Calcutta, August 25, 1997.
12. *Statesman*, Delhi, August 27, 1997.
13. "Faith, heredity, and conversion", Sultan Shahin, *Hindustan Times*, Delhi, May 15, 1995, also reproduced in the appendices.
14. *Times of India*, Delhi, January 2, 1996, letter to the editor.
15. Mirza Faizal, Gorakhpur, letter to the editor, "Love in Islam", *Times of India*, March 24, 1997.

16. "Justice for All", editorial, *Times of India*, August 4, 1997.
17. See *Indian Express*, Delhi, June 24, 1997, for Kamal Siddiqi's report from Islamabad.
18. *Separatism Among Indian Muslims*, Francis Robinson, Vikas, Delhi, p. 375.
19. *Asian Age* and *Economic Times*, Delhi, June 14, 1997.
20. *National Herald*, Delhi, February 24, 1997.

*Chapter 10*

# AN "ISLAMIC" FRANKENSTEIN

Several years ago, an Indian Ambassador, posted in a third country, received an invitation from his Pakistani counterpart addressed to him as "His excellency the Ambassador of Bharat". The spirited Indian envoy, a Muslim having close ties with Khan Abdul Ghaffar Khan, returned it to the sender and addressed him "His excellency the Ambassador of Kabrastan". On the next occasion for the two to meet, the Pakistani envoy asked the Indian why the latter had addressed him as the Ambassador of Kabrastan. Promptly he replied: "The graves of my ancestors are in your country, that is why."

The real reason for the offence was that the Pakistani had called him the Ambassador of "Bharat". The Pakistanis take delight in calling India "Bharat". Normally nobody should feel offended but if the term is used vengefully, it causes offence; as in this case.

"I am Bhatt, AIR's South East Asia Correspondent", I once introduced myself to the Pakistani High Commissioner in Singapore. (Pakistan had not yet left the Commonwealth, only to walk back in sheepishly.) His reply was typical of the Pakistani establishment: "BHUT or BHATT?" Spelling out the two names. If the name was Bhut, it would signify a Kashmiri Muslim; although there are many Bhats and even Bhatts among the latter. Perhaps the High Commissioner would have welcomed me with open arms if I were a Bhut although the presumption that a Kashmiri Muslim would have embraced him was wrong. That was the end of my contact with him as he had no use for me. How was the

High Commissioner to know that right in Delhi, I had often been mistaken for a Kashmiri Muslim. Perhaps that has something to do with other things besides my name.

There is, no doubt, intense rivalry between the diplomats of the two countries but the reaction of this particular gentleman was shocking and an eye-opener to me. As noted earlier, the average Pakistani is warm and friendly but there is an under-current of hostility, perhaps due to the venom of communalism and Pan-Islamic sentiment among them.

The visit of the British Queen to India in October 1997 proved a disaster because the Labour government in that country, recently returned to power after 18 years, had convinced itself that the visit must demonstrate its zeal for solving the Kashmir problem. In the first few years after independence, Britain had burnt its fingers in Kashmir and after that for many years it had stayed its hands. But now the newly empowered Labour leaders, prominent among them, the Foreign Secretary Robin Cook who had accompanied the British Queen to India and Pakistan, felt they could tilt at the windmills in Kashmir (to use an expression chosen by a British diplomat). While in Pakistan, Cook had said, Britain would help to mediate in the Kashmir dispute between India and Pakistan to find, what he called; a just solution.

**Too Many Cooks**

There is a proverb that too many cooks spoil the broth. Here was a single Cook spoiling the broth. Even the mild-mannered Gujral, whose Gujral Doctrine has been widely interpreted as a sign of weakness in Pakistan and elsewhere, reacted strongly to Cook's interventionist statement and said, while in Cairo, that Britain was a third rate power. Both Cook and Gujral later did their diplomatic duty and ate their words but the truth stuck. The reason for Cook spoiling the broth for Queen Elizabeth was, apart from the residual imperial tendency and the desire to meddle in other people's affairs, that Cook was trying to please the Muslims, mainly Pakistanis but some Indians too, settled in Britain who have a whiphand in some 30 British parliamentary constituencies in the Midlands in the U.K. Governments and political parties fall victims to constituency pressures and well considered policies are thrown overboard in the process. In the end, the British had to eat the humble pie but one cannot say that the last word has been said on the subject.[1]

India will have to walk warily to prevent the internationalisation of the Kashmir dispute, which Pakistan would love to see. What matters us here is the attitude of the Pakistani Muslims living in Britain compelling the British government to adapt its policies to meet their wishes. They only act as true Pakistanis, the torch-bearers of the Islamic cause. Isn't Pakistan interfering in such far-flung regions as Bosnia and Chechenya, in Russia, the next door Afghanistan, where its Taliban forces are involved in a life-and-death struggle with other Afghans, and even in the affairs of the Central Asian Republics?

Violence in Islamic societies is endemic. Of the 32 rulers of the Delhi sultanate in the 320 years of its rule, before the Mughal empire was firmly in control, only three succeeded their predecessors without bloodshed. And only 15 of the 32 rulers were destined to die a natural death, the other 17 were murdered. Palace intrigues, often leading to bloodshed, are not unknown in any society, but this record is difficult to beat. The hero of many fundamentalists, Aurangzeb, murdered his eldest brother, Dara Shikoh, when he captured the throne of Delhi (and Agra) and kept his own father Shahjahan, the builder of the immortal Taj, in captivity until he died a forlorn man. He was allowed to look at his beloved Taj Mahal from his captivity in the Fort.

What has happened in Algeria is terrifying. The Islamic fanatics in that country have killed thousands, including women and children, and, in turn, many of them have been killed in thousands by government troops. That has been the fate of the Algerians, democratic and peace-loving, in the past six years after the government "robbed" the fundamentalists of their claim to impose their bloody rule on Algeria. In these years some 60,000 or more people have been killed over 400 in December 1997 in a recent outrage. There may be some force in what they claim—and they have many defenders in this country—but one may well ask: are they entitled to kill women and children and other innocent people just to establish their claim? There is a human right angle here. Are the victims not entitled to human rights? Have only the killers the rights?

**Ethnic Clashes**

In Pakistan, thousands have been killed in ethnic clashes—between the Muslims who migrated to Pakistan from India, still called Muhajirs (migrants) and the Pathans, between the Muhajirs and the ethnic Sindhis, with the Punjabis in the security forces, and in sectarian clashes between the minority Shias and the much larger majority Sunnis, who kill people specially at prayer in mosques. This is no cause for exultation but the truth has to be told that many times more Muslims have been and are still being killed by other Muslims in Pakistan than the Hindus or Muslims in communal riots in India. Islam is a religion of peace by its name but its followers are often found to be bitterly engaged in bloody feuds with fellow Muslims or others. There is another sad fact. Despite the cruel fate of the Urdu-speaking Muhajirs in Pakistan, there is believed to be an under-current of sympathy and appreciation for Pakistan among many Muslims in India. The reason for this is said to be the feeling among some that all Muslims have to hang together.

Alas, Pakistan has become a cess-pool of terrorism and specialises in exporting it to other countries, as the Americans are gradually realising, but the fact is that terrorism is striking at the roots of Pakistani society. Male domination, an important element of conservative Islamic society, has taken deep roots in Pakistan under the cover of projecting the country as a champion of conservatism. Zia-ul-Huq, the military dictator, third in Pakistan, who seized power in 1977 and then killed Zulfiqar Ali Bhutto in a criminal trial of "murder", fanned fundamentalism. Ignorant people talk of so much in common between India and Pakistan, but they forget that 40 years after the first military dictator appeared in Pakistan, in 1958, India is yet to produce a military dictator. With the *Hudood* and *Zina* laws, directed against women, Zia launched a major Islamisation drive in Pakistan, where the soil was not at all unsuitable. "Under them, a woman is only half a witness and four Muslim males are needed to testify against a Muslim male to prove a crime, especially against women. The *Zina* laws specifically deal with adultery and intercourse outside marriage, with punishment ranging from flogging and imprisonment to death by stoning".[2]

Since the *Zina* laws were introduced, crime against women has touched the million mark, according to a pro-Pakistan Indian mediaman.[3] Crime against women is a serious problem everywhere, as in India, and there is no dearth of lawyers ready to ask women in courts highly embarrassing questions about their rapists, over-sexed or sex-starved men, and get them off the hook. But, thank God, there is no such law in India that male witnesses must be produced to prove rape and women must be treated as half a witness. There is no point in trying to balance one country against the other. This is not to deny that there is a genuine feminist movement in Pakistan and prejudices are being fought.

Pakistan's record in human rights is highly unsatisfactory although it appears as the champion of Kashmiri Muslims in international forums. According to Amnesty International's report, "Pakistan's elected governments have, over the last decade, failed to repair the damage done by military rule."[4] The report indicts the government of Benazir Bhutto, dismissed by a President installed by her, Farouk Leghari, (who was subsequently forced to resign by Premier Nawaz Sharif), for many crimes including the practice of political appointment of judges. Heavily madeup Benazir has been much admired by some Indians for her eloquence in saying things she never means. But right under her nose, countless women have suffered humiliation, indignity and jail terms or death. The Amnesty report says: "The *Zina* ordinance allows women to be imprisoned solely on the grounds of their gender, and rape victims to be accused of unlawful sexual intercourse if they cannot prove they were raped."[4] In other words, a rape victim finds it hard to prove that she was raped, because of the difficulty, almost impossibility, of procuring four Muslim males as witnesses, and in the end she might herself be tried and jailed for unlawful sexual intercourse.

**Brave Woman Lawyer**

Reference has been made to the role of the brave woman lawyer, Asma Jahangir, who is also a human rights activist. She has created history by fighting for the rights of poor Christian boys, charged with blasphemy, and of Muslim women in distress. The dichotomy referred to earlier in the case of the Indian Muslims, (looking backwards and forwards) is even more true of Pakistan because more and more women are coming forward in that country to fight the battle against religious bigotry and for upholding the women's right to an honourable existence. But the forces of orthodoxy, having a reciprocal relationship with the political bosses, are extremely powerful. The political parties could be led by women, like Benazir Bhutto or men like Nawaz Sharif. These people have the same votebank problem and find it beneficial to support the fundamentalists and be helped by them.

According to an Associated Press (of America) report from Pakistan, "Pakistan's legal community lives in constant fear of attacks by extremist Muslim groups".[5] The Lahore High Court judge, Arif Iqbal Hussain Bhatti, who acquitted the two Christian brothers arranged before him for alleged blasphemy (writing slogans against Prophet Mohammad) in 1995, was killed by a lone gunman who walked into the retired judge's office and fired pistol shots at him. It was Asma Jahangir who had defended the two Christians before the judge and the United States had put pressure on Pakistan to see that they were not hanged.

The American agency's report from Lahore went on to make the point that "the killing may have been retaliation for a 1995 trial in which Bhatti acquitted the two Christian brothers of blasphemy. Justice Bhatti's ruling sparked protests by the extremist Sunni Muslim group "Guardians of the Friends of the Prophet" and the two brothers were whisked out of the country and granted asylum in Germany". The report also quotes Asma Jahangir that she and Bhatti had lived with regular threats from Sunni extremists since the 1995 trial.[6]

Drug trafficking has already been referred to. That is another major threat to Pakistani society. Many in that country have enriched themselves, at the cost of the nation and the innocent drug victims, by heroin smuggling. A number of Indians are also engaged in the nefarious trade as the drugs often pass through this country on their way to the affluent countries of Europe and north America. But the menace in Pakistan has reached extraordinary proportions. There are a number of honest officers in Pakistan fighting the menace but the evil is too widespread and reaches out to all sections, including the police and the armed forces. Despite death sentences the evil is too rampant because the profits from smuggling are fantastically high. If you buy a kilo of heroin from Afghanistan, a big source or supply apart from Pakistan itself, it costs only around $1,300 but it fetches not less than $75,000 in the illegal trade in the United States. The ratio of the profit margin is a skyrocketing 1:57.[7]

No wonder a Pakistani Air Force officer, Squadron Leader Farooq Ahmed Khan, carried two kilograms of the lethal drug with him when he was taking a Boeing of the Pakistan Air Force to the US to bring back military supplies from that country. He could have made $150,000 for his smuggling if he had not been caught by the Americans, notwithstanding the Superpower and Client state relations that exist between the US and Pakistan.

**Diplomatic Row**

The love-hate relationship between the two countries over drugs is quite interesting. Often there is a diplomatic row when, for example, Pakistan arrested its national working with the Drug Enforcement Agency of the Americans in Pakistan, Ayaz Baluch, apparently in retaliation to the arrest of the PAF Squadron Leader, Farooq Ahmed Khan. But the case of Mir Aimal Kansi was even more interesting. The man had been working for the high profile snooping outfit of the US, the CIA, Central Intelligence Agency, of which the Americans are immensely proud, in Washington. Kansi had been on the run after killing two of his American colleagues right at the agency's headquarters in Washington. Another arm of the mighty United States, the FBI, Federal Bureau of Investigation, caught up with Kansi in the North-West Frontier Province, NWFP, in June 1997. They got hold of him in a hotel room and took him to Islamabad and from there by a special plane to Washington. This took them only two days, as the flight took off on June 17.

The Americans do not believe in extradition proceedings specially where a client state like Pakistan is involved. The legal niceties were dispensed with as Kansi was whisked off with the apparent connivance of the Pakistan government. But if American media reports are to be trusted the US government paid Pakistan two million dollars for taking out Kansi in this surreptitious manner. "We are not a country that forgives... we don't forget. We seek retribution", proudly declared Nicholas Burns, US state department spokesman in Washington, celebrating Kansi's return to the country of his crime.[8]

What about two million dollars? This came out in the remarks of the Virginia state attorney, while prosecuting Kansi. The counsel, Robert Horan, said the US should not have paid "the Pakis $2 million as they could sell their mothers for just a few thousand dollars".[9] The remarks naturally evoked a strong reaction in Pakistan. The people of Pakistan are intensely patriotic but they had to gulp the humiliating statement because their government swallowed yet another insult by the Americans. For all external appearances the government fumed and fretted and called in the US Ambassador for a tongue lashing to the foreign office in Islamabad but things became quiet soon afterwards. Incidentally, the people's reaction would give a lie to those, like Gujral's Defence Minister, Mulayam Singh Yadav, who advocate from time to time, including the forum of the Lok Sabha, that there should be a confederation of India, Pakistan and Bangladesh. How would the people allow their freedom to be circumscribed by forming a confederation with a country they consider their enemy, apart from Bangladesh agreeing to join hands with Pakistan from whom they separated in a brutal war?

The Kansi arrest and subsequent illegal deportation to the United States defied all laws of extradition and challenged the sovereignty of Pakistan. A former ISI chief, Lt. Gen. Hamid Gul, who headed one of the most destructive agencies of Pakistan, went to the Lahore High Court over the arrest and whisking off of Kansi to the United States. The Chief Minister of Baluchistan, the province to which Kansi belonged, described the way he was handed over to the Americans as a "condemnable act".[10] Kansi was convicted and sentenced to death and some innocent Americans were killed by his supporters in Pakistan. For a time the Americans stayed away from their vassal state, that is American citizens were advised to keep off Pakistan, but in the end nothing came out of it.

Two million dollars is not a small amount. It is equivalent to ten crores (100 million) of Pakistani rupees at least. Fugitives have to be brought to book and killers must be punished according to law. But there are extradition laws and there is a sovereignty of nations. The ease with which the FBI agents seized Kansi from a hotel and then carried him off to their country without bothering about the niceties of the law is an unprecedented action and in contrast with the repeated Indian pleas to the UAE to allow the deportation of the Bombay (Mumbai) mafia gangs from that country to India. When India seeks these gangsters' return the UAE authorities say they do not know who Dawood Ibrahim and his gang members are.

Incidentally, the fugitives like Dawood Ibrahim, Tiger Memon and others, all wanted in connection with the Bombay blasts of March 1993, in which some 300 people were killed in a day, spend part of their time in Dubai and part of it in Karachi in Pakistan. They can go about as free as larks in Pakistan but when it comes to Kansi the man can be carried off by the Americans without much ado.

**Shia-Sunni Conflict**

Sectarian violence is a recurring phenomenon in Pakistan. In the first eight months of 1997 some 250 persons were killed and well over 3,000 in the years since Pakistan was created. The Sunni-Shia clashes have spread in Pakistan in a big way ever since Islamisation began on a large scale under the Zia regime. Most people, of course, co-exist in a peaceful way, most of the time but the repeated conflict and violence is a matter of great concern to the peaceful citizens. The trouble with violence and the divisive movements like sectarianism is that political parties often take sides. Both the Muslim League of Mian Nawaz Sharif and the PPP of Benazir Bhutto have ingratiated themselves with the organisations of the two sects. First the PPP included the Shia outfit, Tehriq Nifaz Fiqh-i-Jafaria, in the People's Democratic Alliance, fathered by it, and in retaliation the Sunni organisation joined hands with the Pakistan Muslim League of Sharif. The organisation is called the Anjuman Sipah Shahaba. Now it was Benazir's turn to woo the Sunny set-up also and one of its leaders was included in the provincial government of Punjab, which was dismissed along with her own central government.

Now Sharif has got rid of the law under which the President had the powers to seek an uncooperative Prime Minister. In fact,

Sharif has established total Punjabi domination of the government, the presidency, the judiciary and the election commission. No wonder the army, which is an important element of Pakistan, but is basically Punjabi, looks on with favour. But before long it may show its prowess since the army may not tolerate the Prime Minister becoming so strong and powerful.

The religious formations are quite powerful. In the major city of Gujranwala in Punjab Province, the Senior Superintendent of Police, SSP, Mohammad Ashraf Marth, and his driver were killed in broad daylight by unidentified gunmen in May 1997.[12] Obviously the police had been tough with both the religious factions and one of them succeeded in putting the SSP out of action for ever. The most shocking outrage of the continuing armed clashes was reported from Karachi, notorious more for ethnic violence, in November 1997. In the incident, suspected Shia gunmen killed three top clerics of the Sunni faith in a hand grenade attack. The three religious men were proceeding to the prestigious Binouri Sunny seminar on the outskirts of Karachi in a van when motorcycle-born assailants struck.

The three religious leaders killed were: Maulana Sheikh Habibullah, principal of the seminar, Mufti Samiullah, chief of foreign student affairs, and Mohammad Tahir, senior teacher.[13]

Binouri is so big it has students from about 45 countries, among them the Gulf Muslim nations, Britain (obviously Pakistanis and some Indian Muslims settled there), the United States, France and others. Three days prior to the attack on the Sunni leaders, a Shia scholar was killed outside a (Shia) mosque in the western Orangi district of Karachi and apparently the Shias were seeking revenge. I was reminded of the Buddhist Dhammapada verse, ascribed to the Buddha himself, inscribed on the airport entrance in the Laotian capital of Vientiane: "Na hi veren verani shammantih kadachan, Averen hi shammanti esh dhammo sanatano", in this world revenge does not avenge enmity, only forgiveness quietens the fire. The warring Sunnis and the equally fanatical but numerically much smaller Shias had no need for such wise sayings. Of course, the Laotians themselves have not observed the path of non-killing in retaliation taught by the great Buddha. In this case, the trouble between the Sunnis and Shias had spread in a big way from Punjab to Karachi.

**So You Reap**

As you sow so you reap. Pakistan exports terrorism to neighbouring Indian states of the Indian Punjab and Jammu and Kashmir and its ISI is trying to foment trouble even in other areas including the sensitive north-east. In the Indian state of Punjab, terrorism has almost (though not totally) been eliminated and in Kashmir it has been much controlled. But that is no thanks to the ISI of Pakistan which continues to mount pressure even after its shameful failure. Terrorism, however, had a backlash in the country of its birth and it has now fully engulfed it, with the Kalashnikov rifles freely available in Pakistan and in places like Karachi they could even be hired.

The Binouri seminary is one of the biggest Islamic universities in Pakistan. One can understand and even appreciate the promotion of religious institutions in a country wedded to promote Islam. But should these institutions foster violence and fanaticism? India also has quite a few of them, Darul Ulum in Deoband in UP being one of the most prominent. There is no lack of funds for these institutions, including foreign funds from the Gulf. Right in Islamabad the Egyptian government put up a major Islamic university of which the Pakistan President himself is Chancellor. But it is not surprising that the key figure of the American World Trade bombing in New York city was connected with it and the religious leader, Sheikh Omar Abdul Rahman, was also associated with it.

Pakistan's Islamic exuberance has led to the establishment of dozens of religious schools from out of which come many decent young men (women are never admitted to them), but also many terrorists and the Talibans who control many areas of neighbouring Afghanistan, on behalf of Pakistan. These men, the so-called students (Taliban) have been waging war in Afghanistan with American arms supplied by the CIA thorough the ISI, Inter Services Agency of the Pakistan army which often functions on its own. The Americans were helping Pakistan and the Mujaheedins, the religious fighters and forerunners of the Taliban, even before the Taliban came on the scene. The Soviet Union had no business to be of Afghanistan but in the process of fighting their troops the Americans flooded Pakistan with weapons which found their way to the terrorists and the mafia.

The Americans gave Pakistan more than ten billion dollars worth of big and small arms. The arms reached the ISI for the ostensible purpose of equipping the Afghan rebels. The US has played a destructive role in Asia, from Vietnam, Cambodia, where it overthrew a well settled regime in 1969-70, Afghanistan, where even now there is no stability and no peace, in Pakistan, where terrorism is rampant, in Iraq where it is fighting a war, with the alleged support of the United Nations, and elsewhere. It refuses to declare a country like Pakistan, a terrorist state, although it has now recognised that the Pakistani outfit, Harkat-ul-Ansar, which killed four western tourists including an American in July 1995, through its front organisation the Al Faran, is a terrorist body.

The arms the Americans sent to the ISI of Pakistan in a clandestine role (something which the American Congress should be concerned about) did not go to the Afghan rebels a hundred per cent. Some three million Kalashnikov rifles (known in India as the AK 47 rifles) were sold to the drug mafia, the Kashmir terrorists and some to the Punjab terrorists so that they could keep the fires burning. The ISI has many irons in the fire, including the conduct of the terrorist operations in Kashmir and India's Punjab state.

This information has been brought to light by an American organisation, the World Watch Institute[14] in Washington, supposed to be a non-governmental think tank. Most of such bodies are, however, financed in that country by the CIA or some other government agency. Whether it is true or not in the case of the World Watch body, the fact remains that it has at its disposal considerable documented information which could possibly have come from the government.

The Al Faran, under the umbrella of the Harkat-ul-Ansar, first killed a Norwegian tourist as presumably Norwegian blood is cheaper, than British or American. Then they held four tourists, two Britons, a West German and an American, having taken all of them captive while they were holidaying in the Pahlagam tourist spot in the Kashmir valley. The Al Faran wanted to trade the foreigners against some dreaded terrorists captured by the Indian forces, and the US and Britain put pressure on India to either locate the four westerners or hand over the terrorists so that the westerners could be freed. Their families made many trips to

India, went to Kashmir and then went over to Pakistan where they met first Prime Minister Benazir Bhutto and later her successor, Mian Nawaz Sharif. To no avail, of course. They got a lot of sympathy but no trace of their near and dear ones and meanwhile both the United States and Britain continued to bolster the Pakistani regime and the terrorist bodies indirectly. Finally, when every avenue was explored to get back the westerners and it was confirmed that the Harkat-ul-Ansar, had through sheer exhaustion, killed the tourists, being tired of shifting them from hideout to hideout and fed on Indian food all the time, then, in October 1997, the Americans declared the Harkat a terrorist body to which American laws would apply, and, in particular, remittances from America, would not be permitted.

**Pakistan Fountainhead**

The US, however, did not declare the fountainhead of terrorism, Pakistan, a terrorist state, because American interests had to be safeguarded. How, for example, Kansi could otherwise be whisked off from a client state? If the Indian have to bear the burnt of the ISI venality let it be. After all the Americans put up with insults from the Saudi Arabian government which would not allow US troops, stationed in that country, to wear any insignia of Christianity because the Saudis do not permit any religion other than Islam to be practised, whether it is Christianity or Hinduism. It is more vital to have good foreign policy ties with Saudi Arabia. What are a few Christian insignia worth where major foreign policy gains are concerned?

Harkat-ul-Ansar is based in Pakistan and it was to the Pakistani Prime Minister, one after the other, that the families of the four tourists appealed for mercy and the latter even made statements and noises of sympathy. The Americans stopped at Harkat-ul-Ansar and the British are more concerned about the support of Pakistanis in the Midlands than about the life of a single Briton.

A virtual arms bazar has sprung up in Pakistan. The generosity of the CIA and the ignoble role of the ISI, which received the American arms, has ensured that the bazar is never starved of the deadly weapons. As already noted, weapons can be had for hire. Just as you can hire a video or video camera you can hire a gun in

Pakistan, kill off someone and then return the weapon to the owner for hiring out to another person. No wonder the Sunnis and Shias are at each other's throat and the ethnic conflict goes on in Karachi almost as an endemic affliction. The MQM, a partner of Nawaz Sharif in his government, has never lacked the weapons it needs nor do its detractors. Needless to add that often normal life goes on undisturbed and the average Pakistani, as much law abiding as anyone else, may be largely unaffected by such activities.

The Taliban has its training in Pakistan and its leaders admit that Pakistanis, apart from the Talibans trained in the country, are fighting[15] and helping to create division and unsettled conditions in that unfortunate but determined nation. No outside power has held down the Afghans for any length of time and the Pakistani leadership and their American backers may have to eat the humble pie in the end. The mighty Soviets found it out in the eighties. Meanwhile the people of Pakistan would go on paying a price for this adventurism. The economy is shattered, terrorism is rampant, fundamentalism is growing and drug-trafficking is going unchecked. The army and the establishment, apart from their participation in these nefarious activities, have been deeply imbued with anti-Indianism. The subjection to Washington is as deep as ever.

The ardour of the Pakistani establishment for capturing Kashmir is undiminished despite the many setbacks the country has suffered since Jinnah ordered the raiders into the beautiful valley of Kashmir on the morrow of the setting up of Pakistan more than fifty years ago. The politicians have blown Kashmir so much out of proportion that they now find it difficult to get out of its tentacles and that goes for the establishment, the foreign office, the civil service and the army. When they seek to place Kashmir on the agenda of the talks with India and when the British and the Americans pressurise India to find a "just" solution to the problem they really mean that Kashmir, or a substantial portion of it, should go to Pakistan. All the glib talk of a dialogue between India and Pakistan and the western ploy that the "people of Kashmir" should be associated with the talks really signify that India should surrender its sovereignty over Kashmir. Can Gujral do it, or would the Indian nation allow him to barter away the territory in a weak display of his non-reciprocity "Gujral" doctrine? Only at his peril can he do it, or for that matter any other government of India.

Pakistan has been led to believe that it can eat grass, as Z.A. Bhutto said, if it wants to grab other people's territory. They really do not care for the people of the valley for which the evidence of what the Pakistani raiders did in September 1947 is enough. Nor do they care for Islam although the battle for the state is being waged in the name of religion. Islam is only a ploy to grab territory although the OIC, a body of Islamic nations, gets more and more embroiled into the Kashmir issue. Pakistan would love that the western powers or the OIC pull its chestnuts out of the fire.

Nawaz Sharif talked of peace with India when his party was out of power. He is said to have won the 1997 election to the Pakistan National Assembly on the peace ticket. Benazir also talked: "If someone could play a Sikh card (meaning Pakistan) someone else (read India) could play a Sind card". She did it when she was in the wilderness and forgot about it when she assumed the office of Prime Minister of Pakistan. Perspicacity, like good sense, comes naturally to people when they are out of office. Once in office, Nawaz Sharif is subject to the control of the army, the discipline of the ISI (in Pakistan the tail wags the dog) and the overlordship of the establishment which drafts all his communications to India. All the three are dead against India and so has the Pakistan Prime Minister to give in to them if he has to remain in power. It is also his lot to give in to Islamic fundamentalism and impose further restrictions on the fair sex. He asks the men broadcasters in Pakistan to keep a safe distance from the women employed there, all in the name of Islam.[17]

The people are fired by the urge to succeed as a nation and somehow they have brought themselves to believe that India is their enemy. If there is a cricket match between India and Pakistan it is taken as a battle which Pakistan must win. The urge to win is, of course, overpowering and defeat means the players must hide themselves for fear of being lynched. When the Pakistan team returned from India in March 1996 after losing the quarter-final match against India at Bangalore, in the 1996 World Cup, the players had to take shelter for fear of being wounded. We have it on the authority of Wasim Akram, former Pakistan captain, that his family received death threats because he was not playing in the match. In the Gadafi stadium in Lahore in November 1997 in the final between South Africa and Sri Lanka, Pakistan having been ousted in the league matches, the fans had hung up a banner "Kashmir is Ours". Pakistan has always looked upon Kashmir as a piece of territory, although it pretends to fight for the rights of the Kashmiris. This banner appropriately summed up how an average Pakistani looks upon the Kashmir issue. Even in matches where Pakistan is not involved you will find the Sharjah crowd of Pakistani supporters shouting "Jitega bhai jitega, Pakistan Jitega", brothers, Pakistan will win.

If Pakistan has developed its nuclear weapons capability the target is India which has gone to sleep after the Pokharan blast in 1974. The Pakistanis and many Muslims in India have convinced themselves that they are the descendants of the people who ruled over India for centuries. They identify themselves with those early invaders or rulers. Somehow they believe that the setbacks that India has caused them in the 1971 war for the liberation of Bangladesh is only a battle in a long war in which they would be victorious. They hold the view that Islam may lose a battle but not a war. Their interpretation of history is often faulty but what you are concerned with is the view held by many in that country and by the establishment and the army.

## NOTES

1. *Independent*, London, a story from which was reproduced in the *Hindustan Times*, Delhi, October 25, 1997.
2. "A dogged chronicler of religious excesses", *Indian Express*, Delhi, October 13, 1997, quoting a Pakistani film maker, Sabiha Sumar.
3. "The tide of false dogma", Chanchal Sarkar, *Hindustan Times*, Delhi.
4. *Indian Express, Ibid*.
5. "Legal community in Pakistan lives in fear", *Times of India*, Delhi, October 12, 1997.
6. *Ibid*.
7. "Pakistan gets tough with drug barons", an Agence France Presse report from Islamabad, *Times of India*, Delhi, May 10, 1997.
8. *Indian Express*, Delhi, "With Pak fugitive's capture, Americans feel avenged", in a despatch from Chidananda Rajghatta, Washington.

9. "US attorney's remark threatens ties with Pak", *Indian Express,* Delhi, August 5, 1997.
10. "Aimal Kansi's arrest challenged", *Hindustan Times,* Delhi, June 25, 1997.
11. Sectarian Violence in Pakistan, Abha Dixit, *Hindustan Times,* Delhi, November 4, 1997.
12. *Hindustan Times,* Delhi, May 7, 1997.
13. Three Pak Sunni leaders killed, *Indian Express,* Delhi, quoting an AFP report from Karachi, November 3, 1997.
14. *Indian Express*, Delhi, October 26, 1997, a report from PTI, Washington.
15. "Pak youth fighting Afghan war", *Indian Express,* Delhi, July 21, 1997.
16. "Sharif's crusade targets Indian music, "*Times of India*, Delhi, November 10, 1997. The Islamabad report also speaks of a ban on girls schools playing Indian film songs at their school fete. Despite the ban on Indian films in Pakistani theatres and film music on the Pakistani government radio and TV, they continue to be popular.

*Chapter 11*

# UNREQUITED LOVE

Buoyed up by Prime Minister Gujral's policy of non-reciprocity, largely unsuccessful, which he immodestly raised to the status of a doctrine named after him, eager do-gooders, more seekers of publicity than genuine lovers of friendship with the neighbour, have made valiant efforts to enter Pakistan but failed. On the eve of the golden jubilee of India's independence and the completion of fifty years of Pakistan's existence as a nation, elements, belonging to an outfit calling itself the "South Asia Fraternity", waited in vain for visas to enter Pakistan. Dilbir Singh, described as the local co-ordinator of the fraternity in Amritsar, anxiously kept vigil for the group to arrive from Delhi to catch the "Samjhauta Express" train to Lahore. There they were supposed to be joined by a much smaller number of eager Pakistanis, probably bitten by the publicity bug like their counterparts from India.

This was not to be. Pakistan has shown no anxiety to reciprocate Gujral's string of unilateral concessions to Pakistanis wanting to visit India. Gujral announced the concessions in March 1997, when he was yet not Prime Minister, but even after two years Pakistan has shown no signs of responding. When Benazir Bhutto was Prime Minister and she had entered office to make friends with India, Pakistan had banned the operation of the Indian Consulate General in Karachi. The plea was that the Consulate General was being used for espionage for the Indian agency RAW and for inspiring trouble by the Muhajirs. These people had gone to Pakistan, which they had helped to come into being (Jinnah himself was a kind of Muhajir), or out of the desire to make a good living in a new country. Several of them were forced out of their homes by the Hindus and Sikhs.

Eventually, Nawaz Sharif came to power after Benazir was dismissed first by the President of Pakistan and then rejected completely by the electorate of the country. Meanwhile, the trouble in Karachi continued proving that the RAW, if it was really active and promoting trouble, did not need the crutches of the Consulate General to carryon its far from glorious work. The charge of Indian interference was not proved but the poor Muhajirs and other Pakistanis wanting to travel to India to meet their near and dear ones whom they had left behind had to travel all the way to Islamabad to get the visas so generously made available by Gujral. Sharif had been elected on a peace ticket and had mouthed many friendly things about India before the poll which brought him to power but he conveniently ignored all that once in office, where he had to bear into mind the wishes of the anti-Indian establishment. There can be no more humanitarian action than allowing the Pakistanis wishing to travel to India and likewise Indians wanting to go to Pakistan to do so. In other words, as many visas ought to be issued by India as possible and an equal number if not more by Pakistan for its citizens wishing to enter India. But Islamabad is not interested at all. It would like to restrict the number of Indians wanting to travel to that country and put all possible roadblocks in the path of its own citizens who have to go to India. The shots are called in that country by the anti-Indian bureaucrats, Sharif may come and Benazir may go. The closure of the Karachi Consulate General is proof of it.

There is, however, no apparent dearth of Indians who would want to stage a kind of bonhomie, a jugalbandhi if you prefer, of Indians and Pakistanis on important occasions like Independence Day but they fail to realise that you cannot clap with one hand. If the Pakistan government is not looking kindly at this activity and does not want its citizens to mix with Indians why should these do-gooders humiliate themselves and India? It is strange that Gujral, who is himself from Punjab although for political reasons he had to declare himself a resident of Patna, and his friends have a peculiar nostalgia although the Punjab state suffered the worst kind of travails during the partition. It is utterly devoid of common sense and one which ignores history altogether.

It is a truism that Pakistan has deep rooted prejudices against India from the days of Sir Syed Ahmed Khan and even earlier (when it was a question between Hindus and Muslims) and carefully nursed by leaders like Jinnah who talked of two nations. Thanks to this hostility, earlier efforts of the likes of Dilbir Singh came to nought. The incident referred to at the start of this chapter was not the first of its kind. Groups of do-gooders, publicity hunters and those actuated by nostalgia have even earlier tried to cross the Wagah border, near Amritsar, by road or in the Samjhauta Express which is the only rail connection between the two countries and mostly takes Muhajirs from Pakistan back to their country of adoption and some Indian relatives of theirs to Pakistan. The authorities in Islamabad have frustrated the attempts of such groups to enter Pakistan.

Gujral has opened the gates wide open to the Pakistanis, and many avail of this opportunity, but Mian Nawaz Sharif who entered office on the peace card came soon under the grip of the anti-Indian establishment. It was futile to hope that he would be different from the corrupt Benazir Bhutto who seemingly amassed a lot of wealth some of which has been frozen by the Swiss government after the Sharif regime provided them with proof of the culpability of Benazir. The Americans went all out to boost her when she was in power but the people of Pakistan could see that a certificate from the White House in Washington was not good enough for a Pakistani politician.

**The "Gujral Doctrine"**

Sharif went to the extent of rejecting the "Gujral doctrine" and refused to agree to his proposal for mutual defence cuts. He told a London-based British Television on the eve of the golden jubilee of Pakistan's first fifty years that the two countries must first resolve their outstanding differences. Naturally, he would like to have Kashmir on the Indian platter but he forgot that even Gujral dare not give him that gift. He told the London TV network that "this (mutual defence cuts) is not possible, unless India and Pakistan sit down and take a decision to resolve outstanding differences including the Kashmir issue." The debate continues whether the egg came first or the chicken.

The so-called dialogue between India and Pakistan, with Gujral on one side and Sharif one the other, was unnatural because Gujral was in office at the head of a disunited front, supported from outside by the Congress party which withdrew the support, as feared, and could not make any firm commitment, although he tried to behave as though he could. While Gujral was not on any sure ground neither was Sharif in a position to take any steady position. What with the Pakistani army in the background and his quarrels with the President, the Judiciary and the Election Commission, he did not have the time or the opportunity to make a serious effort to resolve any outstanding differences with India. The anti-Indian establishment in the meantime went through the motions, including the fanning of fires in the OIC.

No doubt, Pakistan's foreign debt, now estimated at 62 billion dollars, is still mounting but then it knows that the United States will bail it out in a situation like the one it may find itself which South Korea faced in December 1997. For the Indian do-gooders any major occasion is good enough to wave the flag of friendship. Wagah is conveniently located as it is close to Amritsar. But to their chagrin their counterparts from Pakistan are too much afraid of the wrath of the Pakistani establishment and fail to turn up at Wagah. The border is jealously guarded on both sides and there is no question of it being crossed. A journalist, described by the media, as eminent, who is the leader of the repeated attempts to cross the border, said that it was his dream to act as a bridge between India and Pakistan. He must have kept his light under the bushel because in the years that I have known him (he was a little behind me in the information service) the startling fact had never come to surface. He is, in fact a "refugee" from Pakistan.

The need for the people of India and Pakistan to come together in the real spirit of fellow feeling and camaraderie can hardly be overstressed but gimmicks and stage shows must be distinguished from a heart-to-heart 'milan'. Reciprocity is essential in all dealings between nations, no matter what any "doctrine" may say, as the father of that doctrine is compelled to admit that occasionally. In the aftermath of the second world war, the United States launched the Marshall plan under which massive economic and military assistance was provided to several European nations because it wanted them to stand up to the blandishments of Stalin, the Soviet boss, because it wanted a strong anti-Communist bloc, not because the United States was overly concerned with the economic conditions of Britain, Yugoslavia or any other country. It is chimerical to talk of non-reciprocity in Indo-Pakistan relations or in the relations of other neighbours of India.

The affection practised by India for the Pakistani cine and music stars and starlets was unilateral even before Gujral came on the scene; of course; the flow became much more of a onesided torrent when Gujral was in power. We have been witness to the influx of a host of them, the Bakhtiyar girls, Somy Ali and Anita Ayub, the pseudo-actor like Mohsin Khan, and the late "sufi" singer, Nusrat Fateh Ali Khan. The Ghazal singer Ghulam Ali never seems to be away from India and even Mehdi Hasan, who incidentally is prominent in Pakistan in keeping out Indian artists and singers like Lata Mangeshkar, Asha Bhonsle and every single Indian musician, dancer, actor and actress has often been to India.

Nusrat made India his second home and sang songs for films, invoking Allah, before his death. None of the prominent Indian artists like Lata Mangeshkar, Pankaj Udhas, Ustad Bismillah Khan and others can enter Pakistan. The qawali is a form of praise of God but it has been reduced to the singing of love songs and the like. Nusrat specialised in this vogue. He could get away with making allegations against Indian music composers of plagiarism and the like because the Indian media are free and many of them love sensationalism. Later, he kept quiet because he knew which side his bread was buttered. His making the qawali into pop music was even lauded instead of being assailed by the Indian media.

Video and audio cassettes, cable TV and satellite channels bring to the crazy Pakistani audiences Indian films and music, denied to them by the government ban on Hindi films being shown in theatres. Indian actors and actresses are household names in that country despite the theatre ban. In popular plays, a woman may call herself Sridevi or Madhuri Dikshit or a man may identify himself with Akshay Kumar which only goes to prove the popularity of these cinema artists of India in Pakistan.

The barriers created by the Pakistani rulers are thus being crossed by the people themselves. The point about the presence of the Pakistani artists is that an exchange of performers is eminently desirable but it should not be onesided. There should be a mutuality about it and Indian artists should have equal or near equal access to Pakistan and the audiences in that country. Nusrat recognised it but did nothing while he was alive and people who were supporting here him talk of goodwill but so long as it is onesided, goodwill has no meaning.

For years All India Radio has been broadcasting in its Urdu service directed to Pakistan film songs and other light music, which brings to the Pakistani lovers of Indian music songs of Lata, Mohammad Rafi, Kishor Kumar and Mukesh, apart from news bulletins. The service is also heard in India; the service became immensely popular because the Pakistani rulers, supported by artists like Mehdi Hasan, would not allow the Radio in that country to play Indian film music. The Gujral doctrine of non-reciprocity comes in here. Incidentally, many listeners in India, used to the Akashvani name of AIR have thought that AIR and Akashvani are different because the Urdu announcers of the Urdu service always call their service as one from All India Radio, the same old Urdu reluctance to refer to the Indian names if there is an element of Sanskrit in it.

Even if Gujral were to make another concession to Pakistan and unilaterally allow films from Pakistan to be exhibited in Indian cinemas, there may not be many takers for them. The real reason is that the Pakistani films are often copies of the Hindi films of Bollywood, many of which, in turn, are copies of Hollywood films. If one is bad enough the other is worse. Only the audiences, both in India and Pakistan, lap up the fare.

**Award for Dilip Kumar**

An interesting development was the announcement by the Pakistan government of an award for the popular actor Dilip Kumar on the occasion of the golden jubilee of Pakistan. He was honoured with the award of 'Nishan-e-Imtiaz'. This caused much satisfaction to his many fans in India and the actor himself said he was "mightily pleased". Mian Nawaz Sharif is known to have harboured a sneaking admiration for Indian actors like Dharmendra and could have been an admirer of Dilip Kumar also. The fact that he is a Muslim, Yusuf Khan, could have made it easy for the Sharif government to confer the award in a highly religion-dominated society. Dilip Kumar has been honoured with the Dadasaheb Phalke Award, which is given for a lifetime of service to the cinema, and with the Padmashri by the Indian government and he continues to be immensely popular with Indian audiences despite his ill-concieved Muslim identity and his open admiration for Laloo Prasad Yadav, who is being prosecuted for corruption.

The cinema crowd in Pakistan was not much enthused over the award and some of them even suggested that the award should be withdrawn. Some actors in Lahore, Pakistan's Bollywood, were quoted by the American Associated Press agency as saying "admit the mistake and withdraw the award".[1] This would be really embarrassing to Mian Nawaz Sharif if an award once announced is withdrawn. If the Pakistani cinema world was unhappy with the award, those at home were equally unhappy that while Dilip Kumar's films were banned, as all Indian movies are; an award was being given to the Indian actor. The old question came up again: Indian actors, actresses and singers and musicians continue to be banned in Pakistan but a single actor was being singled out for honour.

In reality, the Bollywood people should have asked themselves this question when they heaped paens of praise on Nusrat Fateh Ali Khan and allowed him to cart away his money to Pakistan. Just as Pakistani audiences purchase audio and video cassettes of Lata Mangeshkar, Asha Bhosle and popular Indian films, Indian audiences could also have purchased such audio and video cassettes of Nusrat's album if he had cut one in Pakistan. Nusrat by being in India had acquired immense popularity which he could not have got if he had been banned from India.

The Wagah border non-event on August 14, 1997 was the result of Pakistan's blunt refusal to grant visas to the members of the South Asian Fraternity (behind which also Gujral's hand can be seen). As many as 125 of these self appointed ambassadors of goodwill had kept themselves in readiness to spend what they thought would be 'gala' three days and some of the Pakistanis authorities were to arrive for a similar enjoyment in India. The Indians as well as their Pakistani counterparts were stopped in their tracks by the Pakistani authorities. They also put obstacles in the path of those who could have tried to reach the Wagah border. Prohibitory orders were clamped in the area and the Pakistani Rangers (the frontier guards of Pakistan) kept a strict vigil on the Wagah border, ready with their automatic weapons if any żealous Indian tried to cross the border without visas.

For those, who thought the border post at Wagah was another disco, much disappointment was in store as the Border Security Force (BSF), kept out the funsters from the check post. The BSF, however, had a hard time to keep the crowd at a safe distance because some of the fun lovers tried to cross the border without the requisite visas. The BSF are as much responsible for the safety of the border as their Pakistani counterparts on their side. The denial of visas to the Indians and the permission to the Pakistanis who at least wanted to reach the border would indicate that the writ of only the hardcore Pakistanis runs in that country. Perhaps those concerned with Pakistan in India know this very well but during Gujral's short-lived rule, things could have been somewhat different.

Some of the leading newspapers in India were gullible enough to splash the goings on at Wagah as attempts at fraternisation and the gaiety as a kind of celebration but by and large, the fiasco was also noted by many. The wildness and indiscipline on a sensitive border was reported by several leading dailies. Among the papers which carried the fate of the visa-seekers was the *Times of India*, Delhi, which was always soft on Gujral. Notably, the *Times* correspondent was able to quote a western diplomat : "In fact, I am of the view that even if the Kashmir problem is amicably resolved, normalcy will not be marked in Indo-Pakistan relations all that easily."[2]

This author has always held that the Pakistanis trot out Kashmir as an excuse and as a stumbling block to good relations between the two countries. They do not want normal ties to prevail at any time. Kashmir is only an excuse and the diplomat quoted by the paper is right in his assessment that the Pakistanis are always in search of an excuse to keep the ties on the boil. The solution of the

Kashmir problem, according to Pakistan, is, "Kashmir is ours" as the banner in the Gadafi stadium proclaimed. They are against India, meaning the fundamentalists who have a powerful hold on the political bosses; so are some of the media who cater to the receptive audience, and the establishment, the army and the foreign service, which is actually part of the establishment. The politicians are only plaything in the hands of the establishment and the army and always play to the gallery which consists of the fundamentalists. Religion is to be publicly acknowledged, whatever one may do privately, and a Kashmir solution for Pakistan means that the territory would become part and parcel of Pakistan.

**"Kashmir is Ours"**

Can anyone in India agree to this, even if it be a weak Prime Minister like Gujral or the confederationist Mulayam Singh Yadav. Pakistan has been seething with anger against India and is itching for revenge after its humiliation by the Indian army and the other two services in the Bangladesh war. Its army of 90,000 men, with their arms and ammunition, had to be surrender to the Indian armed force as Bangladesh became a sovereign and independent nation and broke away from West Pakistan. One of the consequences was the development of the nuclear bomb, which is targeted on India, and the other was the launching of a proxy war in Kashmir. The terrorism in Kashmir has failed to achieve its goal, although it has done considerable harm to India. It matters little to Pakistan that the clock of progress in Kashmir was put back by a few years and many thousands of people were killed.

As for Pakistan's nuclear capability, we cannot do better than recall Zulfiqar Ali Bhutto's words "we will eat grass if we have to do it but we will build a nuclear bomb." The story of the Islamic bomb is that it was first financed by Col. Gadafi of Libya, partly by Saudi Arabia, which is always keen to support with money all such Islamic enterprises, and then largely by Pakistan's own efforts. The technology was stolen by the Pakistan nuclear scientist. Dr Abdul Quadir Khan, popularly known as A.Q. Khan, originally from Bhopal, India. It has always been India's misfortune to father such characters and then hand them over to Pakistan for destructive purposes. China provided Islamabad with a lot of help in technology and supply of equipment and parts and the United States just looked on, making noises from time to time but never really stopping Pakistan in its nuclear enterprise.

It would be enough to say that Pakistan holds India responsible for almost all its ill and its national and foreign policy is based on the premise that India must be taught a lesson and subjugated. Those of Gujral's persuasion who hold out the hand of friendship and stage periodic shows on the Wagah border and elsewhere are not India's friends. They are helping Dr. A.Q. Khan and the proxy war that Pakistan is spawning in Kashmir.

There are, however, some people in Pakistan who think about the various issues and are able to read between the lines. They do not see a distorted vision always. Manzur Ijaz, a noted columnist of the Lahore newspaper, the *Nation*, Wrote in the *Times of India*, Delhi, that the question being debated in the United States was whether Pakistan was a 'failed state';. (The Americans are naturally perturbed about the safety of their investments). He started by saying that some western intellectuals, devoted to a study of Pakistan, had already concluded that Pakistan was a failed state, or was on its way to failure. He draws some solace from a comparison with the state of affairs in Ranjit Singh's[3] empire, which in his words, had ruled over "most of the area now called Pakistan" but enjoyed sovereignty in a notoriously anarchic era (1799-1839). He drew the conclusion that "if the present disorder continues, one cannot predict with certainty whether the Pakistani state will fail or not."[4]

Ijaz referred in his article to the continuing violent eruptions in Karachi, Pakistan's largest city and its commercial capital. A large number of people were killed even in 1997 in the city. When Benazir Bhutto was Prime Minister, the army had carried out a virtual pogrom in Karachi in 1996. This is apart from the constant Shia-Sunni conflict in Pakistan's major province and in Karachi.

The military has been a kind of sacred cow in Pakistan but the newspapers, which make the most of the freedom they enjoy or do not enjoy, are carrying reports of the corruption and money-making activities of the top brass. Nawaz Sharif took courage in both hands and sacked the corrupt Navel Chief, Admiral Mansoorul Huq, in April 1997. (Actually the chief was made to resign). Notably, there were no investigations and no corruption case was launched but the Admiral's greed had reached monumental proportins and his wings had to be clipped. He was said to be close to the "Mr Ten Per cent" husband of Benazir, Asaf Ali Zardari, who is now facing charges of murder, among other things.

**Onerous Task**

The armed forces of Pakistan have been running the country for twentyfive of the fifty years of its existence. During these long years, they have set up "foundations" which have been running business empires. The profitable activity produces sizable benefits, for "ex-servicemen" and for the officers entrusted with the running of the foundations. The army's trust is called "Fauji", that of the navy "Bahria" and for the air force business venture is called "Shaheen". Critics in India must take into account that the Pakistani armed forces have manifold responsibilities: they have to be in battle readiness "to face the Indian challenge", they have to keep a wary eye on the politicians at home and jump into the fray of politics from time to time, including readiness to stage a coup, and they have to run these foundations. What an onerous task for the men in uniform!

But, as we have noted, critical questions are being raised about the three services from time to time. Issues are being raised by the ordinary people and the media about the widespread corruption in the armed forces. This corruption by the top brass and the middle level officers is apart from the smuggling of heroin which is a major economic activity, jointly carried on by the enterprising business community, the three armed services and the politicians. In a popular play in Pakistan, a 'Thanedar', a police officer who is in charge of an area, is asked by a corrupt person to allow him to smuggle heroin. But the 'thanedar' replies: "If I allow you to smuggle, what will I do myself?"

In the Pakistani paper, *Friday Times*, of May 23-29, 1997, a Lahore resident wrote a letter pointing out that it was not a foreign hand that was destroying the country but the enemy within. "How can we forget the golden years of Gen. Zia and the other rich generals? Who bought ranches and prime real estate from the profits made in the F-16 deal? (From) where did Admiral Mansoorul-Huq (sacked by Nawaz Sharif) get the funds to build his palatial house?... It is about time, the same law applied to all."[5] In other countries, politicians hoodwink the ordinary folks in the name of the weaker sections, minorities and secularism (as in India); in Pakistan; the masses could be hoodwinked in the name of Islam, whether it is the politicians, generals or anybody else out to fool the people.

Yes, the military is often beyond the pale of the ordinary law of the land in Pakistan but the media and sometimes the judiciary show guts and bring into question the corrupt role of the armed forces. The Lahore High Court admitted a writ petition filed by an Islamabad lawyer, Wahabul Khairi, raising questions about the encroachment of the military into areas of economic production. The petitioner asked the armed forces to stay out of business and confine themselves to the defence of the country, their primary duty, and the Court ordered notice to be issued to the Defence Ministry for a reply.

The arrest of the Air Force Officer, Sq. Leader Farooq Ahmed Khan, by the Americans for carrying heroin in a military aircraft in the United States, gave the Pakistani media an opportunity to raise questions about the military's role in the smuggling of heroin. The Army Chief, Gen. Jahangir Karamat, complained of trial by the media. The Auditor General of Pakistan shows the same degree of independence as his counterpart in India, the CAG (Comptroller and Auditor General of India) who displayed remarkable independence in exposing the animal husbandry scam (in which Gujral's friend Laloo Prasad Yadav is being prosecuted) and charged the armed forces with financial irregularities to the extent of 2.5 billion dollars in 1994-95.

Failure at home and the blows which the ISI has suffered in Punjab and Kashmir and partially in the North-East of India, after a more friendly regime of Mrs Haseena Wajed came to power in Bangladesh, has not diminished the ardour of the Pakistani armed forces to pursue their anti-Indian agenda. The armed forces also continue to exercise their authority in the internal affairs of Pakistan whatever the setbacks suffered by them and the loss of their image as the all-conquering force, mostly in their own eyes. Their hostility towards India is evident in the writings of the *Hilal* magazine, a weekly brought out by the armed forces PR wing, actually the ISI. In its April 1997 issue, the paper, the counterpart of the *Sainik Samachar*, a routine type of army magazine, said: "Can they (the elements who want a dialogue with India) forget the gory past and extend a hand of friendship to the criminals of humanity who should be tried in Court for committing unspeakable war crimes? Can they ignore what they read in history books, heard from their ancestors who migrated from India and make friends with (the) Hindus who never accepted Pakistan as a separate Muslim state?"

Can anyone imagine the *Sainik Samachar* writing political nonsense like this piece in the Pakistani *Hilal*? It talks of history books, written by people who are the cousins of the writer of this piece. And who are the ancestors? The Mohajirs in Karachi who were butchered like sheep at Ramzan Eid by the armed forces of Pakistan at the behest of Benazir Bhutto? What can they tell others except the tales of blood they have undergone in Karachi and what others have suffered at their hands?

The Supreme Court of Pakistan recently asked the Pakistan government to rein the ISI, the most dangerous and destructive arm of the Pakistan government and its army. The court asked that there should be parameters to the activities of the political wing of the ISI. In its view, the ISI's political cell violates article 17 of the Pakistani constitution which deals with the people's right to form associations and unions. Under the military dictator, Zia-ul-Huq, the ISI got involved in the task of internal intelligence besides external intelligence and counter-espionage. On the authority of Benazir's Interior Minister, former Air Force Chief, Air Marshal Asghar Khan, told the apex Court that the ISI had collected four million dollars and distributed it among the political parties for the 1990 elections.

**ISI Involved at Home**

The ISI is thus, not merely a thorn in India's side but also in the side of the politicians and the media in Pakistan itself. So much for its growing popularity! It is fully involved in the training and arming of the Taliban and, earlier, the Gulbuddin Hikmatyar forces, fighting against President Rabbani in Afghanistan. The Afghan problem has had a terrible backlash in Pakistan, causing the country to bear the burden of three million Afghan refugees and the gun running in the country at a terrible social cost.

The trouble with the Pakistanis is that they have convinced themselves that they are the strongest Islamic power on earth and the country must interfere in the internal affairs of others in the name of religion. In any case, the Gujral doctrine has led to unrequited love and India's efforts to befriend the Pakistanis have failed to produce the desired response. Most people in the world respect strength, more so the Pakistanis. Firmness, combined with friendship, if it is reciprocated, should be India's policy. Pakistan is, no doubt, beset with a host of difficulties, sectarian violence, wrong headed Islamisation, drug trafficking, the perpetual problem of instability, the ever present threat of a military corps, the burdens of foreign debt and the gun culture and the drain because of the adventurist intervention policy pursued by the rulers. Heroin smuggling has become a cottage industry and even the armed forces are not immune from the corrupting influence it entails. Questions are being asked by not only the American bosses of Pakistan but intelligent Pakistanis themselves also if the country would not fail.

Nobody in India, in his senses, wants to grab Pakistan whatever the *Hilal* magazines produced by the ISI for the armed forces of Pakistan may say. When the Bangladesh war ended on December 16, 1971, the first thing India did, was to declare a unilateral ceasefire in the western sector. That was a loud enough message that India is not interested in dismembering Pakistan but if its own follies lead to it that is a different matter. Recently, in the ballot papers cast for the Sharif-sponsored new President Tarar, there was also one which said "Pakistan Murdabad—death to Pakistan". In India also there could be a fringe element which may be day dreaming about an Indian conquest of Pakistan or the zeal of Gujral's defence Minister Mulayam Singh Yadav for a confederation of India, Pakistan and Bangladesh might be misinterpreted as Indian hegemonism.

A dialogue should be pursued, not because the Americans want it (they would want us to hand over Kashmir to Pakistan which they say is disputed territory) but because the stronger must try to offer a hand of friendship to the less strong. But there is a limit and behaving as the stronger would not cause any harm. While pursuing a dialogue, we have to recognise that the decision makers in Pakistan want to grab Kashmir. (Remember the banner "Kashmir is ours").

But we must bear in mind that only the friendship of the strong would be respected. If the Pakistani rulers go on displaying hostility, as the Foreign Minister Gauhar Ayub openly does, hostility has to be matched by strength. For a long time to come, the Pakistani policy towards India would be one of hostility. That, no doubt, is a reflection of the terrible inferiority complex and the spirit of separatism that rules the hearts of the people who rule Pakistan. One sided bonhomie, not responded by the generality of people, is totally misplaced. Maturity, yes, but maturity does not mean, we close our eyes to dangers that exist.

## NOTES

1. *Indian Express*, Delhi, August 18, 1997 "Pak artistes sore over award to Dilip Kumar".
2. "Pakistan's stand on visas deals blow to Gujral doctrine', *Times of India*, Delhi, August 15, 1997. Note the language of the heading.
3. The Sikh ruler, Maharaja Ranjit Singh, ruled in the late 18th and early 19th century when he founded his kingdom. His capital was Lahore, now in Pakistan, and his armies even captured Kabul.
4. *Times of India*, Delhi, February 14, 1997: "Is Pakistan a failed State?"
5. Quoted in the *Indian Express*, Delhi, June 5, 1997.

*Appendix I*

# FUNDAMENTAL RIGHTS

## SECULARISM: CONSTITUTION OF INDIA

### PART III
### FUNDAMENTAL RIGHTS

*General*

**12. Definition**— In this Part, unless the context otherwise requires, "the State" includes the Government and Parliament of India and the Government and the Legislature of each of the States and all local or other authorities within the territory of India or under the control of the Government of India.

**13. Laws inconsistent with or in derogation of the fundamental rights**— (1) All laws in force in the territory of India immediately before the commencement of this Constitution, in so far as they are inconsistent with the provision of this Part, shall, to the extent of such inconsistency, be void.

(2) The State shall not make any law which takes away or abridges the rights conferred by this Part and any law made in contravention of this clause shall, to the extent of the contravention, be void.

(3) In this article, unless the context otherwise requires,—

(a) "law" includes any Ordinance, order, bye-law, rule, regulation, notification, custom or usage having in the territory of India the force of law;

(b) "laws in force" includes laws passed or made by a Legislature or other competent authority in the territory of India before the commencement of this Constitution and not previously repealed, notwithstanding that any such law or any part thereof may not be then in operation either at all or in particular areas.

[1][(4) Nothing in this article shall apply to any amendment of this Constitution made under Article 368.]

*Right to Equality*

**14. Equality before law—** The State shall not deny to any person equality before the law or the equal protection of the laws within the territory of India.

**15. Prohibition of discrimination on grounds of religion, race, cast, sex or place of birth—** (1) The State shall not discriminate against any citizen on grounds only of religion, race, caste, sex, place of birth or any of them.

(2) No citizen shall, on grounds only of religion, race, caste, sex, place of birth or any of them, be subject to any disability, liability, restriction or condition with regard to—

(a) access to shops, public restaurants, hotels and places of public entertainment; or

(b) the use of wells, tanks, bathing ghats, roads and places of public resort maintained wholly or partly out of State funds or dedicated to the use of general public.

(3) Nothing in this article shall prevent the State from making any special provision for women and children.

[2][(4) Nothing in this article or in clause (2) of Article 29 shall prevent the State from making any special provision for the advancement of any socially and educationally backward classes of citizens or for the Scheduled Castes and the Scheduled Tribes.]

**16. Equality of opportunity in matters of public employment—** (1) There shall be equality of opportunity for all citizens in matters relating to employment or appointment to any office under the State.

(2) No citizen shall, on grounds only of religion, race, caste, sex, descent, place of birth, residence or any of them, be ineligible for, or discriminated against in respect of, any employment or office under the State.

(3) Nothing in this article shall prevent Parliament from making any law prescribing, in regard to a class or classes of employment or appointment to an office [3][under the Government of, or any local or other authority within, a State or Union Territory, any requirement as to residence within that State or Union Territory] prior to such employment or appointment.

(4) Nothing in this article shall prevent the State from making any provision for the reservation of appointments or posts in favour of any backward class of citizens which, in the opinion of the State, is not adequately represented in the services under the State.

[4][(4A) Nothing in this article shall prevent the State from making any provision for reservation in matters of promotion to any class or classes of posts in the services under the State in favour of the Scheduled Castes and the Scheduled Tribes which in the opinion of the States, are not adequately represented in the services under the State.]

(5) Nothing in this article shall affect the operation of any law which provides that the incumbent of an office in connection with the affairs of any religious or denominational institution or any member of the governing body thereof shall be a person professing a particular religion or belonging to a particular denomination.

*Right to Freedom of Religion*

**25. Freedom of conscience and free profession, practice and propagation of religion**— (1) Subject to public order, morality and health and to the other provisions of this Part, all persons are equally entitled to freedom of conscience and the right freely to profess, practise and propagate religion.

(2) Nothing in this article shall affect the operation of any existing law or prevent the State from making any law—

(a) regulating or restricting any economic, financial, political or other secular activity which may be associated with religious practice;

(b) providing for social welfare and reform or the throwing open of Hindu religious institutions of a public character to all classes and sections of Hindus.

*Explanation I*— The wearing and carrying of *kirpans* shall be deemed to be included in the profession of the Sikh religion.

*Explanation II*— In sub-clause (b) of clause (2), the reference to Hindus shall be construed as including a reference to persons professing the Sikh, Jaina or Buddhist religion, and the reference to Hindu religious institutions shall be construed accordingly.

**26. Freedom to manage religious affairs**— Subject to public order, morality and health, every religious denomination or any section thereof shall have the right—

(a) to establish and maintain institutions for religious and charitable purposes;

(b) to manage its own affairs in matters of religion;

(c) to own and acquire movable and immovable property; and

(d) to administer such property in accordance with law.

**27. Freedom as to payment of taxes for promotion of any particular religion**— No person shall be compelled to pay any taxes, the proceeds of which are specifically appropriated in payment of expenses for the promotion or maintenance of any particular religion or religious denomination.

**28. Freedom as to attendance at religious instruction or religious worship in certain educational institutions**— (1) No religious instruction shall be provided in any educational institution wholly maintained out of State funds.

(2) Nothing in clause (1) shall apply to an educational institution which is administered by the State but has been established under any endowment or trust which requires that religious instruction shall be imparted in such institution.

(3) No person attending any educational institution recognised by the State or receiving aid out of State funds shall be required to take part in any religious instruction that may be imparted in such institution or to attend any religious worship that may be conducted in such institution or in any premises attached thereto unless such person or, if such person is a minor, his guardian has given his consent thereto.

*Cultural and Educational Rights*

**29. Protection of interests of minorities**— (1) Any section of the citizens residing in the territory of India or any part thereof having a distinct language, script or culture of its own shall have the right to conserve the same.

(2) No citizen shall be denied admission into any educational institution maintained by the State or receiving aid out of State funds on grounds only of religion, race, caste, language or any of them.

**30. Right of minorities to establish and administer educational institutions—** (1) All minorities, whether based on religion or language, shall have the right to establish and administer educational institutions of their choice.

[5][(1A) In making any law providing for the compulsory acquisition of any property of an educational institution established and administered by a minority, referred to in clause (1), the State shall ensure that the amount fixed by or determined under such law for the acquisition of such property is such as would not restrict or abrogate the right guaranteed under that clause.]

(2) The State shall not, in granting aid to educational institutions, discriminate against any educational institution on the ground that it is under the management of a minority, whether based on religion or language.

## NOTES

1. Ins. by the Constitution (Twenty-fourth Amendment) Act, 1971, s. 2.
2. Added by the Constitution (First Amendment) Act, 1951, s. 2.
3. Subs. by the Constitution (Seventh Amendment) Act, 1956, s. 29 and Sch., for "under any State specified in the First Schedule or any local or other authority within its territory, any requirement as to residence within that State".
4. Ins. by the Constitution (Seventy-seventh Amendment) Act, 1995, s. 2.
5. Ins. by the Constitution (Forty-fourth Amendment) Act, 1978, s. 4 (w.e.f. 20-6-1979).

*Appendix II*

# FAITH, HEREDITY & CONVERSION

SULTAN SHAHIN

Five-year-old Harshit is in love with six-year-old Fatima. Though a philanderer, he appears quite serious in this case. Innocent and touching as their childhood affair is, it suffers from adult vices. They are not prepared to accept each other as they are. Male chauvinist Harshit wants Fatima to put a bindi on her forehead. Fanatically, Muslim Fatima wants him to convert to Islam. Left to herself, this is what Mani Ratnam's heroine in *Bombay* would have demanded. Mindless reciters of the Holy Quran do not sacrifice their religion for the sake of love. They blackmail their lovers into conversion to Islam.

Islam specifically forbids any kind of compulsion in matters of religion. The Quran is very clear on this point: *La Ikraha fid Deen*. And yet Muslims suffer from a kind of mania for conversion. The conversion mania is virtually a part of the Indian Muslim psyche. It all starts from early childhood. If you were to be born in a Muslim family, you don't need to use your mind for the rest of your life. Your religion, your philosophical outlook is all pre-determined. You need not know God to believe in Him. You need not read the Quran in a language you can understand to be a firm believer in its being the final word of God. Indeed the less you know about the teachings of Islam, the more devout a Muslim you would be considered. And may God have mercy on you, if you try to follow the Islamic instruction to think, think and think and acquire knowledge. Even if you do think and acquire some knowledge, please be careful not to talk about what you think. For you will not only get ex-communicated, you may even be done to death. Even being born in secular India is no real help. Vote-bank politics has ensured that a thinking Muslim, who is bound to be in a microscopic minority, remains unprotected.

All that one needs to be a good Muslim in India is a king-sized ego. A very negative ego. An ego that tells you that you belong to a chosen community, the *ummat-e-Muhammadi.* While the rest of humanity will go to hell, literally, no matter how many good deeds the non-Muslims do, you will go to heaven eventually, no matter how many evil deeds you do. If you are evil and a Muslim all that you need fear is a brief stint in hell. The fact that you belong to the community of God's beloved Prophet Muhammad will ensure that you eventually reach heaven where you will be allowed to indulge in all the pleasures that are forbidden on earth. You can drink as much wine as you want. You can fornicate with as many women as you desire. Indeed, God is reduced to a supplier of wine and women for the Muslim residents of heaven.

Such a view has nothing to do with Islam. But it has not been difficult to spread this outlook among the ignoramuses that constitute the overwhelming majority of Muslims. Most of them cannot read at all. Those who can read the Quran, read it in its original Arabic version which they do not understand. Those who can read and understand have a vested interest in spreading this un-Islamic view. Even a scholar of Maulana Mohammad Ali Jauhar's standing is credited with the celebrated remark that even the worst Muslim is better than Mahatma Gandhi, for the former would eventually go to heaven and the later will not.

With such a world-view, it is not surprising that a Muslim would do anything to ensure a room in heaven. He is told that converting even one Kafir (non-believer) to Islam would ensure his place in heaven, no matter what else he keeps doing in the world. No wonder that though Islam specifically prohibits forcible conversion, an average Muslim would keep seeking a place in heaven through this easiest of routes. And the easiest of preys are the ones who have had the misfortune of falling in love with such Muslims. Or those who happen to work for them. Or those who depend on them in any way.

I speak from personal experience. The very day I was born, a Maulvi Saheb was called to recite some verses of Quran into my ears. I was supposed to have been converted to Islam. No one sought my opinion. My mother tells me, I protested violently against this intrusion into my privacy. But to no avail. Fortunately, this forcible conversion did not leave a lasting impact. As I grew a little older, I started resenting upon being forced to pray to a God I did not know or understand. This was when I started my dialogue with God, although it remained a monologue for a long time. As I stood up for namaz, I would close my eyes and express the following sentiments: "Dear God, I do not believe in you. I do not even know if you exist. I don't think at the moment I am even capable of understanding you. But if you do exist and can hear me, please understand that I am not a hypocrite. I am standing for prayer only out of fear of being scolded and beaten up. I do not have the physical strength to stand up to these ignoramuses who are forcing me to do something which I do not understand. But please don't consider me a hypocrite. And, above all, if you do really exist—reveal yourself to me, let me know you, understand you and pray to you." I used to pray along these lines very fervently and my father thought I was a very devout Muslim.

My next experience of forcible conversion came much later. My best friend in London had to convert to Islam in order to marry his lady love. Everybody in Surayya's family was delighted that she had finally landed a berth in heaven. Raj couldn't care less. Lies came to his lips easily. The Imam from Birmingham mosque asked him several times if he had studied Islam and understood what he was doing. Raj assured the Maulana that he was a willing convert. I knew better. I hung my head in shame. The dignity of Islam is lowered on all such occasions. But to this day Surayya doesn't understand why I, a Muslim, should be unhappy about it, why I should continue to call her husband Raj, though she had changed his name.

My next experience was to be even more personally

embarrassing and shameful. As some newspaper readers would recall, I was sacked from the editorship of a magazine on my refusal to force my Hindu wife to convert to Islam. The people, running this magazine are considered the most enlightened, secular elite of the Indian-Muslim community. The Chairman of the Board of Directors is the renowned Islamic scholar and divine, Maulana Ali Mian Nadvi. My successor as chief editor of the magazine is a retired IAS officer and former Vice-chancellor of Aligarh Muslim University, Syed Hamid. My appointment had been confirmed after an interview by the then publisher of the magazine and now Minister of State for External Affairs, Mr. Salman Khurshid. Another person who had interviewed me was the well known economist and former AMU Vice-chancellor, Prof A.M. Khusro. The managing director of the company that runs the magazine is the owner of Shama/Sushma group of publications and a well-known secularist, Mr. Younus Dehlavi. Other people involved were similarly well-placed professionals, business executives and non-resident Indian Muslims. None of them could resist the temptation of buying a cheap berth in heaven.

Coming back to poor Harshit, he is bewildered. He is not conscious of being a Hindu. He doesn't know what conversion to Islam implies. His parents are non-committal. His loving grandfather has, however, given the green signal. Love is the highest of all religions, he say. Any sacrifice is worth making for the sake of love. Fair enough. But make sacrifices for the sake of love, Harshit, not for the sake of marriage. I hope you acquire enough courage to resist emotional blackmail, sagacity to accept others as they are and expect others to accept you as you are.

*The Hindustan Times*, Delhi, May 15, 1995

*Appendix III*

# STATE DEPARTMENT REPORT ON RELIGIOUS FREEDOM, JULY 22, 1997

*(U.S. Policies in Support of Religious Freedom) (29,870)*

Following is the official text of the State Department's report on U.S. Policies in Support of Religious Freedom : Focus on Christians:

That is why our commitment to religious liberty is even more than the expression of American ideals:

**India**

*Current situation*

The State is secular. The constitution provides for religious freedom, and this right is respected in practice. There is no national law to bar proselytizing by Indian Christians, but the Government has refused since the mid-1960s to admit new resident foreign missionaries. Missionaries who arrive now do so on tourist visas and stay for short periods only. As of 1993, there were more than 1,900 registered foreign Christian missionaries.

*U.S. Government actions*

The U.S. Embassy discusses a wide range of issues with the Government of India, including respect for human rights.

**Pakistan**

*Current situation*

Pakistan's constitution establishes Islam as the state religion. Since 1986, Section 259 (c) of the Penal Code has stipulated the death penalty for blaspheming the Prophet Mohammed. According to the Human Rights Commission of Pakistan, police opened one case against a Christian, Ayub Masih, under Section 295 (c) in 1996. This blasphemy provision contributes to inter-religious tension, intimidation, fear, and violence.

The Government permits Muslims to convert to other faiths, but proselytizing among Muslims is illegal. Islamic extremists have assaulted, raped, and even murdered members of religious minorities. In many cases, police fail to take necessary precautions or investigate or prosecute those responsible.

This failure has contributed to a feeling of insecurity in many minority religious communities. In October 1996, in one well-publicized case, 14 (some say 19) Christian families fled the Punjab village Number 35 Eb Arfiwala following the arrest of one member of their community for alleged blasphemy. The families reportedly feared attack by Muslim neighbors angered by the alleged incident. By December, the families had not returned to their homes in the village.

In February 1997, Muslim mobs destroyed homes and churches belonging to Christian in the Khanewal area. Local police failed to take adequate steps to control the mobs and thousands of people were rendered homeless. Following the attack, Prime Minister Nawaz Sharif and other officials visited the affected area, promised reparations for the victims, and publicly voiced support for minority rights.

Discriminatory religious legislation has led to acts of violence directed at Ahmadis, Christians, Hindus, and Zakris. Although the Constitution prohibits discrimination in government employment, religious minorities are reportedly underrepresented at all levels of government service, especially in the senior ranks.

*U.S. Government actions*

The U.S. Government has repeatedly urged Pakistan to repeal the blasphemy law. The issue has been raised with Pakistani officials on several occasions in recent years. Although Pakistan has responded by adopting administrative procedures to soften the effect of the law, the problem remains a matter of concern and the U.S. Government continues to press the issue. The U.S. Government has also expressed concern to the Pakistani Prime Minister and other officials over the February, 1997 Khanewal riot, and urged equal legal protection for religious minorities.

U.S. Embassy and Consulate officials monitor individual cases of persecution and intervene with Pakistani government agencies, when appropriate. In addition, U.S. Embassy officers meet regularly with leaders of religious communities, including Christians.

## Appendix IV

### PARTITION TERMED SETBACK TO ISLAM

# 'JINNAH LET DOWN PROPHET'

VISHAL THAPAR

Terming the 1947 Partition as an "act of withdrawal of Islam from India", eminent academician Prof. Amrik Singh blamed Mohammad Ali Jinnah for causing irreparable damage to Islam by his role in precipitating and accepting the Partition of India.

A former Vice-Chancellor of Punjabi University, Prof. Amrik Singh charged Jinnah with letting down Prophet Mohammad—whom Singh described as the most influential figure in history—by failing to spread his (Prophet's) word and walking out of India.

Prof. Singh presented this provocative hypothesis during a seminar on "Partition in Retrospect" here today. The seminar, which is being organised by the National Institute of Punjab Studies—of which Prof. Singh is the acting chairman and the India International Centre, was inaugurated by Prime Minister I.K. Gujral yesterday.

"Jinnah might have won a famous victory by creating Pakistan, but in the process, he hurt Islam irreparably," contended Prof. Singh. "Islam will continue to exist in India but has been reduced to a state of permanent minority by Jinnah's actions," he told a stunned audience of academics.

Reasoning out his novel hypothesis, the former Vice-Chancellor said the Muslims were a major force in the country before Partition. With the division of the country into three parts, the strength of Muslims had been reduced from 25 per cent to 12 per cent in India. This had emasculated the Muslim presence in India.

Illustrating this state of "emasculation", Prof. Singh pointed out that with a 12 per cent population share, the Muslims should have had 60 members in the Lok Sabha. But today, they did not even have 20, Prof. Singh said, squarely blaming Jinnah for the predicament of the community. "This is how Muslim presence in the country has been emasculated", Prof. Singh postulated.

"Jinnah was only thinking for the day, not the morrow. In fact, he had no vision of tomorrow," charged Prof. Singh.

Historically, Islam has not learnt to function in a society where it is in a minority, the former Vice-Chancellor said, listing Egypt and Lebanon as the exceptions where Muslims had co-existed with the others. Wherever Islam has spread, it has either outrightly triumphed or has been driven out. Citing the example of Spain, he pointed out that Islamists dominated the country for 200 years, before they were driven out. But contrary to history, Islam opted out of India thanks to Jinnah, who thus did singular disservice to the community.

Earlier, Leader of the Opposition in the Pakistani Senate and former Home Minister in the Benazir Bhutto Government, Mr. Aitzaz Ahsan, set the tone for the seminar by asserting the "Inevitability of Pakistan" and describing all the remorse and angst over the Partition as unwise and uncalled for.

Basing his paper, "A primordial Divide" on his book, *The Indus Saga*, Mr. Ahsan put forth the hypothesis that the concept of Pakistan pre-exists Islam and that the creation of a separate Pakistan was "not an accident of history."

The primordial divide between India and Pakistan lay in the basic cultural and civilisational distinction between the Indus Valley, which constitutes the heart of Pakistan, and the Gangetic Plain which is quintessentially India. The Indus Valley was always separate and was integrated with the Gangetic Plain only under the rule of Chandragupta Maurya, the Mughals and the British.

Even as this hypothesis was roundly debunked by most participants, the Pakistani Leader of the Opposition described the terming of Pakistan as a temporary event by nostalgists and the depiction of Pakistan as a country irresistably drawn towards India as a fanciful idea. Since the occurrence of Partition was a fact, the people of India and Pakistan should regard it as a settled issue.

*The Hindustan Times*, New Delhi, August 30, 1997

*Appendix V*

# SOME NAIPAUL VIEWS

Vidiadhar Suraiprasad Naipaul is regarded as one of the best writers in English. Born in Trinidad 65 years ago and now living in England Naipaul is of Indian descent. His ancestors went to Trinidad from eastern Uttar Pradesh. Among his over two dozen books, some are about India and he has expressed views otherwise also which are highly significant. In an interview, published in two parts, in the *Times of India*, Delhi, on January 23 and 24, 1998, he said in reply to Rahul Singh's question about an earlier interview of his to the paper, after the demolition of the Babari mosque:

"I can see how what I said then could be misinterpreted. I was talking about history, I was talking about a historical process that had to come. I think India has lived with one more extended event that began about 1000 A.D., the Muslim invasion. It meant the cracking open and partial wrecking of what was a complete cultural, religious world until that invasion.

"I don't think, the people of India have been able to come to terms with that wrecking. I don't think they understand what really happened. It's too painful. And I think this BJP movement and that masjid business is part of a new sense of history, a new idea of what happened. It might be misguided, it might be wrong, to misuse it politically, but I think, it is part of a historical process. And to simply abuse it as Fascist is to fail to understand why it finds an answer in so many hearts in India."

The interviewer asked him: "Couldn't it be just communal prejudice?" Naipaul's reply was : "It could become that. And that has to be dealt with. But it can only be dealt with if both sides understand very clearly the history of the country. I don't think, Hindus understand what Islam means and I don't think the people of Islam have tried to understand Hinduism. The two enormous groups have lived together in the sub-continent without understanding one another's faiths."

The interviewer, one of those who are more concerned to bring out statements against the Hindus, asked him, among others, to compare India and Pakistan: Naipaul replied: "No, they can't be compared. The difference is no longer religion. The difference is of education, the nature of intellectual life. I suppose, the difference is freedom, the difference is the institutions are more rooted in one place, somewhat sham in the other place."

*Appendix VI*

# SUPREME COURT JUDGMENT ON HINDUTVA

*The following is part of the unanimous judgment of a three-member Bench of the Supreme Court comprising Justices J.S.Verma, N.P. Singh and K.Venkatswami, dated 11th December 1995:*

**16.** It cannot be doubted that a speech with a secular stance alleging discrimination against any particular religion, and promising removal of the imbalance, cannot be treated as an appeal on the ground of religion as its thrust is for promoting secularism. Instances given in the speech of discrimination against any religion causing the imbalance in the professed goal of secularism, the allegation being against any individual or any political party, cannot be called an appeal on the ground of religion forbidden by sub-section (3). In other words, mention of religion as such in an election speech is not forbidden by sub-section (3) so long as it does not amount to an appeal to vote for a candidate on the ground of his religion or to refrain from voting for any other candidate on the ground of his religion. When it is said that politics and religion do not mix, it merely means that the religion of a candidate cannot be used for gaining political mileage by seeking votes on the ground of the candidate's religion or alienating the electorate against another candidate on the ground of the other candidate's religion. It also means that the State has no religion and the State practises the policy of neutrality in the matter of religion.

**17.** In *Dr. M. Ismail Faruqui and Others etc. etc.* v. *Union of India and Others etc.*, (1994) 6 SCC 360 (Ayodhya case), the Constitution Bench, after a detailed discussion, summarised the true concept of secularism under the Indian Constitution as under:

> "It is clear from the constitutional scheme that it guarantees equality in the matter of religion to all individuals and groups irrespective of their faith, emphasising that there is no religion of the State itself. The Preamble of the Constitution read in particular with Articles 25 to 28 emphasises this aspect and indicates that it is in this manner the concept of secularism embodied in the constitutional scheme as a creed adopted by the Indian people has to be understood while examining the constitutional validity of any legislation on the touchstone of the Constitution. The concept of secularism is one facet of the right to equality woven as the central golden thread in the fabric depicting the pattern of the scheme in our Constitution."

**18.** It cannot be doubted that an election speech made in conformity with the fundamental right to freedom of religion guaranteed under Articles 25 to 30 of the Constitution, cannot be treated as anti-secular to be prohibited by sub-section (3) of Section 123, unless it falls within the narrow net of the prohibition indicated earlier. It is obvious that a speech referring to religion during election campaign with a secular stance in conformity with the fundamental right to freedom of religion can be made, if it does not contain an appeal to vote for any candidate because of his religion or to refrain from voting for any candidate because of his religion. When it is said that politics and religion do not mix, it obviously does not mean that even such permissible political speeches are forbidden. This is the meaning and true scope of sub-section (3) of Section 123 of the Act.

**19.** We would now consider the meaning of sub-section (3A) of Section 123. This sub-section also was inserted along with the substituted sub-section (3) by Act 40 of 1961 w.e.f. 20.9.1961. The meaning of this sub-section is not much in controversy. Sub-section (3A) is similar to Section 153-A of the Indian Penal Code. In sub-section (3A), the expression used is "the promotion of, or attempt to promote, feelings of enmity or hatred" as against the expression "Whoever ..... promotes or attempts to promote ..... disharmony or feelings of enmity, hatred or ill-will..." in Section 153-A, I.P.C. The expression feelings of enmity or hatred is common in both the provisions but the additional words in Section 153-A, I.P.C. are 'disharmony ..... or ill-will'. The difference in the plain language of the two provisions indicates that mere promotion of disharmony or ill-will between different groups of people is an offence under Section 153-A, I.P.C. while under sub-section (3A) of Section 123 of the R.P. Act, it is only the promotion of or attempt to promote feelings of enmity or hatred, which are stronger words, that is forbidden in the election campaign.

**20.** The provision is made with the object of curbing the tendency to promote or attempt to promote communal, linguistic or any other factional enmity or hatred to prevent the divisive tendencies. The provision in the I.P.C. as well as in the R.P. Act for this purpose was made by amendment at the same time. The amendment in the R.P. Act followed amendments made in the Indian Penal Code to this effect in a bid to curb any tendency to resort to divisive means to achieve success at the polls on the ground of religion or narrow communal or linguistic affiliations. Any such attempt during the election is viewed with disfavour under the law and is made a corrupt practice under sub-section (3A) of Section 123.

**22.** The decision in *Ziyauddin Burhanuddin Bukhari* v. *Brijmohan Ramdass Mehra & Ors.* 1975 (Suppl.) SCR 281, lends assurance to the correctness of the construction made by us of the these provisions. The returned candidate Bukhari was the candidate of Muslim League while the defeated candidate Shauket Chagla was the Congress candidate at the election. Both were Muslims. The returned candidate Bukhari in his appeal to the voters said that Chagla was not true to his religion while he himself was a true Muslim and that Chagla was neither a good Hindu nor a true Muslim. The clear implication of the appeal was that Chagla was not true to his religion whereas Bukhari was, and, therefore, the voters should prefer Bukhari. In short, the appeal for votes was made on the ground that Bukhari was a staunch believer of the

Muslim religion as against Chagla who was not. It was this clear appeal based on the ground of the candidate's religion which was held to constitute the corrupt practices defined by sub-sections (3) and (3A) of Section 123 of the R.P. Act.

**23.** The next question now relates to the constitutional validity of these provisions on the meaning ascribed to them.

**24.** Sub-section (3A) of Section 123 is undoubtedly a provision made in the interests of public order or incitement to an offence because the promotion or attempt to promote feelings of enmity or hatred between different classes of the citizens of India on any of the grounds specified therein, apart from creating divisive tendency, would also be prejudicial to the maintenance of public order and may amount to incitement to commission of offences. The freedom of speech and expression guaranteed to all citizens under Article 19 (1) (a), which is the basis of the constitutional challenge to this provision, is subject to clause (2) of Article 19 which permits the making of any law imposing reasonable restrictions on the exercise of this right in the interests of public order or incitement to an offence. For this reason, no further attempt was made to press the argument of challenge to the constitutional validity of sub-section (3A) on the construction we have made of that provision.

**25.** The question now is of the constitutional validity of sub-section (3) of Section 123. We have already rejected the argument that the element of prejudicial effect on public order is implicit also in sub-section (3) as it is in sub-section (3A). According to Shri Ram Jethmalani, unless this element also is read into sub-section (3), it is violative of Article 19(1)(a) inasmuch as clause (2) of Article 19 does not save its validity under any of the other heads specified therein.

**26.** We have construed sub-section (3) of Section 123 as a restriction only to the extent that votes cannot be sought for a candidate on the ground of his religion, etc. and similarly there can be no appeal to refrain from voting for any person on the same ground. In other words, an appeal to vote for a candidate or not to vote for him on the ground of his religion, etc. is the restriction imposed by sub-section (3). This restriction is in the law enacted to provide for the conduct of elections, the qualifications and disqualifications for membership of the Houses, the corrupt practices and other offences at or in connection with such elections. The right to contest the election is given by the statute subject to the conditions prescribed therein. The restriction is limited only to the appeal for votes to a candidate during the election period and not to the freedom of speech and expression in general or the freedom to profess, practise and propagate religion unconnected with the election campaign.

**27.** It is true, as argued by Shri Jethmalani, that the freedom of speech and expression guaranteed to all citizens under Article 19 (1) (a) is absolute subject to the reasonable restrictions imposed by any law saved by clause (2) of Article 19, under one of the heads specified therein. The heads specified in clause (2) of Article 19 are, therefore, several and they are intended to cover the entire area with which the absolute freedom to say anything which the speaker may like would not extend, in keeping with the standards of a civilized society, the corresponding rights of others in an orderly society, and the constitutional scheme.

**28.** The expression "in the interests of" used in clause (2) of Article 19 indicates a wide amplitude of the permissible law which can be enacted to provide for reasonable restrictions on the exercise of this right under one of the heads specified therein, in conformity with the constitutional scheme. Two of the heads mentioned are: decency or morality. Thus, any law which imposes reasonable restrictions on the exercise of this right in the interests of decency or morality is also saved by clause (2) of Article 19. Shri Jethmalani contended that the words 'decency or morality' relate to sexual morality alone. In view of the expression "in the interest of" and the context of election campaign for a free and fair poll, the right to contest the election being statutory and subject to the provisions of the statute, the words 'decency or morality' do not require a narrow or pedantic meaning to be given to these words. The dictionary meaning of 'decency' is "correct and tasteful standards of behaviour as generally accepted; conformity with current standards of behaviour or propriety; avoidance of obscenity; and the requirements of correct behaviour" (*The Oxford Encyclopedic English Dictionary*); "conformity to the prevailing standards of propriety, morality, modesty, etc.; and the quality of being decent" (*Collins English Dictionary*).

**29.** Thus, the ordinary dictionary meaning of 'decency' indicates that the action must be in conformity with the current standards of behaviour or propriety, etc. In a secular polity, the requirement of correct behaviour or propriety is that an appeal for votes should not be made on the ground of the candidate's religion which by itself is no index of the suitability of a candidate for membership of the House.

**30.** Thus, seeking votes at an election on the ground of the candidate's religion in a secular State, is against the norms of decency and propriety of the society.

**31.** In our opinion, the saving in clause (2) of Article 19 permits the imposition of reasonable restrictions on the exercise of the right conferred by Article 19 (1) (a) by making any law in the interests of decency or morality; and sub-section (3) of Section 123 of the R.P. Act, as construed by us, has the protection of clause (2) of Article 19 under the head 'decency' therein. This conclusion is reached by us even if it is assumed that the provision is not saved merely as a condition subject to which the statutory right of contesting an election is available to the candidate. The fact that the scheme of separate electorates was rejected in framing the Constitution and secularism is the creed adopted in the constitutional scheme, are relevant considerations to treat this as a reasonable restriction on the freedom of speech and expression, for maintaining the standard of behaviour required in conformity with the decency and propriety of the societal norms. Viewed at in any manner, sub-section (3) of Section 123 cannot be held to be unconstitutional. This view is also in accord with the nature of right to contest an election, as understood in *Jamuna Prasad Mukhariya and Others* v. *Lachhi Ram and Others*, 1955 (1) SCR 608.

**32.** The argument assailing the constitutional validity of sub-section (3) and /or (3A) of Section 123 is rejected.

**Meaning of 'Hindutva' and 'Hinduism'**

**33.** The next contention relates to the meaning of 'Hindutva' and 'Hinduism' and the effect of the use of these expressions in the election speeches.

**34.** We have already indicated the meaning of sub-section (3) of Section 123 of the R.P. Act and the limit of its operation. It may be said straightaway that any speech wherein these expressions are used, irrespective of their meaning, cannot by itself fall within the ambit of sub-section (3) of Section 123, unless the speech can be construed as an appeal to vote for a candidate on the ground that he is a Hindu or to refrain from voting for a candidate on the ground of his religion, i.e., he not being a Hindu. We have also indicated that mere reference to any religion in an election speech does not bring it within the net of sub-section (3) and /or sub-section (3A) of Section 123, since reference can be made to any religion in the context of secularism or to criticise any political party for practising discrimination against any religious group or generally for preservation of the Indian culture. In short, mere use of the word 'Hindutva' or 'Hinduism' or mention of any other religion in an election speech does not bring it within the net of sub-section (3) and/or sub-section (3A) of Section 123, unless the further elements indicated are also present in that speech. It is also necessary to see the meaning and purport of the speech and the manner in which it was likely to be understood by the audience to which the speech was addressed. These words are not to be construed in the abstract, when used in an election speech.

**35.** Both sides referred copiously to the meaning of the words 'Hindutva' and 'Hinduism' with reference to several writings. Shri Jethmalani referred to them for the purpose of indicating the several meanings of these words and to emphasise that the word 'Hindutva' relates to Indian culture based on the geographical division known as Hindustan, i.e., India. On the other hand, Shri Ashok Desai emphasised that the term 'Hindutva' used in election speeches is an emphasis on Hindu religion bearing no relation to the fact that India is also known as Hindustan, and the term can relate to Indian culture.

**36.** The Constitution Bench in *Sastri Yagnapurushadji and Others* v. *Muldas Bhudardas Vaishya and Another,* 1966 (3) SCR 242 held thus:

> "Who are Hindus and what are the broad features of Hindu religion, that must be the first part of our enquiry in dealing with the present controversy between the parties. The historical and etymological genesis of the word "Hindu" has given rise to a

controversy amongst Indologists; but the view generally accepted by scholars appears to be that the word "Hindu" is derived from the river Sindhu otherwise known as Indus which flows from the Punjab. "That part of the great Aryan race", says Monier Williams, "which immigrated from Central Asia, through the mountain passes into India, settled first in the districts near the river Sindhu (now called the Indus). The Persians pronounced this word Hindu and named their Aryan brethren Hindus. The Greeks, who probably gained their first ideas of India from the Persians, dropped the hard aspirate, and called the Hindus "Indoi" (*Hinduism*, Monier Williams, p.1).

The Encyclopedia of Religion and Ethics, Vol. VI, has described "Hinduism" as the title applied to that form of religion which prevails among the vast majority of the present population of the Indian Empire (p. 686). As Dr. Radhakrishnan has observed; "The Hindu civilization is so called, since its original founders or earliest followers occupied the territory drained by the Sindhu (the Indus) river system corresponding to the North West Frontier Province and the Punjab. This is recorded in the *Rig Veda*, the oldest of the Vedas, the Hindus scriptures which give their name to this period of Indian history. The people on the Indian side of the Sindhu were called Hindu by the Persian and the later western invaders" (*The Hindu View of Life*, Dr. Radhakrishnan, p. 12). That is the genesis of the word "Hindu."

When we think of the Hindu religion, we find it difficult, if not impossible, to define Hindu religion or even adequately describe it. Unlike other religions in the world, the Hindu religion does not claim any one prophet; it does not worship any one God, it does not subscribe to any one dogma; it does not believe in any one philosophic concept; it does not follow any one set of religious rites or performances;

in fact, it does not appear to satisfy the narrow traditional features of any religion or creed. It may broadly be described as a way of life and nothing more.

. . . The term 'Hindu', according to Dr. Radhakrishnan, had originally a territorial and not a credal significance. It implied residence in a well-defined geographical area. Aboriginal tribes, savage and half-civilized people, the cultured Dravidians and the Vedic Aryans were all Hindus as they were the sons of the same mother. The Hindu thinkers reckoned with the striking fact that the men and women dwelling in India belonged to different communities, worshipped different gods, and practised different rites (*Kurma Purana*, *ibid*, p. 12). Monier Williams has observed that "it must be borne in mind that Hinduism is far more than a mere form of theism resting on Brahmanism. It presents for our investigation, a complex congeries of creeds and doctrines which in its gradual accumulation may be compared to the gathering together of the mighty volume of the Ganges, swollen by a continual influx of tributary rivers and rivulets, spreading itself over an ever-increasing area of country and finally resolving itself into an intricate Delta of tortuous steams and jungly marshes.... The Hindu religions is a reflection of the composite character of the Hindus, who are not one people but many. It is based on the idea of universal receptivity. It has ever aimed at accommodating itself to circumstances, and has carried on the process of adaptation through more than three thousand years. It has first borne with and then, so to speak, swallowed, digested, and assimilated something from all creeds." (*Religious Thought & Life in India*, Monier Williams, p. 57.)

We have already indicated that the usual tests which can be applied in relation to any recognised religion or religious creed in the world turn out to be inadequate in dealing with the problem of Hindu religion. Normally, any recognised religion or religious creed subscribes to a body of set philosophic concepts and theological beliefs. Does this test apply to the Hindu religion? In answering this question, we would base ourselves mainly on the exposition of the problem by Dr. Radhakrishnan in his book on Indian Philosophy. (*Indian Philosophy*, Dr. Radhakrishnan, Vol. I. pp. 22-23). Unlike other countries, India can claim that philosophy in ancient India was not an auxiliary to any other science or art, but always held a prominent position of independence... "In all the fleeting centuries of history", says Dr. Radhakrishnan, "in all the vicissitudes through which India has passed, a certain marked identity is visible. It has held fast to certain psychological traits which constitute its special heritage, and they will be the characteristic marks of the Indian people so long as they are privileged to have a separate existence." The history of Indian thought emphatically brings out the fact that the development of Hindu religion has always been inspired by an endless quest of the mind for truth based on the consciousness that truth has many facets. Truth is one, but wise men describe it differently. (..) The Indian mind has, consistently through the ages, been exercised over the problem of the nature of godhead, the problem that faces the spirit at the end of life, and the interrelation between the individual and the universal soul. "If we can abstract from the variety of opinion", say Dr. Radhakrishnan, "and observe the general spirit of Indian thought, we shall find that it has a disposition to interpret life and nature in the way of monistic idealism, though this tendency is so plastic, living and manifold that it takes many forms and expresses itself in even mutually hostile teachings". (..)

. . . Naturally enough, it was realised by Hindu religion from the very beginning of its career that truth was many-sided and different views contained different aspects of truth which no one could fully express. This knowledge inevitably bred a spirit of tolerance and willingness to understand and appreciate the opponent's point of view. That is how "the several views set forth in India in regard to the vital philosophic concepts are considered to be the branches of the self-same tree. The short cuts and blind alleys are somehow reconciled with the main road of advance to the truth." (..) When we consider this broad sweep of the Hindu philosophic concepts, it would be realised that under Hindu philosophy, there is no scope for ex-communicating any notion or principle as heretical and rejecting it as such.

The development of Hindu religion and philosophy shows that from time to time saints and religious reformers attempted to remove from the Hindu thought and practices elements of corruption and superstition and that led to the formation of different sects. Buddha started Buddhism; Mahavir founded Jainism, Basava became the founder of Lingayat religion, Dnyaneshwar and Tukaram initiated the Varakari cult; Guru Nanak inspired Sikhism; Dayananda founded Arya Samaj, and Chaitanya began Bhakti cult; and as a result of the teachings of Ramakrishna and Vivekananda, Hindu religion flowered into its most attractive, progressive and dynamic form. If we study the teachings of these saints and religious reformers, we would notice an amount of divergence in their respective views; but underneath that divergence, there is a kind of subtle indescribable unity which keeps them within the sweep of the broad and progressive Hindu religion. . . . It is somewhat remarkable that this broad sweep of Hindu religion has been eloquently described by Toynbee. Says Toynbee: "When we pass from the plane of social practice to the plane of intellectual outlook, Hinduism too comes out well by comparison

> with the religions and ideologies of the South-West Asian group. In contrast to these, Hinduism has the same outlook as the pre-Christian and pre-Muslim religions and philosophies of the Western half of the old world. Like them, Hinduism takes it for granted that there is more than one valid approach to truth and to salvation and that these different approaches are not only compatible with each other, but are complementary". (*The Present-Day Experiment in Western Civilisation*, Toynbee, pp. 48-49).
>
> The Constitution-makers were fully conscious of this broad and comprehensive character of Hindu religion; and so, while guaranteeing the fundamental right to freedom of religion, Explanation II to Art 25 has made it clear that in sub-clause (b) of clause (2), the reference to Hindus shall be construed as including a reference to persons professing the Sikh, Jaina or Buddhist religion, and the reference to Hindu religious institutions shall be construed accordingly."
>
> (at pp. 259-66)

**37.** In a later Constitution Bench decision in *Commr. of Wealth Tax, Madras & Ors.* v. *Late R. Sridharan by L. Rs.*, (1976) Supp. SCR 478, the meaning of the term 'Hinduism' as commonly understood is stated thus:

> ".... It is a matter of common knowledge, that Hinduism embraces within self so many diverse forms of beliefs, faiths, practices and worship that it is difficult to define the term 'Hindu' with precision. The historical and etymological genesis of the word 'Hindu' has been succinctly explained by Gajendragadkar, C.J. in *Shastri Yagnapurushdasji & Ors.* v. *Muldas Bhundardas Vaishya & Anr.* (A.I.R. 1966 S.C. 1119).
>
> In Unabridged Edition of Webster's Third New International Dictionary of the English language, the term 'Hinduism', has been defined as meaning 'a complex body of social, cultural and religious beliefs and practices evolved in and largely confined to the

Indian subcontinent and marked by a caste system, an outlook tending to view all forms and theories as aspects of one eternal being and truth, a belief in *ahimsa*, *karma*, *dharma*, *sansara* and *moksha*, and the practice of the way of works, the way of knowledge, or the way of devotion as the means of release from the bound of rebirths; the way of life and form of thought of a Hindu.'

In *Encyclopaedia Britannica* (15th Edition), the term 'Hinduism' has been defined as meaning 'the civilization of Hindus (originally, the inhabitants of the land of the Indus River). It properly denotes the Indian civilization of approximately the last 2,000 years, which gradually evolved from Vedism, the religion of the ancient Indo-Europeans who settled in India in the last centuries of the 2nd millennium B.C. Because it integrates a large variety of heterogeneous elements, Hinduism constitutes a very complex but largely continuous whole, and since it covers the whole of life, it has religious, social, economic, literary, and artistic aspects. As a religion, Hinduism is an utterly diverse conglomerate of doctrines, cults, and way of life... In principle, Hinduism incorporates all forms of belief and worship without necessitating the selection or elimination of any. The Hindu is inclined to revere the divine in every manifestation, whatever it may be, and is doctrinally tolerant, leaving others—including both Hindus and non-Hindus—whatever creed and worship practices suit them best. A Hindu may embrace a non-Hindu religion without ceasing to be a Hindu, and since the Hindu is disposed to think synthetically and to regard other forms of worship, strange gods, and divergent doctrines as inadequate rather than wrong or objectionable, he tends to believe that the highest divine powers complement each other for the well-being of the world and mankind. Few religious ideas are considered to be finally irreconcilable. The core of religion does not even depend on the existence or non-existence of God or on whether there is one God or many. Since religious truth is said to transcend all verbal definition, it is not conceived in dogmatic terms. Hinduism is, then, both a civilization and a conglomerate of religions, with neither a beginning, a founder, nor a central authority, hierarchy, or organization. Every attempt at a specific definition of Hinduism has proved unsatisfactory in one way or another, the more so because the finest Indian scholars of Hinduism, including Hindus themselves, have emphasized different aspects of the whole.'

In his celebrated treatise *Gitarahasaya*, B.G. Tilak has given the following broad description of the Hindu religion:

"Acceptance of the Vedas with reverence; recognition of the fact that the means or ways of salvation are diverse; and realisation of the truth that the number of gods to be worshipped is large, that indeed is the distinguishing feature of Hindu religion."

In *Bhagwan Koer* v. *J.C. Bose & Ors.*, (1904 ILR 31 Cal. 11), it was held that Hindu religion is marvellously catholic and elastic. Its theology is marked by eclecticism and tolerance and almost unlimited freedom of private worship...

This being the scope and nature of the religion, it is not strange that it holds within its fold men of divergent views and traditions which have very little in common except a vague faith in what may be called the fundamentals of the Hindu religion."

(at pp. 481-82)

**38.** These Constitution Bench decisions, after a detailed discussion, indicate that no precise meaning can be ascribed to the terms 'Hindu', 'Hindutva' and 'Hinduism', and no meaning in the abstract can confine it to the narrow limits of religion alone, excluding the content of Indian culture and heritage. It is also indicated that the term 'Hindutva' is related more to the way of life of the people in the sub-continent. It is difficult to appreciate how in the face of these decisions the term 'Hindutva' or 'Hinduism' *per se*, in the abstract, can be assumed to mean and be equated with narrow fundamentalist Hindu religious bigotry, or be construed to fall within the prohibition in sub-sections (3) and/ or (3A) of Section 123 of the R.P. Act.

**39.** Bharucha, J. in *Dr. M. Ismail Faruqui and Ors. etc. etc.* v. *Union of India & Ors. etc.* 1994 (6) SCC 360, (Ayodhya case), in the separate opinion for himself and Ahmadi, J. (as he then was), observed as under:

> "... Hinduism is a tolerant faith. It is that tolerance that has enabled Islam. Christianity, Zoroastrianism, Judaism, Buddhism, Jainism and Sikhism to find shelter and support upon this land..."
>
> (at page 442)

**41.** In *Kultar Singh* v. *Mukhtair Singh*, 1964 (7) SCR 790, the Constitution Bench construed the meaning of sub-section (3) of Section 123 prior to its amendment. The question there was whether a poster contained an appeal to voters to vote for the candidate on the ground of his religion; and the meaning of the word 'Panth' in the poster was significant for the purpose. It was held as under:

> "It is true that a corrupt practice under S. 123(3) can be committed by a candidate by appealing to the voters to vote for him on the ground of his religion even though his rival candidate may belong to the same religion. If, for instance, a Sikh candidate were to appeal to the voters to vote for him, because he was a Sikh and add that his rival candidate, though a Sikh in name, was not true to the religious tenets of Sikhism or was a heretic and as such, outside the pale of the Sikh religion, that would amount to a corrupt practice under S. 123(3), and so, we cannot uphold the contention that S. 123(3) is inapplicable because both the appellant and the respondent are Sikhs... The corrupt practice as prescribed by S. 123 (3) undoubtedly constitutes a very healthy and salutary provision which is intended to serve the cause of secular democracy in this country. In order

that the democratic process should thrive and succeed, it is of utmost importance that our elections to Parliament and the different legislative bodies must be free from the unhealthy influence of appeals to religion, race, caste, community, or language. If these considerations are allowed any sway in election campaigns, they would vitiate the secular atmosphere of democratic life, and so, S. 123(3) wisely provides a check on this undesirable development by providing that an appeal to any of these factors made in furtherance of the candidature of any candidate as therein prescribed would constitute a corrupt practice and would render the election of the said candidate void.

In considering the question as to whether the distribution of the impugned poster by the appellant constitutes corrupt practice under S.123(3), there is one point which has to be borne in mind. The appellant had been adopted as its candidate by the Akali Dal Party. This Party is recognised as a political party by the Election Commission notwithstanding the fact that all of its members are only Sikhs. It is well known that there are several parties in this country which subscribe to different political and economic ideologies, but the membership of them is either confined to, or predominantly held by, members of particular communities or religions. So long as law does not prohibit the formation of such parties and in fact recognises them for the purpose of election and parliamentary life, it would be necessary to remember that an appeal made by candidates of such parties for votes may, if successful, lead to their election and in an indirect way, may conceivably be influenced by considerations of religion, race, caste, community or language. This infirmity cannot perhaps be avoided so long as parties are allowed to function and are recognised, though their composition may be predominantly based on membership of particular communities or religion. That is why we think, in considering the question as to whether a particular appeal made by a candidate falls within the mischief of S. 123(3), courts should not be astute to read into the words used in the appeal anything more than can be attributed to them on its fair and reasonable construction.

That takes us to the question of construing the impugned poster. The principles which have to be applied in construing such a document are well settled. The document must be read as a whole and its purport and effect determined in a fair, objective and reasonable manner. In reading such documents, it would be unrealistic to ignore the fact the when election meetings are held and appeals are made by candidates of opposing political parties, the atmosphere is usually surcharged with partisan feelings and emotions and the use of hyperboles or exaggerated language, or the adoption of metaphors, and the extravagance of expression in attacking one another, are all a part of the game, and so, when the question about the effect of speeches delivered or pamphlets distributed at election meetings is argued in the cold atmosphere of a judicial chamber, some allowance must be made and the impugned speeches or pamphlets must be construed in that light. In doing so, however, it would be unreasonable to ignore the question as to what the effect of the said speech or pamphlet would be on the mind of the ordinary voter who attends such meetings and reads the pamphlets or hears the speeches. It is in the light of these well-established principles that we must now turn to the impugned pamphlet."

(at pp. 793-95)

**42.** The test applied in the decision was to construe the meaning of the word 'Panth' not in the abstract but in the context of its use. The conclusion reached was that the word 'Panth' used in the poster did not mean Sikh religion and, therefore, the appeal to the voters was not to vote for the candidate because of his religion. Referring to an earlier decision in *Jagdev Singh Sidhanti* v. *Pratap Singh Daulta and Ors.*, 1964 (6) SCR 750, it was reiterated as under:

> "... Political issues which form the subject-matter of controversies at election meetings may indirectly and incidentally introduce considerations of language or religion, but in deciding the question as to whether corrupt practice has been committed under S. 123(3), care must be taken to consider the impugned speech or appeal carefully and always in the light of the relevant political controversy...."
>
> (at page 799)

**43.** Thus, it cannot be doubted, particularly in view of the Constitution Bench decisions of this Court that the words 'Hinduism' or 'Hindutva' are not necessarily to be understood and construed narrowly, confined only to the strict Hindu religious practices unrelated to the culture and ethos of the people of India, depicting the way of life of the Indian people. Unless the context of a speech indicates a contrary meaning or use, in the abstract, these terms are indicative more of a way of life of the Indian people and are not confined merely to describe persons practising the Hindu religion as a faith.

**44.** Considering the terms 'Hinduism' or 'Hindutva' *per se* as depicting hostility, enmity or intolerance towards other religious faiths or professing communalism, proceeds from an improper appreciation and perception of the true meaning of these expressions emerging from the detailed discussion in earlier authorities of this Court. Misuse of these expressions to promote communalism cannot alter the true meaning of these terms. The mischief resulting from the misuse of the terms by anyone in his speech has to be checked and not its permissible use. It is indeed very unfortunate, if in spite of the liberal and tolerant features of 'Hinduism' recognised in judicial decisions, these terms are misused by any-one during the elections to gain any unfair political advantage. Fundamentalism of any colour or kind must be curbed with a heavy hand to preserve and promote the secular creed of the nation. Any misuse of these terms must, therefore, be dealt with strictly.

**45.** It is, therefore, a fallacy and an error of law to proceed on the assumption that any reference to Hindutva or Hinduism in a speech makes it automatically a speech based on the Hindu religion as opposed to the other religions or that the use of words 'Hindutva' or 'Hinduism' *per se* depict an attitude hostile to all persons practising any religion other than the Hindu religion. It is the kind of use made of these words and the meaning sought to be conveyed in the speech which has to be seen and unless such a construction leads to the conclusion that these words were used to appeal for votes for a Hindu candidate on the ground that he is a Hindu or not to vote for a candidate because he is not a Hindu, the mere fact that these words are used in the speech would not bring it within the prohibition of sub-section (3) or (3A) of Section 123. It may well be, that these words are used in a speech to promote secularism or to emphasise the way of life of the Indian people and the Indian culture or ethos, or to criticise the policy of any political party as discriminatory or intolerant. The parliamentary debates, including the clarifications made by the Law Minister quoted earlier, also bring out this difference between the prohibited and permissible speech in this context. Whether a particular speech in which reference is made to Hindutva and /or Hinduism falls within the prohibition under sub-section (3) or (3A) of Section 123 is, therefore, a question of fact in each case.

**46.** This is the correct premise in our view on which all such matters are to be examined. The fallacy is in the assumption that a speech in which reference is made to Hindutva or Hinduism must be a speech on the ground of Hindu religion so that if the candidate for whom the speech is made happens to be a Hindu, it must necessarily amount to a corrupt practice under sub-section (3) and/or sub-section (3A) of Section 123 of the R.P. Act. As indicated, there is no such presumption permissible in law contrary to the several Constitution Bench decisions referred herein.

# INDEX